Not Paying the Rent

Neil Wilcock · Edgar Federzoni dos Santos
Editors

Not Paying the Rent

Imagining a Fairer Capitalism

palgrave
macmillan

Editors
Neil Wilcock
Leipzig University
Leipzig, Germany

Edgar Federzoni dos Santos
Leipzig University
Leipzig, Germany

University of Vienna
Vienna, Austria

ISBN 978-3-030-78860-5 ISBN 978-3-030-78861-2 (eBook)
https://doi.org/10.1007/978-3-030-78861-2

This Palgrave Macmillan imprint is published by the registered company Springer Nature Switzerland AG
The registered company address is: Gewerbestrasse 11, 6330 Cham, Switzerland

Foreword: Scenario of the Transition to a Terrible World

The Threat of a Globalisation of Rent

The world requires a benign globalisation of profit via globalisation of welfarist structures where labour is again empowered (Elsenhans, 2002, 2019b). The world is headed, however, towards a globalisation of exacerbating inequalities through politically controlled modes of production with increasingly insecure and marginal labour—what I term a globalisation of rent.

The promises of globalisation of profit in the post-World War II setting, through the capitalist mechanism of demand expansion resulting in shared prosperity, have not been kept. It had been expected that intensified trade and capital movements would provide knock-on positive results of growth for all economies that were ready to open their markets and liberalise their economies. Globalisation would give technically backward economies the chance of catching up without hurting the positions of the leading economies of the international division of labour, by ultimately creating equal levels of technical development. Common growth was expected to be the result of industrial specialisation. Specialisation would increase the demand for unskilled labour, the plentifully available factor of production of the periphery, and backward countries were promised that their incomes would increase and full employment would result.

State intervention was not essential for managing the world economy in this idealised form; a loose network of international organisations was sufficient, especially as the economically powerful nations controlled them and agreed on basic political and economic orientation. The increasingly demonstrated inefficiency of centrally planned economies, i.e. real socialism, was expected to peter off remaining antagonisms and converge global economics and politics towards democracy. When the Berlin Wall fell, the perspective emerged that the world was close to the end of history (Fukuyama, 1995); the final victory of peace-loving, internally liberal and democratic market economies against their authoritarian rivals.

With the so-called Great Recession, the rise of new cultural identitarian political movements,[1] often called fundamentalism in the Global South (Elsenhans, 2012), and the rise of neo-populism also in the West, this hope greatly diminished. New rising powers, especially in the Global South (new great powers such as China or India, but also minor powers such as Indonesia or Iran), intensified local conflicts, while a new aspiration of weaker powers to possess nuclear weapons rendered erstwhile optimistic perspectives null and void.

Globalisation did not arrive at the harmonious world it promised and mainstream economics remains at a loss to explain. Mainstream economics does not recognise the two fundamental mechanisms driving globalisation, namely changing the industrial mix through the exchange rate mechanism (explained later), nor rising mass incomes which is the essential condition for stability and growth.

The Character of Globalisation in the Late Twentieth Century

Globalisation in the nineteenth century between the West and the Global South was driven by comparative advantage of the South in raw material production, ultimately by high earnings for raw materials in relation to average productivity in industrial productions in the countries of the Global South. High raw material prices sheltered industries in the West from low wage competition in manufactured products from the Global South.

[1] The term I use to define the rise of political movements in developing societies that mobilise popular support with references to conceptions of cultural or religious identities that arise in conditions of state-led industrialisation failure. Examples include the ruling Bharatiya Janata Party (BJP) in India with its Hindu nationalism, the Islamic Salvation Front in Algeria and the Justice and Development Party (AKP) in Turkey.

Signs of a shift in this configuration of the West being protected by relatively high raw material prices for the Global South appeared in the form of manufactured exports from the rising Asian tigers South Korea, Taiwan, Hong Kong, and Singapore since the 1960s. Already in the nineteenth century some production sites in the then Global South achieved competitiveness in some manufacturing industries, if they were able to keep their exchange rates for their currencies low. For example, Japan and India developed from the 1880s onwards increasingly competitive textile industries based initially on machinery imports, however, in the case of Japan, they demonstrated the capacity of technically backward countries to assimilate most modern technologies, partly because of state intervention, but also on the basis of exchange rates of their currencies below purchasing power parity-cheap labour allowed them to move up the production chain. In difference to India, Japan had no lucrative raw material exports, only productive agriculture. It could keep its exchange rate below purchasing power parity already in the early twentieth century (Morimotu, 1918, p. 144).

In more modern times, globalisation of the last third of the twentieth century was based on a shift of comparative advantage. Cheap labour economies were able to achieve comparative advantage in industrial exports, initially relatively simple labour intensively produced products, but increasingly also in technically more demanding products—thereby moving up the development chain. These economies were never as capable in production as the industrial world, but their earnings from raw materials often never had existed such as the case of South Korea, Taiwan, Hong Kong and Singapore. More commonly, specialisation on raw materials had become a development dead end with the exception of oil.

There was no need to defend high-cost producers in the West or politically safe countries of the South from cheaper competitors.[2] Production from the cheapest resources available could be extended without limits. This maintained low inflation rates as many products of the South were low-cost imports which substituted increasingly expensive Western raw materials. Prices could fall to level of the cheapest supplier as raw material rents disappeared.[3] The shift of the Global South to comparative

[2] Again, this does not apply in the case of countries with a high oil production.

[3] Raw material production implied specialisation on products with low price and income elasticity of demand in the West, because industry is raw material saving and private

advantage in industrial exports, initially of relatively simple products, is the result of the disappearance of comparative advantage in raw material exports. It is not necessarily the result of a technical catch-up.

Comparative advantage still exists without competitiveness (Elsenhans, 2002), in fact, "competitiveness" as it continues to be used in political economic discourse is a dogmatic legacy of 1980s neoliberalism. In order to develop competitiveness of production, where a country has comparative advantage, an adjustment of prices is necessary. Comparative advantage is not transformed in competitive advantage[4] via decreasing real wages, but via lower international prices of this labour (Elsenhans, 2004): the real wage represents purchasing power for a basket of limited goods in the currency of that wage, whereas the international price of labour is primarily defined by the exchange rate. If an economy is able to supply additional workers in export industries from a local surplus of wage goods production, it remains competitive as long as the costs of the imported inputs including machinery can be paid for by the additional exports. At its limit, export can accept zero earnings to be reserved for additional labour.[5]

The Western strategies of maintaining repressive political structures had led up to the 1930s of dramatically decreasing per capita production of food in the South (Cullather, 2010, p. 33). With declining legitimacy of Western rule in the Global South, especially after the breakout of the Cold War, the South had to be preserved from famine. The Green Revolution led to massive increases in food production especially in the highly populated countries of Asia. They started to produce an internal surplus of food for feeding additional export workers and these food surpluses

households expand their demand for food less rapidly than their rising incomes. This is basically the outcome of the mechanism described in the progressive critique of the deterioration of the terms of trade.

[4] The distinction between comparative and competitive advantage should be noted: comparative advantage is in regard to advantage derived from specialisation such that a trading relationship between economies of different capabilities can take place in both economies interest, whereas competitive advantage is in regard to an advantage derived on in a single market in opposition to other competing economies.

[5] As long as additional labour is supplied its wage goods from localproduction of otherwise not exportable goods, any earnings from exports above the cost of imported imports contributes to the overall incomes of a backward economy with high levels of unemployment. Hence, the importance of an expanding internal market for any development to occur.

became the physical counterpart of the additional wages paid to additional workers who found employment in the newly rising export industries.

With a secured internally produced food supply, an increasingly large number of countries in the Global South could transform comparative advantage into competitive advantage. There were huge differences in international costs of labour, wages in export-oriented manufacturing of the Global South at the official exchange rate were only 1/20 of the wages businesses had to pay in the old industrial countries in the same production lines. However, real wages between 1880s Indian textile industry and 1990 East Asian countries in relation to the industrial West remained relatively stable around 1/5 to 1/7.[6] It proves that exchange rates—not the real wages—determine cost competitiveness.

With the exception of the city states (Hong Kong, Singapore—comparable cases were also dynamic in countries with high poverty like Mumbai and Chennai), the successful export-oriented manufacturers opted for profound interventions in favour of the economically weakest part of the society, namely the marginalised landless rural poor through land reforms. Where such reforms did not take place, new comparative advantage had limited multiplier effects on employment beyond the directly created jobs in manufacturing industries. So-called shared growth contributed to additional growth. Where this mechanism was absent, labour was not empowered by the capitalist mechanism of profit being defended by rising mass incomes, and entrepreneurial spending on net investment which would expand markets rarely materialised. Ultimately, mass consumption, which can only be sustained through an empowered labour class, creates the incomes necessary for selling consumption goods at earnings higher than the wages paid directly or indirectly to labour (Elsenhans, 2015, pp. 1–11).

Quite independently of their ideological orientations, China, South Korea and Taiwan demonstrated that successful export-oriented manufacturing depends on social and economic reforms in favour of the majority.[7] They disproved the contention of mainstream economics that low wages promote accumulation and growth.

[6] Morris (1965, p. 22), Lokanathan (1935, p. 358), Lafay (1996, p. 948), Strack et al. (1997), and Oonk (2001, p. 425f).

[7] Grabowski (2018, p. 357), Kay (2002, p. 1091), Speare (1974, p. 306), and Shih (1968, p. 306).

Successful export-oriented manufacturing countries, however, are increasingly under competition from newly emerging exporters and manufacturers. The new entrants become competitive on the basis of the same mechanism of devaluation but the low number of jobs in export-oriented industries (at least initially) implies that the social conditions of empowerment of labour are still worse than in the successful newly industrialising countries (Le Monde 23 January 2011, p. 13, 17 September 2010, p. 10). This new competition limits the negotiating power of labour in those countries of the Global South where export-oriented manufacturing already had a larger impact on the local labour markets. It shows that success in one country will lead to further delocalisation of productions, hence conjoined policies for creating high levels of employment globally are required.

As well, the rise of newly industrialising countries will go at least temporarily with rising demand for raw materials and hence new possibilities of raw material rents. Resource-rich exporters of manufacturers will experience rising exchange rates which forces them to either intensify state intervention in order to protect their perhaps already high level of industrialisation or to go for a new raw material-oriented growth model with limited incentives for industrial exports due to an exchange rate too high for industrial expansion but instead favourable to owners of current resources further enrichment, i.e. local rentiers. Brazil is a such a case of no deliberate policy for keeping the exchange rate low at levels where industry can increase its exports (Araújo et al., 2012, p. 442; Coxhead, 2007, p. 1111).

New competition and the danger of Dutch Disease are factors that launch a collective drive into austerity, foregoing the potential development through investment in manufacturing and skilling of their workforce, which would allow them to move up the industrial chain of production.

The Convergent Option of Rent-Seeking

To the difference of nineteenth-century globalisation, the Global South has become competitive in a large variety of production lines that are important for employment in the West. The mechanism that operates is once more specialisation according to comparative advantage. A country specialises in the products where its advance is highest or where its backwardness is lowest, not where its advance is high. According to comparative advantage, as mentioned previously, absolute levels of productivity are not decisive.

Suppose there is a new technology where leading economies and less advanced economies have no experience of learning-by-doing. The more advanced economy will certainly be superior but the degree of its advance in productivity in relation to a less advanced country will be less than in previous high technologies: in a previous high technology, only the leading economies have had training on the spot. In the new technology both the leading and less advanced economies are lacking this factor of productivity. If the leading country is not able to transfer its advance due to learning-by-doing hundred per per cent to the new technology, the leading economy has to specialise on older products according to the laws of comparative advantage.[8] In such a situation, even in a leading economy there is no possibility to avoid specialisation on non-dynamic products without intervening in the market process. If austerity does not work sufficiently, also leading countries which are firmly committed to free trade, will opt for industrial policies and protectionist measures, starting with state subsidies for national systems of innovation, which the old powers are increasingly doing.

Moreover, productivity outstripping production growth, which is implied in austerity policies, translates as losses of jobs (Gindin and Panitch, 2012, p. 290f.; Erber and Hagemann, 2012, p. 39). This was starkly illustrated during the 1980s experiment with neoliberalism in the UK, as Ian Gilmour writes, "[G]reater productivity is only of limited use unless it leads to higher production; producing relatively less while doing it more efficiently merely increases unemployment and redistributes

[8] This may appear far-fetched as the new technology will be associated with the previous leading economies, however, as was the case in the Tiger economies, they were able to develop in electronics at cost advantage to the West. It appears as if the cost of production in the new technology in the incumbent leading country is too high. The instinctive reaction in the eyes of industrialists and governments is to keep real wages low to reduce production costs, hence to opt for austerity. But the cause for this lack of competitiveness is the exchange rate, which for leading economies is relatively high because of their relatively high productivity in old technologies.

income from those out of work those still in it" (Gilmour, 1993, p. 85).[9] Most of the job losses in the wake of globalisation are not due to delocalisation of production to low-income sites, but due to *production growing less than productivity*—in other words, an underconsumption crisis.[10] There are possibilities of production, which the effective demand on the market does not bring into operation. While the erstwhile newly developing countries used interventionist trade and industrial policies at the outset, it is less whether competition is weakened but in whose favour this weakening takes place—in favour of labour through making labour scarce via expanding demand, or through reducing market mechanisms by oligopoly in favour of rent-seeking enterprises.

This is the basis of argumentation: trade openness goes with more state intervention. Globalisation produces losers which in the Western world are still able to survive through welfare (Rodrik, 2011, pp. 233–235). The dynamic enterprise sector and the demands of the weaker households will not be averse to increasing state intervention or state toleration of private "oligopolies". For example, mark-up pricing, as criticised by Keynesian and neoclassical microeconomics, is rarely criticised as shown by the evolution of car prices.

Economies which are committed to keeping the export markets of more advanced economies open indulge in rent-seeking. Devaluation is costly and decreases the incomes of the upper income groups as owners of key state resources. The rate of devaluation is important if surplus labour should be absorbed in the labour market. Subsidising directly or indirectly productions which are not yet competitive can help to limit the devaluation rates. Local content rules are one means where exporting enterprises have to use export earnings for purchasing local but not yet competitive products. They will do so as long as they have no better possibilities of employing their resources for investment. This means, that as long as they are earning average profit rates, they will continue to do so. South Korea imposed on its textile exporters the purchase of only locally produced machinery by blocking imports of textile machinery (Mytelka,

[9] For a devastating critique of the ill-considered policies associated with neoliberal beliefs, from a former member of the Margaret Thatcher's cabinet at the time, see Ian Gilmour's "Dancing with Dogma: Britain Under Thatcherism" (1993).

[10] An underconsumption crisis is a recession characterised by unused capacity, unemployment, low final demand, and where pessimistic expectations based on a falling economy block further investment.

1986, p. 258; Haggard, 1983, p. 83). As the price elasticity of demand for Korean textile exports was low, initially higher costs of textile machinery and subsequent higher prices in Korean currency for textile exports did not lead to massive reductions of quantities exported.

In order to fight against the effects of underconsumption crises, the leading industrial economies and the catching-up economies will opt for rent appropriation in order to defend their competitiveness normally imposing increased austerity.

It was Hilferding's (1968, p. 451) contribution to the theory of imperialism showing that if there is a protected internal market of considerable size, external prices can be lower than internal prices. Internal prices have to be higher than average costs and external prices higher than marginal costs, which in case of economies of scale are lower than average costs. Whenever industries operate under decreasing unit costs due to economies of scale, being able to charge a protected part of an enterprise's production with the costs of development of a new technology, additional quantities can be charged at lower prices. In Hilferding's period, this was realised through custom barriers. Today subsidising the development of new technologies can be done through low exchange rates and state subsidies for the technical innovation system, enacting a type of backdoor protectionism. Low exchange rates protect an emerging national industry much better than customs duties, and the resources for financing such measures can be taken from the locally producible surplus which is triggered at least by increasing employment in the wake of devaluation.

As the title of this foreword predicts, instead of a homogeneous world market the international economic system will tend to fragmented markets with all their inefficiencies for overall growth rates, but with the protection they provide to "national" economies in the domains of maintaining presence in the most promising future technologies. Additionally, maintaining acceptable levels of employment so that unemployment does not become dangerous for political stability (a level quite different in different countries).

The International Political System Follows Fragmentation

After the fall of the Berlin Wall, those international relations theories critical of North American realism enhanced the idea of an international society of states and other organisations increasingly ruled by agreed norms of "civilised" behaviour. In a period where the major political power constantly prides itself on its capability of mobilising quite superior military power, the constructivists' idealism seems misplaced.[11] It is however not solely the wickedness of some leaders determining our future course, but the complementary character of a fragmented state system (in the sense of withdrawing from inter-state political collaborations and cooperation on mutual topics) to a fragmented economic system (a likewise withdrawing from free trade on the basis of comparative advantage).

In the race for innovation there is a need to create large markets for mass production, which is maintained by distributing start-up costs on rapidly expanding volumes of production (cf. Hilferding points on imperialism above). The carving out of new colonial empires is difficult given the degrees of mobilisation achieved in all these originally traditional communitarian or tributary modes of production[12] the Western powers opened up for their domination in the second wave of colonialism in the late nineteenth century, e.g. Southeast Asia, Africa. Large markets require to be found today inside the "national" state.

There are today enough large states for creating a multipolar system composed of a limited number of great powers which agree to block access to their club to others. This is achieved either by co-opting them in their clientelist systems or by blocking any attempt of the formation of large states out of smaller ones—a clientelist geopolitics revolving around continental blocs.

The US, India, and China represent already nearly half the world's population. Russia by its size, nuclear status and geopolitical position, and Brazil due to its geopolitical position in Latin America, are candidates for the club of great "bloc" powers. The European Union may become one, after the distracting fulminations of Brexit subside, if it can return to the original idea of deepening supranationality. Much will depend here on Germany being ready to recognise the position of France as the political

[11] Cf. the contributions in honour of Thomas Rise in Zeitschrift für Internationale Beziehungen 24(1), 2017, especially Deitelhoff 2017 and Holzscheiter 2017. The most pertinent points in these articles are the things which go unsaid, namely, there is practically no information about important empirical achievements on the basis of the constructivist paradigm. Cf. also Elsenhans (2019a).

[12] Meaning a pre-capitalist political economy where surplus is extracted by political means.

leader despite Germany's economic weight (Elsenhans, 1999, p. 17) i.e. a return to the configuration which emerged in the wake of 1945.

The emerging bloc powers, in case of a European Union under French leadership also the leading state in the European Union, have nuclear capabilities. Nuclear forces serve as an instrument of politics, not as a military instrument. They serve powers outside the region with limited conventional capabilities in a particular region or powers inside the region facing the threat of intrusion of rival bloc powers to compensate any relative inferiority by the threat of use of nuclear power. These great powers will therefore organise around them zones of influence. In these zones of influence, for geographical reasons, particular dominant powers will exercise hegemonic influence because of conventional superiority (Elsenhans, 2019b, pp. 122–124).

Smaller powers have two options: firstly, they might try to negotiate good terms for their independence by respecting the interests of the respective hegemonic power and uphold some autonomy by maintaining good relations to the rest of the great powers. The great powers from outside the region may support local dissenters in order to keep the regional hegemon from transforming regional hegemony into an increased projection of power on the global level. There is little possibility that the smaller powers within regions can unite for limiting the hegemon and will therefore jealously maintain their sovereignty (think Bangladesh, Vietnam, Mexico, Argentina, Azerbaijan), and even might try to become nuclear themselves (Libya, North Korea, Iran, Pakistan). The tendencies will increase with the experience of increasing projection of power by regional hegemons (China, India, Russia, Brazil, US, European Union).

Such a system will function according to the rules of the Vienna system (1814–1919). The concert of great powers has problems which emerge from the haphazard way the club of great powers was differentiating itself from other large countries. In Asia there are some major countries which do not fit into the opposition between great powers and small powers. In order to improve their status, they will rely on extra-regional support, for instance, Japan or Turkey. The temptation of becoming nuclear will increase for those middle powers and in response the club of great powers will try to unite for thwarting this disruption.

There are areas where no regional great power will emerge. For the foreseeable future, neither Nigeria nor the Republic of South Africa can take up the leading role as a hegemon in sub-Saharan Africa, nor do I see the emergence of an Arab leading power as all other great powers have political problems with Muslim minorities.

The absence of regional hegemons will lead to instabilities. The new state system emerges from an old substrate with many small countries having enjoyed some autonomy under the umbrella of the overarching bipolar conflict and the protection of, an albeit weakening, Third World solidarity. Extra-regional powers will try to limit the rise of rival powers in these weak bellies of the international system as shown by the multitude of conflicts in sub-Saharan Africa and the Middle East. This resembles very much the rise of the powers in Western Europe after the demise of universal monarchy under the leadership of the Habsburgs during the seventeenth and eighteenth centuries until the rationalisation of the European map by the French Revolution and the Napoleonic expansion in the early nineteenth century.

As the main characteristic of the newly emerging system is rivalry despite cooperation between the great powers, the leaderships will try to reduce uncertainty by not working in the direction of destabilising rival powers. There will be a tacit agreement to maintain internal power structures in other leading powers as much as possible.

This international system will be characterised by avoidance of deep structural changes inside their societies and respect for government roles which are economically supported by the privileged access of government to rents which result in further economic marginalisation and erasure.

Alternatives: They Exist but Are Not Chosen

The economic basis of the emerging international system is rent which is increased by concerted austerity. It translates into fragmentation of economic spaces on which regional hegemons are emerging. In the defence of their rents and their political instruments for preserving statehood, these great powers, but also the smaller powers, will jealously maintain sovereignty. To prevent other powers encroaching on their sovereignty, there will be coalitions following the classical theories of a balance of power globally. Systemic maintenance will override all other particular interests, including economic interests. This applies also to new political movements defining themselves as identitarian or civilisational as may be articulated in the wake the crisis of secular nationalism in the rent-ridden economies of the South or of intensified post-materialism in the North where economic priorities are secondary.

This does not exclude the emergence of a heightened heterogeneous international society with many nonstate actors, including powerful international organisations and civil society actors. Their activities will however be restricted in effect by the requirements of the powers, great and small, to maintain their existence.

The alternative would be to empower society, which is the majority (Elsenhans, 2019b, 2019c). Whatever the legal terms of labour's relation with the economic system, it ultimately depends on labour's negotiating power (or lack of) on labour markets, and with increasing productivity through digitalisation, this requires either increasing mass incomes in relation to that productivity increase, or reduced working hours, ideally with both reinforcing each other. This negotiating power depends on scarce labour's capacity to produce a surplus, ipso facto, there is demand; otherwise those surpluses are appropriated as rent. The surplus produced by labour may be appropriated as profit provided that entrepreneurs opt for net investment but it can also be appropriated by as rent through non-market mechanisms if there is no compulsion to compete on open markets.

Profit will be strengthened against rent to the extent labour organisations are able to negotiate a return of surplus in their favour. This can be enhanced by rule-based mechanisms of reduction of discretionary power in the distribution of rents. Democratic delegation of the power of the purse in highly complex economies does not really check the oligarchical tendencies so nicely described for organisations with a true democratic origins like the German labour movement of the late nineteenth century and apply even more so in the future as increasingly centralised power is able exert even stronger influences of goal displacement in their favour (Michels, 1925, p. 182).[13] Green growth can be promoted by very general rules where discretionary power is limited because some production processes are simply banned or complemented by compensatory processes (Elsenhans, 2020).

Increasing consumption, hence basically increasing mass consumption by high levels of employment (scarcity of labour) and political redistribution of incomes, and reduction of working hours where acceptable levels of consumption have been achieved, would reduce rent, and be replaced by profit as the form in which surplus is appropriated on the

[13] Referred to as the Iron Law of Oligarchy.

basis of anonymous market mechanisms. The power of the open market to empower labour has never been accepted by Marxists who remain resistant, but most likely oblivious, to its potential for redistribution under these conditions'.

From what I have described in the contradictions of the international division of labour it is highly improbable that levels of employment are reached in the periphery of the global system, the Global South, where labour becomes so scarce that it is empowered. It is, however, highly probable that in the trajectory to this goal the emergence of rents of new types will strengthen the rent appropriation mechanisms. They may take the form of governmental, even with formal democratic mechanisms of participation, but with oligarchic structures of power. Cynically speaking, leadership will emerge which prioritises the interests of the masses but maintains hierarchy and intensified social control through technology of various means, as China has at present (from surveillance of words in the West[14] to the social credit system in China). "Modernisation" may no longer go with increasing mobility.

By weakening the opposition between capital and labour, mass organisations will be docile and resistance beyond the agreed level will be atomised, as demonstrated in the Third World by the limits imposed by the powerful and the so-called third wave of democratisation, whether it is Mexico ever since its "bourgeois revolution", Morocco in the 2010s or in the near future Algeria. Crowds on the street may be more active than ever before, but they have no programmes of redirecting the basic structures of the economic systems. Citizens may be more active and protesting than ever, yet less able to translate this into real change. New technology, like Twitter and Telegram, has proved a formidable tool for protesting but remains vapid as a platform of governance in any sense, as that still requires imagination, ideas and committed organisation.

Next generations probably will look back to our period of the second half of the twentieth century being of high social innovativeness never reproduced afterwards, a sort of Axial era (sixth century B.C. to seventh century A.D.) of the end of the twentieth century.

The intellectual struggle may play its role in avoiding that denouement. The bourgeois revolution is, however, not the result of intellectual

[14] There has been a failure to heed Karl Popper's warning never to be goaded "into taking seriously problems about words and their meanings".

enlightenment, the idea of equality dates at least from the Axial period of Jaspers (1949). The intellectual interpretation of the rise of capitalism has been notoriously long, for example, the insistence on the necessity of massive accumulation of capital when it turned out later on that the capital output ratio in capitalism does not increase (Helmstädter, 1969, pp. 54–60; 2002; Kendrick, 1961, p. 166). With great regret, it is highly improbable that intellectuals can change the course of history, especially if they do not tackle the fundamental problem of empowerment of labour but instead talk only on the possible results of such empowerment—formal democratic participation. I am sceptical whether there will even be an attempt to reconstruct political economy as an instrument of legitimation of the struggle of labour, let alone victory in that subsequent struggle.

Hartmut Elsenhans
Leipzig University
Leipzig, Germany

Bibliography

Araújo, E., Bruno, M. and Pirmentel, D. (2012). Regime cambial e mudança estrutural na indústria de transformação brasileira. Evidências para o período (1994–2008). In: *Brazilian Journal of Political Economy* 32, no. 2: 424–445.

Chang, H.-J. (2003). Kicking Away the Ladder: The "Real" History of Free Trade. In: *Foreign Policy* in Focus, Silver City, NM: Interhemispheric Resource Center.

Coxhead, I. (2007). A New Resource Curse? Impact of China's Boom on Comparative Advantage and Resource Dependence in Southeast Asia. In: *World Development* 35, no. 7: 1099–1119.

Cullather, N. (2010). *The Hungry World: America's Cold War Battle Against Poverty in Asia*. Cambridge, MA: Harvard University Press.

Deitelhoff, N. (2017). Billiges Gerede und leeres Geschwätz. In: *Zeitschrift für Internationale Beziehungen* 24, no. 1: 130–142.

Elsenhans, H. (1999). Introduction. In: H. Elsenhans (Hg.), *A Balanced European Architecture: Enlargement of the European Union to Central Europe and the Mediterranean* [Une architecture européenne équilibrée. L'ouverture de l'Union Européenne vers l'Europe centrale et la Méditerranée]. Paris: Publisud, pp. 5–18.

Elsenhans, H. (2001). *Das Internationale System zwischen Zivilgesellschaft und Rente*. Münster: Lit.

Elsenhans, H. (2002). Macroeconomics in Globalization: Productivity, Wages, Profits, and Exchange Rates in an Era of Globalization. In: *Brazilian Journal of Political Economy* 22, no. 85: 53–78.

Elsenhans, H. (2004). Globalisation, Devaluation and Development. In: *Rajasthan Economic Journal* 27, no. 1: S.1–14.

Elsenhans, H. (2012). The Rise of New Cultural Identitarian Movements in Africa and Asia in the Emerging Multipolar System. In: *Comparative Studies of South Asia, Africa and the Middle East* 32, no. 3: 642–661.

Elsenhans, H. (2015). *Saving Capitalism from the Capitalists: A Contribution to Global and Historical Keynesianism.* Beverly Hills, CA, London, and New Delhi: Sage.

Elsenhans, H. (2019a). Constructivism: The Political Economy of Political Correctness in a Constructivist IR Zoo. In: *Pakistan Horizon* 72, no. 2: 19–38.

Elsenhans, H. (2019b). The Impending Threat of Globalisation of Rent and the Defence of Capitalism by Labour. In: *International Studies* 56, no. 2: 109–128.

Elsenhans, H. (2019c). Rising Mass Incomes as a Condition of Capitalist Growth. Preserving Capitalism Through the Empowerment of Labor in the Past and the Present. In: *Journal of Post Keynesian Economics* 36, no. 2: 1–36. https://doi.org/10.1080/01603477.2019.1672560.

Elsenhans, H. (2020, forthcoming). Green Growth or the New Frontier of Capitalism: A Kaleckian Approach. In: T. Hickmann and M. Lederer, (Hgs.), *Entwicklung, Verwaltung, Umwelt und Klima - Sozialwissenschaftliche Perspektiven aus Theorie und Praxis. Eine Festschrift für Harald Fuhr*. Baden-Baden: Nomos.

Erber, G. and Hagemann, H. (2012). *Zur Produktivitätsentwicklung Deutschlands im internationalen Vergleich.* Wiso Diskurs. Bonn-Bad-Godesberg: Friedrich - Ebert - Stiftung.

Fukuyama, F. (1995). Reflections on the End of History: Five Years Later. In: *History and Theory* 34, no. 1: 27–43.

Gindin, S. and Panitch, L. (2012). *The Making of Global Capitalism: The Political Economy of American Empire*. London: Verso.

Grabowski, R. (2018). Food Staple Production and Alternative Development Paths: India and China. In: *Journal of the Asia Pacific Economy* 23, no. 3: 357–373. https://doi.org/10.1080/13547860.2018.1469588.

Gilmour, I. (1993). *Dancing with Dogma: Britain Under Thatcher*. London: Simon & Schuster.

Haggard, S. M. (1983). *Pathways from the Periphery: The Newly Industrializing Countries in the International System*. Berkeley, CA: Dissertation.

Helmstädter, E. (1969). *Der Kapitalkoeffizient. Eine kapitaltheoretische Untersuchung*. Stuttgart: Gustav Fischer.

Helmstädter, E. (2002). *Kapitalstock, Kapitalintensität, Kapitalkoeffizient in Preisen von 1995 (1960–2000), Kapitalkoeffizient nach Wirtschaftsbereichen in Preisen von 1985 (1960–1989)*. Gesis Historische Statistik ZA 8533, B O1b, B02. Wiesbaden: Gesis. Online verfügbar unter https://histat.gesis.org/histat/de/project/tables/454B76E29642F3D8D2C857029285A565/3.

Hilferding, R. (1968). *Das Finanzkapital. Eine Studie über die jüngste Entwicklung des Kapitalismus [1909]*. Frankfort on the Main: Europäische Verlagsanstalt.

Holzscheiter, A. (2017). Was vom Arguing übrigblieb. Der Nachhall der kommunikativen Wende in den Internationalen Beziehungen. In: *Zeitschrift für Internationale Beziehungen* 24, no. 1: S.143–159.

Jaspers, K. (1949). *Vom Ursprung und Ziel der Geschichte [1949]*. Frankfort on Main: Fischer.

Kautsky, K. (1914). Der Imperialismus. In: *Neue Zeit* 32, no. 2: 908–922.

Kay, C. (2002). Why East Asia Overtook Latin America: Agrarian Reform, Industrialisation and Development. In: *Third World Quarterly* 23, no. 6: 1073–1102.

Kendrick, J. W. (1961). *Productivity Trends in the United States: A Study by the National Bureau of Economic Research*. Princeton, NJ: Princeton University Press.

Lafay, G. (1996). Les origines internationales du chômage européen. In: *Revue d'économie politique* 106, no. 6: 943–963.

Lenin, V. I. (1964). Imperialism, the Highest Stage of Capitalism: A Popular Outline [1917]. Lenin Collected Works (22). In: V. I. Lenin (Hg.), *Collected Works 22*. Moscow: Progress Publishers, pp. 187–304.

Lokanathan, P. S. (1935). *Industrial Organization in India*. London: Allen & Unwin.

Michels, R. (1925). *Zur Soziologie des Parteiwesens in der modernen Demokratie. Untersuchungen über die oligarchischen Tendenzen des Gruppenlebens*. Leipzig: Kröner.

Morimotu, K. (1918). *The Standard of Living in Japan: John Hopkins University Studies in Historical and Political Studies*. Baltimore, MD: Johns Hopkins University Press.

Morris, M. D. (1965). *The Emergence of an Industrial Labor Force in India: A Study of the Bombay Cotton Mills, 1854–1947*. Berkeley, CA and Los Angeles: University of California Press.

Mytelka, L. K. (1986). The Transfer of Technology: Myth or Reality? In: Carol Cosgrove and J. Jamar (Hgs.), *The European Community's Development Policy: The Strategies Ahead*. Conference Organised at the College of Europe, Bruges, 4–6 July 1985. Brugge: De Tempel, pp. 243–281.

Oonk, G. (2001). Motor or Millstone? The Management Agent System in Bombay and Ahmedabad, 1850–1930. In: *Indian Economic and Social History Review* 38, no. 4: 419–452.

Rodrik, D. (2011). *The Globalization Paradox: Why Global Markets, States, and Democracy Can't Coexist*. Oxford: Oxford University Press.

Shih, C.-S. (1968). Economic Development in Taiwan After the Second World War. In: *Weltwirtschaftliches Archiv* 100, no. 1: S.112–134.

Speare, A. (1974). Urbanization and Migration in Taiwan. In: *Economic Development and Cultural Change* 22, no. 2: 302–319.

Strack, D., Helmschrott, H. and Schönherr, S. (1997). Internationale Einkommensvergleiche auf der Basis von Kaufkraftparitäten. Das Gefälle zwischen Industrie- und Entwicklungsländern verringert sich. In: *IFO-Schnelldienst* 50, no. 10: 7–14.

Hartmut Elsenhans is a German political scientist and Emeritus Professor of International Relations at the University of Leipzig. He has been affiliated with Wolfgang Goethe University Frankfurt, Philipps University Marburg, Constance University, the Université de Montréal; Jawaharlal Nehru University, India; Quaid-e-Azam University, Islamabad; Columbia University and University of California, Berkeley. He has published over 400 articles and 40 books, with the latest two being a retrospective of his articles on rent-based capitalism entitled *Development, Capitalism, and Rent: The Political Economy of Hartmut Elsenhans* and *Capitalism, Development and the Empowerment of Labour, A Heterodox Political Economy*.

Acknowledgements

Neil is chiefly indebted to Corina Scholz for the academic, psychological, and friendship support in completing international organisation chapters, which were improved immeasurably by her inputs. This book follows on from their co-authored "Hartmut Elsenhans and a Critique of Capitalism: Conversations on Theory and Policy Implications" (Palgrave Macmillan, 2016), and while it was the original intention to do a second publication together, I sense Corina choose wisely in taking on a more editorial role this time around. Neil was fortunate to find the next best co-author available in Edgar to fill her considerable boots. A special mention to Ross MacDermott for looking over the final drafts and Alan Fletcher for his phone calls of customary humour. As ever, Neil would like to thank his family, Mum and Dad for more than can be mentioned, as well as brothers Martin and Colin.

Edgar would like to thank Neil Wilcock for making him the irresistible offer of co-authoring this book. All the sleepless nights and missed weekends during sunny lockdown days are owned to Neil and his intellectual restlessness, which he now partakes in at unsociable distance. Edgar warmly thanks his girlfriend Gina Gerstl for the immense patience and support in all five love languages for him to complete this book. Especial thanks to her for not having killed him after the 98th consecutive time he said "I can't have dinner tonight, sorry". Above all, thank you, dear reader, for already having made this far into the book!

Both authors owe warm thanks to Ryan Crowder for responding at short notice to lend his keen eye for detail to the chapters, and Xenia Pilipenko for offering some wonderful testimonies that we would have loved to use but could not possibly get away with.

We should like to thank the staff at the Economics Catalogue at Palgrave Macmillan for trusting in this publication and being flexible to our requests.

We feel honoured to have such strong responses to the original chapters, which confirms we picked wisely. We thank each of the response authors for their timely and stimulating inputs, namely Professor Salvatore Babones, Dr. Hannes Warnecke-Berger, Dr. Fabricio H. Chagas-Bastos, Vinicius Neves dos Santos, and Thiago Elert Soares.

We are deeply grateful to Professor Hartmut Elsenhans for the intellectual inspiration and academic guidance, and for being kind enough to provide a foreword for this text, which in his imitable style combines theoretical insights with the practical realities of pertinent economic forces.

Naturally, however, the errors are all our own.

Contents

Notes on Contributors

Salvatore Babones is Associate Professor at the Univerisity of Syndey. He is the author or editor of ten books and more than two dozen academic research articles. His two main areas of academic research are the political economy of the greater China region and the methodology of quantitative modeling in the social sciences. He also publishes extensively on American social and foreign policy.

Fabricio H. Chagas-Bastos is Assistant Professor at the Department of Political Science at the University of Copenhagen, and a Marie-Curie Fellow.

Thiago Elert Soares is a sustainable development professional with work experience at the United Nations University (UNU) in Germany and the *Deutsche Gesellschaft für Internationale Zusammenarbeit* (GIZ) in Rwanda. He holds a MSc in Development Studies from the London School of Economics and Political Science (LSE) as a Chevening Scholar and a MPP from the Hertie School in Berlin as a Helmut-Schmidt Scholar.

Edgar Federzoni dos Santos holds a joint master's degree in Global Studies from the University of Leipzig and the University of Vienna, focusing on Brazilian development. He has been a prominent practitioner for almost a decade at one of the leading international organisations specialising in policy development. He has implemented development actions in South America, West Africa, Eastern Europe, the Middle East, and Central Asia.

Vinicius Neves dos Santos has a master's degree in international relations from the University of São Paulo and is an expert in international cooperation from the Complutense University of Madrid. He has worked for ten years with international trade and negotiations at the Federation of Industries of the State of São Paulo and was a professor in the postgraduate programme in international relations at the Anhembi Morumbi University in São Paulo.

Hannes Warnecke-Berger is Senior Researcher at the University of Kassel, Germany. He is a political scientist and the author and editor of various books and articles, including *Politics and Violence in Central America and the Caribbean*, and *Politics and History of Crime and Violence in Central America*. His most recent publication is editor of *Development, Capitalism, and Rent: The Political Economy of Hartmut Elsenhans*.

Neil Wilcock is a practitioner at one of the leading international organisations specialising in policy development. He has delivered specific development projects in Eastern and Southern Africa, Southeast Asia and South America. He holds a joint master's degree in Global Studies from the University of Leipzig and the University of Wroclaw, Poland. As a researcher, he concentrates on global political economy, with this book directly following on from his last publication, *Hartmut Elsenhans and a Critique of Capitalism: Conversations on Theory and Policy Implications*.

Part I

CHAPTER 1

Introduction

Neil Wilcock and Edgar Federzoni dos Santos

Synopsis

Not Paying the Rent: Imagining a Fairer Capitalism makes the case that global development can only be realised through full employment capitalism and free from rent economics. This book will propose a development-focused transition through international organisations. The shift will be proposed in a convoy model of globalisation[1] and underpinned by international organisations defending freedom, prosperity, and peace. The terms rent, capitalism, development, labour marginality, and convoy model of globalisation which are crucial to this explanation will be defined later in the introduction.

This book follows on from a previous publication by one of the co-authors, "Hartmut Elsenhans and a Critique of Capitalism: Conversations

[1] Wilcock and Scholz, 2016, *Hartmut Elsenhansand a Critique of Capitalism*, Chapter 5.

N. Wilcock (✉) · E. Federzoni dos Santos
Leipzig University, Leipzig, Germany
e-mail: neil.wilcock.07@aberdeen.ac.uk

E. Federzoni dos Santos
University of Vienna, Vienna, Austria

N. Wilcock and E. Federzoni dos Santos (eds.), *Not Paying the Rent*,
https://doi.org/10.1007/978-3-030-78861-2_1

on Theory and Policy Implications" (Wilcock and Scholz, 2016) which was a series of interviews on development with Professor Hartmut Elsenhans. Elsenhans is a primary source of inspiration for the book directly and indirectly. Indirectly from his theories on global capitalist development (as the multiple references will attest), and directly, through initial guidance on the books' contents. Elsenhans' scholarship is diverse and varied, having published numerous books on development theories to Algerian independence to social movements. This book seeks to extrapolate on those theories in directions previously uncovered by Elsenhans in a single volume, namely the economic history of Brazil and policy recommendations international organisations could adopt that foster world economic development. Elsenhans' theory on the global development, which we have applied, sketches paths to development for the least well-off countries without inhibiting growth of others through a convoy model of globalisation.

Contents of the Book

Professor Hartmut Elsenhans has written the foreword entitled, "The scenario of the transition to a terrible world", which imagines the nightmare scenario where rent economics flourishes as inequalities are not tackled but exacerbated. Elsenhans conceptualises this as the continued globalisation of rent in captured markets protected by undemocratic institutions amid a surplus of unused labour. Elsenhans' career has aimed to rewrite economic history in a Keynesian perspective, which before the *General Theory* was not possible as there was no link between history and theory in economics. As Joan Robinson (1979, p. 74) writes "In history, we learned that the mainspring of development was technical inventions; in theory, most of the exercises were in terms of a 'given state of knowledge'...[Keynes] opened up a great field for an analytical survey of economic history". Elsenhans has been able to conduct political economic analysis that replaces timeless equilibrium[2] with historical development. We meekly follow in its footsteps in Part I in the case of

[2] The reintroduction of *time* was a cornerstone of the Keynesian Revolution, such that the world in which humans live with the complications of ever-changing dynamics and forces interact took economics "away from theology towards science" (Robinson, 1979, p. 73).

economic history of Brazil, and hope to add to a field of study that is in need of investment and accumulation itself!

The book is split in half: Part I takes the economic historical development of Brazil as a case study, outlining the political economic path it has undergone since its birth in the sixteenth century through its course of permanent rent and occasional development. In the final chapter of this first part, ideas to enhance the prospects of a prosperous and democratic evolution in Brazil are explored. The case study of Brail is intended to show how rentism has thwarted over centuries the political and economic policies required to create a more prosperous economy and equitable society. The chapters will explore why Brazil despite its huge natural resources and potentially large internal markets never became a high-income country, what relationship this has to the historical weakness of fully functioning capitalism and the prevalence of rent, and what can be done to tackle the structural conditions which have resulted in one of the potentially richest countries in the world becoming one of the most unequal. The intention of these chapters is to "stick our finger in the wound" and get to the nub of the issues affecting Brazil's structurally problems related to economic development.

Part II explores the potential role for international organisations (IOs) in managing economic development without rent. It argues for measures that embolden their capacities to make a positive impact on development. It will specifically address how international organisations can effectively defend a rule-based globalisation in an anti-globalisation age. IOs can contribute in the fight against the rent-based capitalism of captured markets protected by undemocratic institutions amid a surplus of unused labour.

We go beyond the classic realpolitik, which marks the political dynamics within international organisations, to recommend ambitious solutions to world development. The international organisations directly addressed are intended as a hook on which to hang the main political economic policies and more tangibly sketch future development internationally. The final chapter muses on the role the multitude of modern social movements can play in that same mission.

Instead of relying on deconstructions and only criticisms, we want to leave the reader without doubt about our positions and the means we propose to reach them. Whatever we may be accused of, it is not exhausting a single idea. The link between the two parts is the proffering of potential transformations, nationally and internationally, to arrive at the same goal of open, equitable and prosperous development. In Part I, Brazil will exemplify how such a transformation may occur at the national level. Part II will look at development through the politically managed entities underpinning a rule-based organisation.

Style of the Book

A response article by different authors will follow each chapter. Therefore, there will be one response to the case study of Brazil and one for each of the international organisations' chapters, making it five responses. The responses directly follow the chapter, reacting to its strengths, weaknesses, illuminations, blind spots, and others. The responses come from scholars specialising in the themes in question. As will be evinced from the response articles, we have encouraged musings and criticisms to our chapters, as they strengthen the discussion and improve the reading experience. We aimed for the chapter and response dynamic to present ideas in a discursive format such there is simultaneous presentation of a variety of perspectives on the same topic.

Not Paying the Rent intends to be clear, concise, and uninhibited in its message, prioritising solutions over deconstructions. The aim was to have a non-strictly scholarly work, with a more direct and accessible language, but without escaping the need for evidence. As the astute observers of academic status will notice, neither of us have an academic title to our name. We both work as practitioners in international organisations in Vienna and outside formal academia. That distance from institutional academia and all that entails may go some way to explaining the unconventional approaches to content that follows. For example, we were warned against including response authors in the publication as we were told it would "devalue the publication on your academic CV to have other authors than just yourselves". Frankly, we have been far more concerned with providing a book which is through-provoking and enjoyable for the reader than climbing any academic ladder. We are interested in addressing the economics profession as much as that addresses the world, for economic policy well executed can fundamentally improve people's lives.

We hope this publication will add our two cents into contributing to new ideas in macroeconomics. More specifically, we hope it sings in chorus with the growing call to save capitalism for social ends, which is increasingly being recognised in mainstream discourse, e.g. Donald

Sassoon's (2020) "The Anxious Triumph: A global history of capitalism", Robert Reich's (2017) "Saving Capitalism: For the Many, Not the Few", and even the main economics commentator for the Financial Times newspaper, Martin Wolf (2019) in "Why rigged capitalism is damaging liberal democracy" (see also "Rentier Capitalism: Who Owns the Economy, and Who Pays for It?" by Brett Christophers, albeit not a mainstream publication).

For the remainder of the chapter, we will set out the themes that are crucial to understanding the *Not Paying the Rent*. Only then can the interplay among rent, capitalism, development, convoy model of globalisation, and labour marginality make sense in argumentation. Herein follows those definitions and a primer of rent in development economics.

The Threat of Rent to Economies

In the 1987 film Wall Street, Michael Douglas portrays Gordon Gekko, the stereotypical Manhattan financier with slicked-back hair, braces, gold watch, and the arrogance to match. The film showcases the greed and excesses of the 1980s in a financial system that does active harm rather than good to the variety of industries the system is theoretically there to support. Gordon Gekko epitomised a corrupt financial system. One of his loud rants to his subordinates sums up his role in the wider economy:

> The richest one percent of this country owns half our country's wealth, five trillion dollars. One third of that comes from hard work, two thirds comes from inheritance, interest on interest accumulating to widows and idiot sons and what I do, stock and real estate speculation. It's bullshit. You got ninety percent of the American public out there with little or no net worth. *I create nothing. I own.* We make the rules, pal. [Italics added]

While the film does not name-check rent, it is the type of economic exchange and its real-world implications Gordon Gekko characterises: non-productive investments over valuable production, a labour surplus unable to find work, the separation between assets and their financial values, an elite earning huge amounts while the masses are excluded from those returns, political guarantees on securing those terms of wealth, and using the economic surplus not for productive reinvestment but niche products. The young stockbroker that worked for Gordon Gekko, played by Charlie Sheen, rediscovered his conscience to scupper a hostile takeover by his boss which would have resulted in the asset stripping of the airline his father (played in the film by his real father Michael Sheen) ran the labour union for. In the final scene, the working-class father drives his repentant son to the New York Supreme Court House for financial crimes:

> Carl Fox [Father]: You told the truth and gave the money back. All things considered in this cockamamie world, you're shooting par…
> Bud Fox: Dad, I'm going to jail and you know it.
> Carl Fox: Yeah, well, maybe that's the price, son. It's gonna be hard on you, that's for sure. But maybe in some kind of screwed-up way, it's the best thing that could've happened to you. *You stop going for the easy buck and produce something with your life. Create instead of living off the buying and selling of others.* [Italics added]

Gordon Gekko who was portrayed as the turbo-capitalist with the catchphrase "greed is good" is the ultimate rentier in thwarting economic development by opting for non-productive investments which will make returns on unproductive investment (through venture capitalism) but scupper production (dismantling the airline company). Productive investment is the type of investment which meets a demand so is self-financing, for example, investment in construction is mostly productive as it generates rental income or business rates. The venture capitalism of Gekko may create profits, increase productivity,[3] and be politically backed, but it damages production, employment, and ultimately, economic health. Gekko's investment is unproductive in that they will extract value based on his *ownership* of the assets rather than what the assets will actually do in *competition*. The goal of this type of unproductive investment is usually to take someone else's money, by buying up something they need (land, property, electricity generation, market access) and then hold access to that something hostage while they are paid increasing amounts for it (hence the term, rent).

However, full employment capitalism (hereafter referred to as just capitalism) requires capitalists to use the surplus from their economic activity

[3] Incidentally, the fastest route to productivity increases is through redundancies but as Gilmour (1993, p. 85) writes, "[G]reater productivity is only of limited use *unless it leads to higher production*, producing relatively less while doing it more efficiently merely increases employment and redistributes incomes from those out of work to those still in it" [Italics added].

for reinvestment in production in a bid to increase efficiency amid competition so further expand production. To the difference to this profit-based activity, the surplus Gekko earns can be siphoned off for personal largesse and not rechannelled to further productive investments. In capitalism, labour shares in the surplus gains by increasing its wages proportionately, whereas in a rent-dominated branch or system, labour's gains are disconnected from the surplus.

The financial system which Gekko symbolises in the film is not adding value by promoting economic efficiency or expanding production, instead it is seeking to create wealth from its *ownership* ("two thirds comes from inheritance, interest on interest accumulating…stock and real estate speculation") rather than industries of productive growth in the real economy[4] based on its *competition*. Instead, the bloated financial sector is overwhelmingly redistributing wealth upwards and risks downwards and creating a new means for criminal intent through secrecy, evasion of prudential banking regulations, zero taxes, and worse (Shaxson, 2011, 284).[5] For example, Keynes painted the rentier as a "functionless investor" who sits back and looks on while existing capital grows through someone else's toil.

The rise of financial speculation in recent decades, stems from a lack of real demand in the economy, "Part of the reason for the rich valuations in today's markets…is that more newly-created money is chasing an ever-shrinking pool of investable assets as central banks take assets on to their own balance sheets" (Plender, 2021). That vain search for returns through speculation, and creation of artificial markets like the subprime mortgage scandal in the US rather than investing in productive outputs, points to defects in the capitalist system. Functioning capitalism relies on an empowered labour force which holds up demand through the mass markets it is able to create by its proportionate share of wage in economic growth.

Another characteristic of rentism is the political guarantees the financial sector has extracted which has inversed priorities to favour their

[4] The fracturing of financial prices and their value is a threat to an economy which will eventually lead to an economic crash. For an explanation of the result, see Hartmut Elsenhans in a video entitled "Hayek, Keynes and the Next Economic Crash" by Wilcock and Scholz (2016), https://www.youtube.com/watch?v=IlCK_m2yKik&t=3s.

[5] "Developing countries lost up to a trillion dollars in illicit financial outflows just in 2006 – that is, ten dollars out for every dollar of foreign aid flowing in."

stabilisation ahead of the real economy it is intended to serve.[6] Political guarantees were evident in the UK government's response in the aftermath of the 2008 financial crash when it propped up an overgrown financial system (which caused the crash in the first instance due to overspeculation), instead of shrinking it to proportionate size, criminally convicting the financial crimes and concentrating investments in productive activities. A truly capitalist system is as liable to destroy the capitalist, through competition, as the worker.[7]

The policy response rewarded the recklessness in one of the untold policy scandals of this century in the UK. Between 2008 and 2012, the Bank of England spent around £375 billion on asset purchases, in a policy of so-called quantitative easing (QE) to bolster liquidity in financial markets. In the Bank of England's own analysis paper (2012), it showed QE held up a range of asset prices, which are heavily skewed to the top 5% of households holding 40% of all financial assets:

> *The total increase in household wealth stemming from quantitative easing up to May 2012 is estimated at over £600 billion, equivalent to around £10,000 per person if assets were evenly distributed across the population. But the median household holds only around £1,500 of gross assets, whereas the top 5 per cent of households hold an average of £175,000.*

The QE billions were sucked up by the banks' balance sheets—and the bankers' continuing bonuses—so that their result was largely limited to further inflating asset prices which benefited the richest 5% (Elliot, 2012). The political guarantees asset owners were able to extract through QE was in stark contrast to the austerity measures implemented to public services, public sector wages, and welfare payments which impacted disproportionately those at the lower end of incomes which worsened inequality (which was the underlying reason for the crash in the first place, i.e. a lack of real demand in the economy due to wage stagnation[8]). Although

[6] Nicholas Shaxson's more recent publication "The Finance Curse: How Global Finance Is Making Us All Poorer" (2018) explores the political power and the pernicious effects of a bloated but influential financial sector, exemplified by the City of London.

[7] First explained by Joseph Schumpeter in his explanation of "creative destruction" (1942).

[8] Raghuram Rajan in his book Fault Lines (2011) argues that what led to the crash was not just greedy banks but growing social inequality in the West. When western governments were threatened by growing protests and dissatisfaction with this inequality,

the 2008 response was a high point, this is an established pattern in the UK, from the 1970s "dash to grow" strategy which through monetary policy expansion bolstered the ailing stock market temporarily but not the real economy right up to today in the response to the COVID-19 pandemic which the Financial Times reports "[C]entral banks' asset purchasing programmes [are] increasing wealth inequality and coronavirus [is] adding to social inequality" because they have "derisked public markets, at least in the short term, while taking more risk on their own balance sheets" (Plender, 2021).

The City of London, like the UK property market, exhibits much characteristics of rent-based economy. Policymakers continue to place a high premium on rising stock market prices and property values as sources of growth. Take appreciation of stocks (asset holders) ahead of currency as a long-term trend, "Equities…have outperformed all other asset classes, returning 12.4% a year in the UK since 1925, compared with 6.6% for global bonds and 4.9% for cash" (Wagstyl, 2021). However, the ill-effects of a rent-based system in the UK property are borne out: if prices don't rise, consumption falls; if house prices do rise, inequality rises. Rentism, not capitalism, resides at the heart of why the UK does not have a stable, growing and equitable economy.

Identifying Rent as a Threat to Capitalism

Dating back to the start of the nineteenth century, the concept of rent as a danger to capitalism is not new. It describes the appropriation of surplus from economic activity that is based on power as opposed to profit, the surplus that is based on markets. The significance is that rent leads to hierarchical and closed "non-market" structures whereas profit leads to full employment capitalism:

> *A profit-based scenario would be an independent company operating in a competitive market, for example any clothing, food, or car company. It is responsible to its customers, who are free to prefer the services of another company if they are not satisfied, and if enough customers feel the same way, it will be out of business while others make the profits. This is economic activity*

they simply bought the people off by giving them a mass of cheap money. An amazing statistic supports this, of the growth in real incomes between 1976 and 2007, 58% of it went to the top 1%.

> *determined by the choices on free and open markets, which new companies can enter and old companies can leave. The profit [surplus] the companies earn has to be reinvested in order to stay competitive, due to a capitalist logic.* (Wilcock and Scholz, 2016, p. 13)

Rent-based scenarios lack the compulsion for the surplus to be reinvested to improve efficiencies but instead is used to buttresses a small elite as owners without competition. Any company would prefer to be a private monopoly free from democratic government control and at liberty to remunerate themselves as highly as they chose. As Ian Gilmour (1993, p. 120) writes, "Who after all wants to be competed with? In theory, of course, competition is always desirable, but in practice only for other people". Whereas in capitalism, profit is when the surplus renders the seller wages for a healthy livelihood as well as reinvesting in his current production to stay ahead of competition:

> *The whole theory of overcoming underdevelopment is based on the idea that rent surpluses need to be reinvested but nobody is forced by capitalist logic to reinvest rent. The reason for that is we are not in a true capitalist economy and explains why development is failing.* (Elsenhans in Wilcock and Scholz, 2016, p. 17)

Archetypical rent scenarios are those that earn directly from natural resources, like valuable minerals (e.g. oil) which are easily extracted from the ground while the workers of those same plants do not share in the exorbitant returns:

> *[Rentiers] generate large economic surpluses in their state-controlled and resource-extraction sectors, in industries like telecommunications and oil, but these surpluses tend to be captured by the powerful economic and political elites of the state class.* (Elsenhans and Babones, 2017, p. 36)

Rent scenarios can both exist in smaller arenas (monopoly land ownerships), large parts of economies (financial system in the UK) or come to dominate the entire state, known as rentier states (the oil industry in Kuwait). Rentier states rely on a single product for the existence of the state with the rent being extracted from the most lucrative industry. While those countries, or rather a small national elite within them, have temporarily become rich due to massive natural resource endowments, they are neither capitalist nor high-income countries. Such economies are not capitalist because they do not possess the capitalist means of exchange (free and open markets) to generate high-income levels within the economy as they have never developed a middle class of earners.

Adam Smith contrasted two uses of the surplus in the scenario of the inefficient and efficient landlord: the inefficient landlord (the rentier) is wasteful by using his surplus to entertain large banquets, circus acts, girls for entertainment, and other largesse, whereas the efficient landlord (the capitalist) will invest in the improvement of his land and new technology. The rentier looks to protect his resources rather than expand them as extracting value (rent) under political protections is more lucrative and guaranteed than creating value (profit) from a competitive market.

Capitalism requires an empowerment of labour, meaning labour has negotiating power on the exchange of its work so it secures a proportionate share of the surplus. Empowered labour creates the conditions of mass markets based on mass consumption needs. A working-class capable of withdrawing or negotiating on markets creates the demand for mass consumption. Separation from full employment capitalism exhibits a lack of labour empowerment, without adequate demand to maintain mass consumption patterns.[9]

The compulsion to reinvest in capitalism demonstrates that economic growth and efficiency depend much more on competition than ownership.[10] The reliance on ownership, which characterises rentism, results in captive markets, or worse, unnatural monopolies. Unnatural monopolies restrain competition and keep inefficient producers going. The profits on monopolies are not reinvested in capitalist innovation/accumulation, but instead on the political and social structures that secure the terms of trade. The lack of competition results in consumers facing higher prices than in economies with fair competition. In monopolies, mark-up costs—an indicator of how much higher prices are above the cost of production—are pushed onto the consumer unfairly to maintain mark-ups (the surplus as

[9] Covered in depth in Chapter 5 "An Underconsumption Crisis" in Wilcock and Scholz (2016).

[10] And "when competition is impossible, public monopolies have usually been preferred to private ones which, unless the public interest is to be wholly ignored, have to be subjected to a high degree of regulation" (Gilmour, 1993, p. 120).

rents[11]). In this instance, both the consumer loses out in having to pay higher prices[12] and the economy overall in the rewarding of inefficiency.

Economist Abebe Aemro Selassie (2019) estimates the results of increased competition would double the pace of living standards improvements in sub-Saharan through the lowering of prices for goods and services, "It is competition which equates the margins, distributes resources so as to maximise utility, and generally makes the whole scheme work". Firms' mark-ups tend to be higher in the services sector, among the less-diversified oil-exporting economies and across state-owned enterprises, highly prevalent in Africa. An additional advantage of competition is it acts as a large incentive against corruption rather than a trigger of it "because they must innovate to keep up with competition on the world market".

Development depends less on the availability of resources for investment (in most cases there are resources to use in underdeveloped states), rather the condition of the market where the return is secured. Without that investment triggered off by a high prospect of market return, an economy will be cursed by rent. Sufficient investment is threatened through speculation, excess savings in the case of a recession or negative future expectations.

Marked inequality arises as a result of that surplus not being used on investment for mass market production but for niche products. Mass consumption drives growth and capitalist development while niche purchases impedes it. Many of the wonderful monuments around the world are as much a symbol of brilliance as they are of inequality. The Taj Mahal was constructed by royalty with too much money to feasibly spend that they resorted to encrusting a tower with diamonds instead of being forced to reinvest in productions that could lift the rest of the population from squalor and poverty.

Capitalism as a system is therefore not characterised by the level of overall wealth but by the need for reinvestment, mass markets and mass demand. This rings as true for post-industrialised countries with high per capita income as it is for countries with lower levels of industrialisation. In both cases, a continuous effort to overcome and avoid rent extraction

[11] In German, the economic term for it is actually producer rent (Produzentenrente) as opposed to consumer rent (Konsumentenrente).

[12] Prices being close to production cost reflects a competitive market.

is required to maintain and/or to further capitalism. While criticising the version of capitalism and its unsustainable direction, the harnessing of the productive power of market economies has led to a global reduction in global poverty, the rise in literacy, improvements in health and longevity (MacWhirter, 2020). No-other economic system can provide the motor for integrated global prosperity, and managed better, can be utilised to overcome the survival challenges of this century, notably the environmental threats. To borrow from Keynes (2008, originally pub. 1926):

> *Capitalism wisely managed, can probably be made more efficient for attaining economic ends than any alternative system yet in sight, but that in itself it is in many ways extremely objectionable. Our problem is to work out a social organization which shall as efficient as possible without offending our notions of a satisfactory way of life.*

Overcoming Existing Rent-Based Systems

Overcoming rentism is the process of *state reformation* by mobilising rents in a transformative way. The breaking up of rentism should be aimed at the introduction of free and open markets for labour to become empowered which rent had hitherto blocked. In an early stage of capitalist development, agrarian reform is such an example of reducing the rent available to the owners of capital in favour of the consumption of the poor. At later stages of capitalist development, such state reformation means removing political guarantees on capitalist exchange, for example, not protecting the oversized banking industry after its proven burden on the economy, and instead, exposing productions to competition.[13]

Overcoming rent is a redistribution policy as it appropriates wasteful surplus (rent) and through creating open markets (means to profit) it can lead to mass incomes and mass markets for consumption. Markets operate according to the general power set in which it is embedded, which should be social and democratically managed. Therefore, capitalism aimed at social goals, which will sound like heresy to discourse on the left, actually has the capacity to dissolve privileges and guarantees:

[13] Or democratic control in the cases of natural monopolies, as the Norway example later will explore.

> *The most successful economies of the Global South are those that have been capable of channelling rents into support for employment using market mechanisms instead of macroeconomic state planning. It is, however, not market orientation per se which produces rapid growth but the combination of a large variety of measures for promoting employment of the mass of average skilled labour.* (Elsenhans and Babones, 2017, p. 74)

The discussion on overcoming rent is not only theoretical, mercifully, there are real-world examples to exemplifying it. Japan, South Korea, and Taiwan all overcame rent relations through radical agrarian reforms at the beginning of their economic development and have strong national labour movements which meant that their success in exporting high-tech industries spilled over into the economy at large (ibid.). The key is that rents, which are upholding inequality and blocking a capitalist system, are captured and intentionally used to absorb surplus labour to create sufficient labour demand scarcity.

In the case of Norway in the 1970s, the discovery of a huge natural resource in oil did not lead to a paternalistic rentier state like most others, instead the resource triggered economic development leading it to become the wealthiest country per head of population and among the most equal societies. Norway has escaped the "resource curse" that beset most other oil exporters:

> *Norway faced the same dilemma as every other new oil producer with no experience of the industry: if you rely too much on private foreign companies, too little of the oil wealth benefits the country in the form of government revenue or economic development; if you go too far in the other direction, you risk a bloated, politicised oil sector that evades both accountability to the people and competitive pressures to be efficient...The trick of the Norwegian model was to retain the private sector's competitive drive and its expertise – which Norway sorely needed – by making sure that the regulator was independent enough to rein in the state oil company as well as its private-sector peers.*[14] (Sandbu, 2009)

[14] For a fascinating insight into the Iraqi immigrant, Farouk al-Kasim, who was the main architect of the Norwegian model, see Financial Times profile "The Iraqi who saved Norway from oil" (Sandbu, 2009). Also, search out the television series, Lykkeland (or State of Happiness in English) on the discovery of oil in Norway in the 1970s and the pressures to sell exclusivity rights to the multinationals backed by major Western powers (the US). While the 1983 film Local Hero portrays US investors coming to Scotland in the late 1970s when the country struck oil and depicts how the foreign big businessman

Since 1996, every krone the government has earned from oil has gone into a savings fund known as Norway's sovereign wealth fund. In less than 25 years, it has grown into a $1.2tn giant, owning 1.5% of the world's publicly traded companies, worth more than triple the country's gross domestic product and equivalent to a remarkable $225,000 for each of Norway's 5.3 million citizens (ibid.). Most of the fund's value comes from accumulated gains on bonds, shares and property while regularly covering a sixth of public expenditure. Despite the sovereign wealth fund being set up due to the discovery of oil, none of the oil money has even been spent yet and only invested for the country's resilience and development.

As the Norway example demonstrates, existing rents can be used for increasing growth for the economic welfare of the whole society when lucrative resources are not used for niche products of a small elite but socially and democratically managed in the interests for whom it belongs. At that point economic growth no longer entails merely an expansion of gains for the already advantaged, as growth of that kind does not encompass proportionate increases for all sections of society but just for those in control of the resources. Growth can then serve to increase, not decrease, inequality. Norway is a prime example of economic growth for *development*, as a high standard of living resulted from its economic growth. Development will result from economic growth if resource administration is embedded within institutions aimed towards social goals rather than for a cost-reducing capitalist class:

> *[M]anagers of private market-oriented companies rarely have a view of the overall macroeconomic relations. They see costs—including especially the cost of labour in the wake of wage increases—primarily through the lens of their own profitability. To them, costs are nothing more than a drag on their profits and hence an obstacle to growth, whereas in reality the higher consumption that is made possible by higher wages is strongly beneficial for capitalist growth.* (Elsenhans and Babones, 2017, p. 45)

Evidently, a fair management on capitalism and the social democratic politics needed to enact it are inseparable within a medium to long-term perspective. There is no way of creating a rich, equal and prosperous society without a profitable economy and neither a prosperous economy without its democratic and responsible political management.

are so charmed by the quirky locals they choose not to pursue their money-making venture—the film is aptly a fantasy in Scotland's case.

The Global Relevance for Overcoming Rent

So far, the relevance of overcoming rent has been discussed in the context of national economies at different stages of economic and capitalist development. What is the case for economic development within economies, however, is also the case for economic development at a global scale. Elsenhans takes the profit-rent dichotomy discussed above a stage further in his "convoy model of globalization". The model describes the profit mechanism operating internationally between countries that pushes towards the converging of productivities globally. Without delving into a full explanation of the model (see Chapter 6 of Wilcock and Scholz, 2016), it connotes a mechanism of conjoined economic development for a successful *global economy* rather than just individually successful economies. Such a model of globalisation rests on both the developed economies taking the lead to stimulate the world economy through higher levels of demand while developing economies beginning the processes of catching-up through (green/tech) industrialisation and the resulting mass markets:

> *China is an example of a country that has developed through industrialisation, a devalued currency and increasing wages; it now acts as the leader for less advanced countries like Vietnam and Thailand in that China's increasing internal demand is fuelling their exports as they absorb them.* (ibid., 57)

There is a cascading effect within the development model, hence the "convoy" name, such that economic growth in one country is to the benefit of its contact countries, and not to their detriment as it is often characterised within a "global competition" narrative. There are various levers available to the developing state, such as a deliberate devaluation of the currency in order to become competitive, protection of infant industries, or increasing mass incomes, while leading countries (Germany and Japan today) through their demand provide a stimulus for others' development just as they benefited from others' demand in the past. The significance of such a model is it offers both the possibility of global development through capitalism against the threats from a globalisation led by rentiers.

A Choice Between Two Futures: A Capitalist or a Rent-Based System?

With the continued squeeze on the cost of living because of the Great Recession (2008–2015) and the longest period of wage stagnation since the Napoleonic Wars, people are wondering if capitalism has a future. This seems natural given that the present global economic situation is leaving labour unable to exercise an increasing share in productivity increases (i.e. lack of wage increases) due to labour surplus. While the latest chapter of global economic history has brought about richness and largesse for some, it has brought mass insecurity and poverty for even more. That inequality is not the core tendency of capitalism, as Marxists' believe, but rather signposting its breakdown, and if not stemmed, presaging its demise.

Where Marx is correct is the tendency of capitalism towards highly unequal modes of production and shares of its spoils, a trend towards inequality that has been increasing due to the weakening share of labour. However, political intervention can and has "Saved capitalism from the capitalists" (Elsenhans, 2015). Donald Sassoon argues that capitalism has been (accidentally) saved by progressive political influence, "The socialists wanted the abolition of capitalism but the reforms they advocated tended to strengthen it" (quoted in MacWhirter, 2019). Capitalism could never have created the consumer society of the latter half of the twentieth century without labour influence. Only by electing social democratic governments, which redistributed some wealth and the existence of an organised working class,[15] rescued it from its own excesses (ibid.).

Until today, Marxists cannot acknowledge that capitalism has raised the standard of living of the average worker, instead seeing advances as revealing only more exploitation. When the worker received a television and a car, it was said at the time, it is only yet more time he will need to invest to pay for their upkeep. Marxists also turn a blind eye to the constantly declining differences in life expectancy between the rich and the poor between the 1870s and the 2010s which coincides with mass consumption expansion (Mortimer, 2020).

Lenin stated that socialism had the best chance of succeeding the more an economy prospered productively and equitably. Marxists will repel at the proposition that market relations and economic growth can

[15] Marx predicted the organised working class would be the agents of capitalist destruction.

be complementary solutions instead of redistribution. We contend both expanding market relations and redistribution (by overcoming rent) are complimentary for social ends. The level of economism within society indicates that we can only rescue capitalism *and socialism* from within the current system—transformation rather than revolution.

One possible future is dominated by rent, which upholds existing inequalities and resists change from within. A portent of that future dominated by rent is the elevation of financial investments over the real economy in the last 30 years. A rent-based system will still have "markets" in name, but they will be deeply entrenched in "non-market" structures and a pseudo-democracy devoid of ideological choice. Liberals may then finally recognise the importance of strengthened labour in maintaining capitalism and socialists accept the value of competition. In a cheeky antithetical nod to Fukuyama's "End of History" (1993) prediction in the hegemony of liberal democratic capitalism, Elsenhans paints an alternative future in "Saving Capitalism from the Capitalists" (2015, p. 201):

> *[G]overned by ruling classes with very well-ordered selection principles not so different from the civil service of the ancient Chinese Empire…This ideological turn will put capitalism out of mind, and in the end describe it as a temporary phase of disorderly growth of technology which could have been brought about also without these disturbances…a new and stable tributary mode of production will appear as the end of history.*

There needs to be an innovative restoration of capitalism to protect it from itself, otherwise we are sleepwalking into a globalisation of rent, solidified market imperfections of an overinvestment in financial resources, political patronage, luxury not mass spending, labour surplus, markets with increasing barriers to entry and spending on product differentiation and marketing. All of which will ultimately result in hierarchical and unaccountable systems of power.

To avert this dystopia, it is incumbent on the developed states to absorb global demand that is in effect a starting point in a cooperative convoy model of global development. Otherwise, globalisation is at risk of losing the benefits of full employment capitalism, namely prosperity, equality, and freedom. Social democratic politics and the working classes must once again (accidentally) save capitalism from itself.

Bibliography

Bank of England. (2012). The Distributional Effects of Asset Purchases (12 July 2012), Accessible at: https://www.bankofengland.co.uk/-/media/boe/files/news/2012/july/the-distributional-effects-of-asset-purchases-paper.

Christophers, B. (2020). *Rentier Capitalism: Who Owns the Economy, and Who Pays for It?* London: Verso.

Elliot, L. (2012). Britain's Richest Gain Most from Quantitative Easing. In: *The Guardian Newspaper* (23 Aug 2012), Accessible at: https://www.theguardian.com/business/2012/aug/23/britains-richest-gained-quantative-easing-bank.

Elsenhans, H. (2015). *Saving Capitalism from the Capitalists: World Capitalism and Global History*. New Delhi: Sage.

Elsenhans, H. and Babones, S. (2017). *BRICS or Bust? Escaping the Middle-Income Trap*. Stanford: Stanford University Press.

Fukuyama, F. (1993). *The End of History and the Last Man*. New York: Avon Books.

Gilmour, I. (1993). *Dancing with Dogma: Britain Under Thatcherism*. London: Pocket Books.

Keynes, J. M. (2008). *Laissez-faire and Communism*. Whitefish, MT: Kessinger.

Macwhirter, I. (2019). Iain Macwhirter on Two New Books About Capitalism. In: *The Herald Newspaper* (14 July 2019), Accessible at: https://www.heraldscotland.com/life_style/arts_ents/17756767.review-anxious-triumph-global-history-capitalism-fully-automated-luxury-communism-manifesto/.

Macwhirter, I. (2020). Book Review: Can the Slowdown Lead to a Better Society? In: *The Herald Newspaper* (25 April 2020), Accessible at: https://www.heraldscotland.com/life_style/arts_ents/18405123.book-review-can-slowdown-lead-better-society/.

Mortimer, I. (2020). The Best of Times…the Worst of Times. In: *BBC History Magazine* 21, no. 12 (December 2020): 66–72.

Plender, J. (2021). Debt Dangers Hang Over Markets. In: *Financial Times* (8 January 2021), Accessible at: https://www.ft.com/content/91efe8fa-857c-438a-a0f3-96dfb8e7daaa.

Rajan, R. G. (2011). *Fault Lines: How Hidden Fractures Still Threaten the World Eonomy*. Princeton: Princeton University Press.

Reich, R. B. (2017). *Saving Capitalism: For the Many, Not the Few*. London: Icon Books.

Robinson, J. (1979). *Collected Economic Papers*. Oxford: Blackwell.

Sassoon, D. (2020). *The Anxious Triumph: The Making of Global Capitalism, 1880–1914*.

Shaxson, N. (2011). *Treasure Islands: Uncovering the Damage of Offshore Banking and Tax Havens*. New York City: Palgrave Macmillan.

Shaxson, N. (2018). *The Finance Curse: How Global Finance Is Making Us All Poorer*. London: Vintage.

Schumpeter, J. (1942). *Capitalism, Socialism, and Democracy*. New York: Harper & Bros.

Selassie, A. A. (2019). Boosting Competition for Faster Growth in Africa. In: *New Vision, Ugandan Newspaper* (28 October 2019), Accessible at: https://guardian.ng/opinion/boosting-competition-for-faster-growth-in-africa/.

Sandbu, M. (2009). The Iraqi Who Saved Norway from Oil. In: *Financial Times* (29 August 2009), Accessible at: https://www.ft.com/content/99680a04-92a0-11de-b63b-00144feabdc0.

Sandbu, M. (2020). There Will Be Shocks: Yngve Slyngstad, Norway's $1tn Man. In: *Financial Times* (20 November 2020), Accessible at: https://www.ft.com/content/db3246a1-1a33-4448-899c-c3680a85cac1.

Wagstyl, S. (2021). Wildebeest Investors and the Dangers of the Herd. In: *Financial Times* (15 January 2021), Accessible at: https://www.ft.com/content/328959a6-4013-4880-a321-f5fae122f5cf.

Wilcock, N. and Scholz, C. (2016). *Hartmut Elsenhans and a Critique of Capitalism: Conversations on Theory and Policy Implications*. London: Palgrave Macmillan.

Wolf, M. (2019). Big Read: Why Rigged Capitalism Is Damaging Liberal Democracy. In: *Financial Times* (18 September 2019), Accessible at: https://www.ft.com/content/5a8ab27e-d470-11e9-8367-807ebd53ab77.

CHAPTER 2

Inherited Underdevelopment?

Edgar Federzoni dos Santos and Neil Wilcock

Introduction

Human history flows in only three directions: revolution, reform, and status quo. Few words in politics spark more anxieties than revolution. It often reminds us of force and violence, and it has, indeed, shed a tremendous amount of blood around the world. Some revolutions have freed oppressed peoples; others have oppressed free peoples, while others still have served as an unlawful rotation of elites in power. Without value judgement, however, revolution is an inevitable experience for a species with an ever-changing understanding of reality and its role in the world.

Reform, on the other hand, is incremental and just not as appealing. Those who see a revolution-based history as being the only possible outcome (i.e. Marxists) dismiss reforms and reformists and accuse them of impeding real emancipation. Nevertheless, reform is, by far, the most

E. Federzoni dos Santos (✉) · N. Wilcock
Leipzig University, Leipzig, Germany

N. Wilcock
e-mail: neil.wilcock.07@aberdeen.ac.uk

E. Federzoni dos Santos
University of Vienna, Vienna, Austria

N. Wilcock and E. Federzoni dos Santos (eds.), *Not Paying the Rent*,
https://doi.org/10.1007/978-3-030-78861-2_2

dominant form of political change. Regimes, systems, and governments commonly adapt to shifting historical, political and economic contexts by promoting small alterations in policies and legal frameworks. Revolution is not always necessary, sought or possible, while reforms are easier to implement, favoured by the powerful and less likely to attract widespread reactions or opposition. Not unrarely do failing regimes opt for promoting reforms as an attempt to boost their survival. Modern authoritarian regimes also favour incremental adjustments in electoral, constitutional, judicial, and legislative mechanisms, as opposed to tyrants of the past who more abruptly seized power. Constant reform is, however, necessary as new problems and solutions arise, even if it is palliative that does not bring the essential change required.

Status quo is the least acknowledged but potentially more damaging and undesirable than the other two forms. Nevertheless, what does status quo mean? In this book, it will mean the planned maintenance of practices, laws, policies, mechanisms, structures, institutions or elites, across time, detached from and/or disregarding historical and contextual changes. Obviously, no polity has ever remained entirely static through time. However, structures might change so little that the practical outcomes of their forces upon society are virtually the same, decade after decade, even century after century. As recent examples one can see Russia and Turkey. The status quo is, therefore, a concept more directly related to outputs than to inputs.

Even the strongest of structures succumb to the pressure of historical changes. The French Revolution inspired the revolts in the Americas that resulted in the end of colonisation in that Continent. The Industrial Revolution forced the fall of mercantilism and with it vanished four centuries of absolutism in Europe. In other words, it takes deliberate, active force and resources to counteract historical transformations. The more time structures act to maintain the status quo, the stronger is the force needed to accomplish it. Epitomising this phenomenon are rulers who seek firmly to stay in power and, over time, evolve governments into authoritarianism, then occasionally into totalitarianism, to preserve their structures of control.

Reforms are often necessary, revolutions are sometimes crucial, but what then is the advantage of avoiding the vicissitudes of time and keeping the status quo? None, except for the influential decision-makers benefitting from its maintenance. Brazil has never really had a nation-wide revolution; it does all its catching-up (when it has done so) through reform, but it is most guilty of strenuously protecting its status quo. Let us elaborate further on that.

Status Quo and Underdevelopment in Brazilian History

The year was 1500 when the Portuguese officially took possession of some parts of the territory in today's Brazil and 1530 when they started colonising that same territory. While it is a long time ago it is also how far back some structures have existed, almost entirely intact.

Determined not to invest many resources from the indebted national treasury, Portugal hesitated for 30 years to establish any form of government in or to send colonisers to the newly conquered lands. The rule over the territories was limited to a few missions per decade to trade brazilwood (hence the country's name) with some indigenous peoples and to bring prisoners who would be abandoned there for years so that they learn the language of the indigenous populations to help the Portuguese find and negotiate more products during their subsequent expeditions. The disinterest of the Portuguese was such that the French found themselves mostly unimpeded to navigate all along the Brazilian coastline, ally with many of the local tribes and run a more voluminous and recurrent trade route with Brazil than the Portuguese would manage. After several unsuccessful attempts to supersede the French in trading with its own colony, King John III of Portugal ordered the establishment of a system of hereditary captaincies to impose his presence and power.

In this system, the king's entrusted noblemen received the concession of large strips of land to invest their private funds in business ventures in *Terra de Santa Cruz* (Brazil's former name). The king would allow the hereditary captains to exploit the land, resources, and the labour of the local peoples in return for taxes on profits. The expectation was that, without spending a single nugget of gold, the kingdom would produce new for-export products, primarily sugar from the sugarcane, which enjoyed high demand and meagre supply in Europe at the time. Thus, the first act of the first Brazilian government was the establishment of a rent-based, non-developmental, pre-capitalist, and exploitative system. A government was established of landowners of swathes of land in control of the most productive assets for export.

To explain what is meant in theoretical terms, "Rent is defined by the power-based means from which it is collected, which is in contrast to profit – the other type of surplus – which is collected on the basis of competition. Under the conditions of competition, capitalist producers are forced to reinvest their profits in order to remain competitive, which serves as a motor for growth, as opposed to rent-based economies where the so-called 'capitalists', more accurately rentiers, are under no duress to reinvest their surplus as, owing to a power relation, they have guaranteed returns" (Wilcock and Scholz, 2016, p. 12). Rent is therefore incongruent with development, as it yields no investments, no innovation, no expansion of formal internal mass markets, no generation of mass income, and no general improvement in life quality. Instead, it rewarded a tiny elite in control of the extraction of resources used for their entrenchment of ownership (and control) of the lucrative state asset.

The colonial relationship determined that the *metropolis*[1] had a trade monopoly with the colony, and therefore, all economic output from the captaincies must be taken solely to Portugal. With this, the coloniser profited twice: first with the taxation over the production, and second by accumulating precious metal from the export of colonial products. The colony's economy was, then, entirely isolated and fully immersed in the European mercantilist system.[2] The captaincies model, however, did not thrive as expected. Only the Pernambuco and Sao Vicente captaincies prospered to the point where the captains would have solid returns on their investments. All the other captaincies either failed to control or enslave the locals, were attacked by locals, had their lands invaded by the French or the Dutch or had gone bankrupt due to mismanagement. Even in this context, the captaincies system was still advantageous to Portugal given that any economic output, no matter how small, came at no cost to the Crown's and was generally lucrative at the end of the day.

At the same time, a few European commoners moved to and settled in the new world outside the designs of the Kingdom of Portugal. These individuals had no royal-assigned lands, no slaves and no intention to produce for export. Many ventured in search of gold and silver; others

[1] Metropolis is the term used to designate the central government, or the coloniser, in a colonial system. The metropolis of colonial Brazil was Portugal, just like the metropolis of the 13 American colonies was England (and later UK).

[2] There is a lengthy historiographical debate around whether the Portuguese colony was or not more resembling of the feudal system instead of mercantilism, but this discussion is beyond the concerns of this book. We will focus more on the practical effects of the system in the economy than on conceptual labels.

allied with local tribes by marriage; and others founded villages in the countryside or the jungle, outside of the immediate reach of the hereditary captains. As Portugal did not have a direct political and military presence in *Terra de Santa Cruz*, it became impossible to inspect remote areas away from the captaincies' capital towns. This means that the outlier settlers lived independently from the metropolis and created, together with the indigenous, an informal, independent internal market that was based on small entrepreneurs, ownership of the means of production, labour empowerment, no slavery and free production, and trade systems among themselves. By the seventeenth century, this informal economy was already more extensive than the formal, exploitative rent-based economy (Caldeira, 2017, pp. 100–101).

Comparatively, the US and Canada experienced a different type of colonisation: settler colonisation.[3] As the main characteristic of this form of domination, colonisers would send a sizable contingent of settlers to live and work freely in the colony. The landownership was private and of small to medium size which incentivised the settlers to move as they lacked it at home. Although there was slavery in the US, it was not a tenet of the settler colonisation. Production targeted the internal market and the polyculture, and the Thirteen Colonies mostly enjoyed economic and trade autonomy, with very few exclusive ties with the UK. The colonies were politically free and self-governing, being allowed to organise themselves and elect their local leadership. As opposed to *Terra de Santa Cruz* (Brazil's early name), the colonial US also had freer communications, more robust infrastructure, and better dissemination of ideas. The impact on society and the economy alike was remarkable. By 1812, the US had 50 universities, whereas Brazil opened its first in 1909. Even the rest of Latin America, which also experienced an exploration-based form of colonisation, had 31 universities already by 1828. The first printing press

[3] It is important to be clear that the argument here is not one of a good or bad colonisation. All forms of colonisation involve violence, abuses, murder, and imposition of non-existent racial superiority. The story of colonisation in the US and Canada is no different from that of Brazil when it comes to the disregard and genocide of local populations and violent invasion of their territory. Instead, the argument posed here is solely to point out that varying historical factors necessarily lead to diverging outcomes. Colonial Brazil and the US experienced contrasting economic systems, which led them on different paths. For the specific and targeted economic analysis proposed here, the factors in place in the US were more conducive to an early economic development than in Brazil.

only arrived in Brazil in 1808, when the Portuguese royal court moved to the country. Until then, books and newspapers were mostly forbidden.

Additionally, the US had rail and road networks integrating the cities of the interior since the early years of settlement. In Brazil, there were no trains until the nineteenth century, and Portugal forbid the construction of roads between villages and cities to curb the growth of the informal, internal market. Only routes from the plantations to the ports were allowed. As a result, by the end of the eighteenth century, the US and Brazilian economies had a similar size, yet, by the end of the nineteenth century, the US economy was already 15 times larger than Brazil.[4] This is the outcome of more than three centuries of maintenance of a monopolistic rent-based status quo that brought benefits to a handful of rentiers at the expense of development for the country. The economic model had not been viable since the seventeenth century, but it was only in the nineteenth century, specifically in 1850, that the newly established Brazilian Empire revoked the hereditary captaincies law and enacted another providing for a private land-for-purchase framework. Nor, however, can this action be seen as an attempt to modernise as only the same wealthy noblemen could afford to buy land, which in turn lead to familiar outcomes: extreme concentration of the means of production, little-to-no investment, no innovation, no competition, and no generation of mass incomes and exploitation of labour. By this point, there had been 350 years of virtually stable economic and political structures and elites imposing non-developmental policies.

Brazil and its elites resembled a prototypical rent-based situation, "When the rentiers base themselves at the centre of state productions, they constitute a 'state class' from which they secure access to those rents and insulate themselves from competition" (Wilcock and Scholz, 2016, p. 12). In other words, the wealth accumulated through the direct interference or facilitation of the government comes without effort. Profit becomes a concession of the State, in effect a political extraction of surplus and complete reversal of the profit mechanism in functioning capitalism. "Profit earners have to go for investment. This is in stark contrast to those who receive rent, where the compulsion to stay competitive is not there: the guaranteed revenues hinder the necessary economic diversification to

[4] Interview of Jorge Caldeira to Instituto Millennium, 2018. Accessed at: www.institutomillenium.org.br/blog/jorge-caldeira-fala-sobre-o-livro-historia-da-riqueza-no-brasil-no-podcast-rio-bravo.

overcome underdevelopment, so they are more interested in their position in a power relation" (Wilcock and Scholz, 2016, p. 16).

There was no room for entrepreneurship and increasing investments in the Brazilian colonial formal economy, as Lisbon siphoned all production and capital gains via taxes, returning almost nothing to the colony that produced them. Worse, the money generated went mostly to the pockets of the royalty in Lisbon and their representatives in Brazil. With resources in the hands of a selected few used for private pleasures, little was left for infrastructure, production of consumer goods, public services, nor the creation of formal internal markets—the basis of a fully functioning capitalist development. This practice is seen throughout Brazilian history. For example, figures show that by the mid-nineteenth century, already after formally splitting from Portugal, the Brazilian emperor pocketed as much as 18% of the country's GDP for his own personal projects (Caldeira, 2017, p. 224).

By definition and practice, labour exploitation and slavery are inconsistent with economic development, activities that prevailed throughout Brazilian history. Brazil was the country to receive the most enslaved people in human history, around five million of them. Indeed, slavery was the motor of economic growth in the entire Americas. Slaves are low-cost assets (they only cost their bare subsistence: crude nourishment, health maintenance and accommodation to keep the person alive and well enough to work) who produce large outputs and, as a result, enable their masters to profit greatly. In reality, however, slavery constitutes an instance in which the causality between growth and development is broken. Generally, an increase in the production of material wealth (growth) is accepted as a prerequisite for an improvement in a population's welfare and living standards (development), particularly in poor countries, but should not be considered as the final goal. Improvements in infrastructure, public services, education, health, purchasing power, and more that characterise development require investments. No nation has significantly transformed its social reality without economic growth. China, Brazil and South Korea saw a human development (HDI) increment of roughly 25% from 1990 to 2017. In the same period, China's GDP grew 3,023%; South Korea's, 575%; and Brazil's, 94%. It is tempting, therefore, to affirm that growth necessarily raises development.

Nonetheless, one cannot help but notice the mismatch between the economic and HDI growth rates in the three countries. As a comparison, the Chinese economic revolution of 3000% economic growth produced the same HDI progress as Brazil, despite its 94% growth rate only. It shows there is no direct proportional causation between economic growth and economic development. That is case in every slavery-based economy: growth does not precede development. As Elsenhans and Babones explain it: "in the absence of a strong pressure from below, the main challenge facing the BRICS countries is that economic growth will serve and empower the rent-seeking classes of the new rich before the mass of the population comes to be empowered through labour scarcity" (Elsenhans and Babones, 2017, p. 105). In other words, growth expresses the absolute increase in material wealth in a territory, disregarding the application and destination of such new resources, and not meaning it is available for the benefit of society. In historically rent-based and elite-serving systems such as Brazil, more commonly than not, wealth generation tends to concentrate in the hands of oligarchic groups.

In an ideal capitalist economy, entrepreneurs sell and profit, reinvesting their extra capital in production, innovation, and technology, consequently raising worker income. With an increase in incomes and an expansion of the market, consumption increases and incentivises more production, profit, investments, technical and knowledge advancements. And the cycle is repeated. However, in slavery-driven Brazil, capital gains went to buying more slaves to explore vaster portions of land, which brought about profits only to the landowner and the royalty. And an entirely different cycle is repeated. Capitalism depends on workers to earn in proportion to productivity gains, but slavery breaks such binds. Individuals who have no salaries, no freedom and no consumer choice do not form a market. Actually, slaves were not meant to create any market—instead, they exist by political desire. They were officially referred to as *instrumentum vocale*, Latin for talking tools, and were stripped of any citizenship or rights and did not have their humanity recognised, neither as individuals nor as members of society. They were the equivalent to pieces of equipment in the means of production. In short, economic systems anchored to labour exploitation necessarily live off rent. Moreover, the profit of the capital owners who exploit the work of others does not come from market competition, but instead from political power. In the case of Brazil, the Portuguese Crown, and later the independent Brazilian empire, maintained slavery as a means to work the vast territories of the countryside cheaply and to perpetuate the power of landowners, the fulcrum of the regime.

Brazil's history of thwarted development coincides with the account of labour scarcity needed for realised development:

> Labour that is scarce is able to link incomes to productivity increase and so share in the spoils of growth. Only scarce labour can negotiate better wages and thereby equalise lower class incomes, and it can only become scarce in the first place when there are mass demand and consequently, mass markets. Mass markets require entrepreneurs to reinvest their surpluses in order to remain competitive. The surplus not being limited means vast sums are appropriated through nonmarket means because investment spending is not required – the control of those lucrative markets through political power is a case of rent. (Wilcock and Scholz, 2016, pp. 36–37)

The driver here is the same as in the relationship between supply and demand. If the supply of labour is low, the relative demand for it will be high, and the value of work increases. Societies with a limited workforce experience higher wages and more dynamic consumer markets, which elevate production, profit, investments and, again, wages. This scenario also promotes technological advancement, as owners of the means of production will tend to seek alternatives to increase productivity without depending on increasingly scarce labour. All these factors together foster growth and development concurrently. Contrarily, low incomes and weak internal markets mark countries with labour surpluses (supply far outstripping demand). These systems only succeed if they direct their products overseas, as they need a market outside of their own to consume their home-grown goods.

Slavery impedes labour scarcity and promotes a labour surplus. As workers are unable to choose where to work, how much to work, or even whether to work at all, the number of slaves is only limited by landowner's financial capacity to purchase them. Along with the massive surplus from sugar, gold, rubber, and later coffee, Brazilian rentiers had enough resources to acquire a high number of slaves. In this context, the outlook of political or economic structures that could spark development was especially meagre.

One may argue that the US proved the contrary: that slavery could kick-start, sustain, and even boost economic development. The slavery-grown products in the Southern US were the basis for the industrial revolution of the colonies of the North. Shipping companies, manufacturers, and bankers alike needed cheap inputs from the South to thrive. However, the Northern economy was autonomous from the South and developed fully without slaves. It had a sizeable consumer market, small to medium-sized properties, and was industrialising quickly. Profits were invested and reinvested in technology and competitiveness. The South was, at the same time, reliant almost solely on raw agricultural products and the exploitation of labour and land. With a considerable surplus of cheap labour and lacking internal competition, the South behaved more like a rent-based economy, which was very distinct from the fast-developing capitalist North.

On the other side of the Atlantic, the UK had been pressuring countries, since the eighteenth century, to abolish slavery. With the advent of the industrial revolution and the beginning of capitalism in Europe, England needed progressively larger markets to consume its products, and slavery was an immense obstacle to this goal. Brazil was the last country in the Americas, in 1888, to formally abolish slavery[5] as resistance by its domestic rentiers finally succumbed to international and internal pressures. The 388-year history of slavery in Brazil is yet another hallmark of how forcibly maintaining the status quo (despite political, economic, social, and historical pressure) prolongs structures suffocating development.

In Brazil of 2021, much has changed. Brazil is no longer a colony nor a kingdom, and slavery is now illegal. The country has had a significant internal market since the 1950s, but some structures have been resisting the pressures of time and produce the same practical negative impacts on development as in the past. By 2018, there were 2,400 farms with more than ten thousand hectares (100 km^2, or 14 thousand football fields each), corresponding to only 0.04% of the total number of rural properties across the country, and occupying 51.8 million hectares (518 thousand km^2), or 14.8% of the productive area of Brazilian fertile land. This means that two thousand *latifundios*[6] occupy a space greater than 4 million other rural properties (Pina, 2018). Of all rural properties in Brazil, 62.4% are unproductive (Vezzali, 2006), whose owners profit by speculating on the appreciation of the land in the real estate market or by

[5] The first was Haiti in 1793, and by 1850, 84% of the countries of the region had already abolished slavery.

[6] Name given in Spanish and Portuguese, mainly in Latin America, to designate massive land properties (at times, larger than European countries) owned by only one person or family.

illegally extracting natural resources—notably through logging activities in the Amazon—thus, eliminating the need for investments, technological advancements, and labour expansion. At the same time, small and medium rural properties are the most productive ones, generating 97.5% of the jobs in the agricultural and livestock sectors as opposed to *latifundios* that only employ 2.5% (Vezzali, 2006). Being productive also forces these small entrepreneurs to compete in the market and to invest to stay economically viable. Simultaneously, estimates show that about 369,000 people would remain in a situation of labour exploitation in Brazil (Global Slavery Index, 2018). Most of these peoples work in the agricultural sector in regions where *latifundios* exist—unsurprisingly, the least developed areas of the country (in terms of both GDP and HDI). Such facts reflect the legacy of the rent-based system in Brazil, the political priority to maintain a status quo, and the inability to transform the economy towards development.

As an empirical example, a comprehensive study in 2012 analysed the possible effects of the colonial legacy in the formation of Brazilian municipalities on their current conditions of land and income inequality and the quality of institutions. In particular, the researchers employed area, latitude, longitude, and date of foundation to identify the municipalities belonging to the captaincies. Next, they estimated whether this historical characteristic of the municipalities is correlated with current institutions of municipalities considering various controls, such as the proportional area of the captaincy, having belonged to the cycles of sugarcane and gold, to be at the coast, distance from Portugal, soil type, amount of rain per year, altitude, average temperature, and municipal socioeconomic variables. The results suggest in a robust manner that the municipalities that belonged to the captaincies are associated with a greater concentration of land as measured by the Gini index (increase in half of the standard deviation), with a lower level of local public expenditure and less political persistence (stability) (Mattos et al., 2012).

A Tropical Country Left Out in the Cold

Another chapter of history that was detrimental to development was Brazil's deliberate isolationism. As mentioned, Portugal forced onto all its land possessions a Colonial Pact that segregated each from the rest of the world. The various Portuguese colonies around the world were only authorised to trade with Portugal; everything entering or leaving their borders was required first to have the king's consent. Businesses and economic and social activities that did not fit with the interests of the metropolis were not allowed to take place, and those who did not represent the king should not enjoy any autonomy or freedoms. Brazil was entirely alienated from the nascent globalisation of the age of discovery (fifteenth and sixteenth centuries) and the first industrial revolution. The most critical technological achievements of the West, namely metallurgy and shipbuilding, made it possible for the European nations to expand their economic activities throughout the known world.

Portugal coerced Brazil into playing by the same rules. There was no chance for the colony to be ahead of the game. Brazil had, from its early days, the potential to harbour a big population, create a significant internal market, use its incommensurable natural riches, and take advantage of the most ethnically diverse population in the world to build cultural ties across the globe, thus enabling mass exchange of ideas, goods, and technology. However, none of that was allowed.

The extension of the Portuguese Empire in the Americas was unprecedented in the European nation's history. By the eighteenth century, Portuguese settlers had already traversed the Tordesilhas Line,[7] invaded Spanish legal possessions, and gained rights over each by *uti possidetis*.[8] Most of this vast area was difficult to access, and Portugal had little interest in it except for enslaving indigenous people whom they encountered on the way, and used to extract natural resources. By and large, Portugal concentrated its activities on the coast. Plantations, roads, towns, infrastructure, and the presence of the State were found almost exclusively around the ports, with Brazil merely an export brand-name. Nearly the complete in-land countryside area belonged to the informal economy, neglected by the central government.

Changes arose when in 1693 gold and silver were discovered in Minas Gerais, a region 400 km from the coast. It was the largest gold reserve

[7] A Treaty signed by Portugal and Spain (1494) to divide the newly discovered world outside Europe between the two naval powerhouses. This legal instrument aimed at avoiding that both countries entered a war or claimed each other's territories and colonies.

[8] Latin expression and legal term meaning "may you continue to possess such as you do possess". In other words, if a person or people possess de facto a piece of land, even if not recognised by the authorities, on time, they can keep the land just for already being there.

known in the world at the time and would finance the Portuguese nobility's extravaganzas for over a century—a prime example of the use of surplus from natural resources for the production and acquisition of niche products for the elite rather than mass consumption goods for the population. By the seventeenth century, the revenues from the Brazilian economy already accounted for around 80% of Portugal's total state budget, mostly spent in the metropolis. In the middle of the seventeenth century, cotton started being produced at large scales, so that Portugal could export it to meet the needs of England's potent textile industry. All producers, however, were again positioned around the ports. Similarly, the sugarcane and coffee producers, in their own economic cycles, had their main hubs close to the coast.

It was only in 1890, 390 years since the discovery, that the first economic cycle embraced the interior of the country. Latex finally brought some wealth to the Amazon region. So not only was the Brazilian economy insulated from the international markets, but it was also kept apart from its own interior for virtually four centuries. Furthermore, at each economic cycle, all investments were to be pulled, almost entirely, from one region to another, depending on where the new precious raw material was found or could be cultivated. In other words, the economic success of a given area commonly followed the collapse of another. There was little economic interdependence and interconnection among the captaincies (and later provinces). Until the nineteenth century, by virtue of their de facto separation, the regions could not stimulate one another's development, similar to the US case.

One sees, then, a matter of a triple isolation policy: (1) Brazil isolated from the rest of the world; (2) the coast isolated from the countryside; and (3) every region isolated from every other region. This situation resulted in a fragmented economy, and a late sense of nation, which sparked several regional rebellions and constant social unrest and instability. Factors unconducive to sustained growth, let alone development.

The Brazilian colonial economy functioned based on monoculture and on-demand production[9] Whichever raw materials the economic powerhouses needed to buy, Brazil ran to provide. This explains why the fragmented country lived off cycles, always between sharp rises and subsequent crashes. It depended on the demand for imports of a given

[9] Excepting from the brazilwood that occurred naturally and never needed to be cultivated.

time, never having a significant internal market that could sustain stable economic activity. The monoculture-based economy lasted for six large cycles (brazilwood, sugarcane, gold, cotton, rubber, and coffee) or as many as 445 years (from 1500 to 1945).

A Change Is Gonna Come...but Not So Fast

One must acknowledge, however, that in 1808 several significant changes came along. Escaping the Napoleon armies, the Portuguese royal family and all its court's nobility set sail to Brazil under the protection of the British Royal Navy. At this point, the differentiation between colonised and coloniser ceased to exist. It was not the end of the colonial period, but it was undoubtedly the first relevant paradigm shift in Brazilian history. Brazil had been upgraded to a kingdom and for once enjoyed the benefits of being the centre of an empire. The taxation collected in Brazil had to be spent in Brazil. The ports opened to trade with the entire known world. Roads between cities and provinces started to pop up. Science began to flourish. The population grew faster and produced more, and the internal market joined the formal economy, which expanded like never before. Was a new era of development on the horizon?

Well, not so fast. Indeed, broader investments in the country coupled with the elimination of the Colonial Pact caused a developmental leap, as expected. However, the rent-based mercantilism founded on slavery and wealth concentration continued concurrently. Rio de Janeiro was the new Lisbon, where the most significant portion of the new taxpayer money stayed near the royal family. The Northern Brazilian region, for example, felt almost no impact of the transfer of the royal family to the country. In fact, just as before their arrival, no sense of belonging or a feeling of national unity was gained. In the nineteenth century alone, Brazil faced 32 uprisings and independence insurrections, ranging from struggles for more freedoms, political autonomy/participation, state modernisation, investments, and regime change, among other claims. In such an unstable environment, the economy fell short of its growth potential, as well as development not being a state aspiration. In comparison, Brazil saw an average annual growth rate of GDP per capita of 0.36% per year between 1800 and 1860, and of 0.40% for the period 1860 to 1910, compared with 2% for neighbouring Mexico from 1860 to 1910 (Abreu and Lago, 2010). Despite the contextual transformation, the practical outcomes of post-1808 Brazil remained wearily similar to those of pre-1808: a rigid, non-developmental environment; a pre-capitalist, captured economy; pervasiveness of rentiers' extractive economic and political power; and, above all, insufficient generation of mass incomes.

Following the defeat of Napoleon in Europe, the Portuguese king was forced to return to his country of origin and ordered to downgrade Brazil once more to the status of a mere colony, leaving his son behind to govern in his name. Still, the new Brazilian elite in Rio de Janeiro would not accept to be returned to a peripheral status after 13 years of economic and political protagonism. Thus, under pressure, the Princess Regent, D. Maria Leopoldina, signed the decree of independence of Brazil on 2 September 1822, which was confirmed by the Prince Regent, D. Pedro I of Brazil, son of the D. John VI of Portugal, on 7 September 1822. The separation came peacefully, and Portugal recognised the new country in 1825 after an agreement to pay a one-off indemnity of two-million pounds sterling to the former coloniser, roughly 50% of the Brazilian annual export volume.

The independence provided a great chance to break from the unproductive, anti-developmental structures of the colonial past. Nevertheless, Brazil was born governed by a European elite that mimicked the politics of the *Ancien Régime*: a physiocratic absolutism founded on slavery, rent, and a resource-absorbing nobility. Before independence, John VI of Portugal knew that his colony had grown much larger than the metropolis, and the breakup was imminent. He instructed Prince Pedro to proclaim himself as the Monarch in such a situation swiftly, and so he did. Pedro was crowned as the first emperor of Brazil in December of 1822, having as the only reference for politics and economy that of the Mercantilist Kingdom of Portugal. From the outset, he attempted to recreate in Brazil the glorious past, the golden times of the feudalism from centuries before in Europe. In sum, instead of modernisation, the inhabitants of the most recent American State witnessed a drastic return to the core of a worn down, failing system.

Pedro adopted an anti-industrial policy that crushed many businesses. To him, the wealth of a country could only be in its natural resources and agriculture, hence physiocracy.[10] The emperor saw nascent industries as an artificial and unsustainable entity of a soon-to-be-dead economic model. Additionally, entrepreneurs and industrialists were considered as

[10] An economic theory that the wealth of nations derived solely from the value of "land agriculture" or "land development".

a parallel power that defied the primacy of the State. This anti-industrial decree saw, once more, all aggregate savings upheld in the slavery sector, undermining industrial innovation or any production diversification that could be detached from primary exports. Ultimately, as there was no room for other activities to prosper it condemned Brazil to the failed economic cycles of the past. Competition was simply not allowed. The government represented only a family-run enterprise with favours to close friends. In return, the slave-owner rentiers financially sustained the regime that guaranteed their survival, and an incestuous, symbiotic relationship was perpetuated.

As Jorge Caldeira puts it, with the national government serving only ever more restricted interests, society reacted to its traditional way: effective progress continued to be made informally, in the secular realm of personal relationships. The market was made inside the houses, through relationships of trust, through the payments without money—because the laws provided for only a few economic transactions in a restricted circle. Political civility depended on tolerant coexistence between people, on customs that supported, in addition to economic exchanges: parties to socialise, ethnic mixtures and religious syncretism (Caldeira, 2017, p. 283). "The dilemma between meeting the needs of society (even if this was the society of landlords and slaves) and the defence of the king's monopolies placed the government (…) like a car tied to two locomotives, each pulling in one direction. The result was immobility, with long and sterile parliamentary discussions on how (…) not to break the mercantilist chains that tied them to the centre of power" (Caldeira, 2017, p. 288).

Repeatedly, it is a tale of how the mercantilist elite contorted themselves and society to protect the status quo. Until its very end (1889), the monarchy, both in colonial and post-colonial times, fought to resist the pressures to change. The structure in place thwarted free labour, income generation, mass consumer market, democracy, investment in productions, and, therefore, development. Brazil was one of the last nations to break free from its colonial ties in America. By the time it did so, all its neighbours were already republics, founded by their local population, competing to catch up in the industrial and capitalist revolution. In opposition, Brazil started as a white European stronghold, ruled by monarchs, imposing a pre-capitalist system averse to industrialisation. Such a long-standing anachronism anchored in anti-developmental structures inevitably led Brazil on a path that has limited its capacity to fulfil its potential.

Nevertheless, not all hope is lost. A more profound transformation came between 1888 and 1889, with the abolition of slavery and the proclamation of the republic, respectively. In the short term, without reliance on enslaved labour, the production costs rose, productivity decreased, and landlords no longer had collateral assets for bank loans. Banks mostly accepted slaves as a collateral, but not land without slaves. Unable to preserve its supporting elite's economic viability, the monarchy collapsed one year after the abolition of slavery. The republic was proclaimed on 15 November 1889 through a military *coup d' état* led by a monarchist general under the pressure of the landowners, urban cultural elite inspired by the French Revolution, and discontented military. As a common divisor, all considered themselves Brazilian and opposed the influence of the European *Ancien Régime* in their country. The great novel aspiration of this era was the will to catch up with the great powerhouses of the time, in the modern world context. It was only then that one could say that an original Brazilian national plan for modernisation and development came into being.

Bibliography

Abreu, M. P. and Lago, L. A. C. (2010). *A economia brasileira no Império, 1822–1889*. Rio de Janeiro: PUC Rio. Accessible at: www.econ.puc-rio.br/uploads/adm/trabalhos/files/td584.pdf.

Caldeira, J. (2017). *História da Riqueza no Brasil – Cinco Séculos de Pessoas, Costumes e Governos*. Rio de Janeiro: Sextante.

Elsenhans, H. and Babones, S. (2017). *BRICS or Bust? Escaping the Middle-Income Trap*. Stanford: Stanford University Press.

Global Slavery Index. (2018). Accessible at: www.globalslaveryindex.org/2018/data/country-data/brazil/.

Mattos, E., Innocentinni, T. and Benelli, Y. (2012). Capitanias hereditárias e desenvolvimento econômico: herança colonial sobre desigualdade e instituições. In: *Pesquisa e Planejamento Econômico* 42, no. 3 (December), Accessible at: http://ppe.ipea.gov.br/index.php/ppe/article/viewFile/1428/1124.

Pina, R. (2018). No Brasil, 2 mil latifúndios, ocupam área maior que 4 milhões de propriedades rurais. In: *Brasil de Fato* (26 July), Accessible at: www.brasildefato.com.br/2018/07/26/no-brasil-2-mil-latifundios-ocupam-area-maior-que-4-milhoes-de-propriedades-rurais.

Vezzali, F. (2006). *Especial Latifúndio – Concentração de terra na mão de poucos custa caro ao Brasil* (11 July), Accessible at: https://reporterbrasil.org.br/

2006/07/especial-latifundio-concentracao-de-terra-na-mao-de-poucos-custa-caro-ao-brasil.
Wilcock, N. and Scholz, C. (2016). *Hartmut Elsenhans and a Critique of Capitalism: Conversations on Theory and Policy Implications*. London: Palgrave Macmillan.

CHAPTER 3

Overcoming Underdevelopment?

Edgar Federzoni dos Santos and Neil Wilcock

Irineu Evangelista de Sousa, the Viscount of Mauá, had become the symbol of industrialisation and progress in monarchic Brazil. Despite the stringent laws against private industry, the Viscount managed to build a private empire. He was a powerful banker, constructed the first railroad, had a shipyard, an iron plant, installed gas street lighting in Rio de Janeiro and the first submarine telegraph cable between South America and Europe. Out of the ten largest private companies in Brazil, he owned eight. His enterprises and mounting economic influence raised an eyebrow in the Imperial Palace. The emperor was a physiocrat who thought the real wealth of a country could only possibly come from agriculture. The meaning of order to the mandatary was one in which the State is the thinking head, with society as the functional body to the designs and commands of the head. Mauá bluntly went against the

E. Federzoni dos Santos (✉) · N. Wilcock
Leipzig University, Leipzig, Germany

N. Wilcock
e-mail: neil.wilcock.07@aberdeen.ac.uk

E. Federzoni dos Santos
University of Vienna, Vienna, Austria

N. Wilcock and E. Federzoni dos Santos (eds.), *Not Paying the Rent*,
https://doi.org/10.1007/978-3-030-78861-2_3

political establishment of his time and quickly became a symbol of a new capitalist bourgeoisie struggling to thrive and break the shackles of absolutist mercantilism. He did not live to see a new regime bloom in the country, as he died just a few weeks before the downfall of the monarchy. Perhaps fitting for the time, he passed his last days bankrupt, following the stringent anti-capitalist regulations imposed by the emperor.

In 1889, the same bourgeoisie of which Viscount of Mauá was part, allied with a discontented army and weakened landowners, promoted a *coup d'état* to install a republican government. They meant to break with the status quo once and for all and kick start a new era of Brazil-driven interests and economic prosperity. Did they achieve their goal? If so, how? These are the questions that this chapter will discuss.

The previous chapter showed examples of how rigid structures from the colonial/imperial times sowed long-lasting economic inequalities in Brazil: the high concentration of land in the hands of few, disparities in regional development policies, dependency on single-crop cycles, political instabilities in the countryside, the economic dominance of coastal cities, and a deficient rule of law. All are phenomena whose roots trace back from before the republic. The transformations of the Republican era did not suffice to wipe out the old structures of power in the economy, society, and politics. Changes occur at differing speeds and produce divergent outcomes throughout the country. The declaration of the republic did not cause the same changes to Rio de Janeiro as it did, for example, to the Rio Grande do Sul (South), Amazonas (North) or Pernambuco (Northeast). It is fundamental to acknowledge that the analyses of the events in this chapter will attempt to take into consideration the contextual discrepancies but will mostly focus on the lowest common denominators that affected the whole nation.

When discussing politically induced transformations in Brazilian history, one must recognise that they did not take place consistently, steadily, and continuously in the same direction. The accounts of this chapter could tell of a boom in economic development and modernisation of political institutions in one decade, only to be followed by a lull in the next. Economic indicators, repeatedly, fluctuate between modern and premodern levels over the course of the twentieth century, especially in the heyday of the republican era (1889–1930). The reader should not forget the events of the previous chapter. Even if knowing that a national revolution has occurred in the late nineteenth century, this does not guarantee that a systemic change followed suit in all layers of society.

This chapter, however, will break down and focus on the factors that have led to a rapid development in Brazil in the early twentieth century. It will acknowledge but not elaborate an extensive analysis on the factors that rendered negative economic results. Isolating these economic enabling factors is fundamental to draw evidence-based, developmental recommendations in the coming chapters.

Something New Under the Sun

In the first decades of the republican regime, Brazil witnessed unprecedented figures in its economy. By 1889, there were fewer than one thousand industries in the country, by 1907 the census already counted 3.25 thousand of them, and in 1920 over 13 thousand companies were registered. Equally, industrial labourers increased from 6.4 to 12.8% of the workforce in the first 20 years of the twentieth century (IBGE, 1990, p. 74), and this despite a population 113% larger across the same period. The first conclusion one can derive from these indicators is that the physiocrats lost space in politics. Even many of the landowning elites started diversifying their businesses and investing in industries. The growth of industrial output points to the fact that an internal consumer market had expanded. Such progress was only possible after the abolition of the law requiring special governmental authorisation to open a private company, representing a historical rupture. No longer was the State suffocating the means of production. The elite backing the republican government was considerably more liberal and urban than the old feudal class. This new reality caused investments to gravitate more towards cities and around a new bourgeoisie interested in expanding domestic production and trade. In 1900, consumption stood at 16 Gwh, whereas by 1930, it achieved the 1,367 Gwh mark, representing an increase of 8,544% (IBGE, 1990, p. 493).

If in the colonial and imperial periods intraregional integration was not desired and mostly disallowed, subsequent years reversed that trend. Investments in infrastructure advanced significantly led by the rapid expansion of railroads. By 1890, there were less than 10 thousand kilometres of railways, only to see this figure more than tripled in 1930. Even more notable is the growth of transported goods by train in the same period, which leapt from 4 million tonnes in 1904 to 25 million in 1929 (Caldeira, 2017, p. 513). It shows unprecedented production output growth and infrastructure development. One of the main reasons for these economic increases was the fast expansion of the monetary base. At the beginning of the 1900s, the government broke the former policy in which currency should only be available to those individuals and businesses working with the Crown or under its auspices, thereby releasing vast amounts of currency into the domestic market.

Consequently, producers and traders from the countryside, formerly in the informal economy, finally had the chance to join the formal economy and be able to exchange products and services with anyone else in the country. The Brazilian economy was finally starting to connect with itself, especially the then isolated states of the countryside. Availability of money also facilitated the acquisition of consumption goods and ultimately spurred productive investments. Despite the inflationary side-effects, it was undoubtedly a game-changer as it repositioned Brazil from a mercantilist to a capitalist system. As money flooded the market, national entrepreneurs could now sate their thirst for capital by resorting to bank loans and do what was previously prohibited: invest in production goods destined for the Brazilian domestic market and ultimately create a profit mechanism.

Such a switch from the informal to the formal economy caused the country to look a lot more like the US over a century earlier. Regional markets began to create synergies, trading with each other on a larger scale, bringing them closer than ever before and incentivising business across state borders. Similar to how the cotton from the southern US sustained the industrial revolution of the north, which in turn re-fed the South's economy through increased demand for its raw products, south-eastern Brazil had ignited an accelerated phase of industrialisation that fomented the production of food and raw materials of the country's northeast. It was the first time in Brazilian history that one region's economy had significantly spurred growth in another, other than from the country's capital.

The reorganisation of the State contributed to yet another historical change: federal states, instead of provinces, would become autonomous to manage their economic and fiscal policies. It represented more than just a new political subdivision of the national territory: it marked the end of the total, direct control of the central government in Rio de Janeiro over the other regions. As mentioned in the previous chapter, that earlier total control had enabled the Crown to seize resources and financial means from the countryside for the king's will. With autonomy, the federal states kept most financial means for investments in their territories, considerably altering the geography of power and development.

What followed was a boom of investments in human resources and infrastructure, especially away from the coast and export-producing states. The state of Pará in the north, for example, which was traditionally an outlying region from the political centre, saw its public budget soar from 3.2 thousand *contos de réis*[1] in 1888 to 25 thousand in ten years. Most of these resources stayed in the state and were used to create a public education network and financed the distribution of land to farmers through a programme designed to attract migrant workers (Caldeira, 2017, pp. 354–355). More precisely, investments in education, professional training, and immigration incentives went from near 0 to 62% of the state budget in just seven years, while infrastructure spending expanded to 35% in the same period.

These numbers are revealing of burgeoning economic activity in that state, and other states of the time corroborate the trend. Sao Paulo city, the capital of the state of Sao Paulo, had a population of 47 thousand inhabitants in 1887, but just 13 years later more than 240 thousand people resided in the city. As the capital did not grow coffee, people were moving from rural to urban areas to work in the flourishing industrial sector (Caldeira, 2017, pp. 354–355). Notably, the textiles industry of Sao Paulo reached an entirely new standing in the late nineteenth and early twentieth centuries, hence the heightened demand for food, cotton, and other raw materials from the northeast. The overall tax income of all the federal states combined duly enlarged,[2] jumping from 196,787 *contos de réis* in 1908 to 1,270,970 in 1928.[3]

Along with the extra money in circulation and a promising domestic market, the Brazilian economic elite rapidly overcame the tight grip of the physiocrats. Despite remaining a primarily agrarian country, industrialisation in Brazil saw a clear spike in imports of industrial goods and machinery: from 1 to 5.5% of the annually imported goods between 1880

[1] The old currency of Portugal and Brazil.

[2] The combined income contracted only in 1911, 1913 and 1914, during the First World War.

[3] Instituto Brasileiro de Geografia e Estatística (IBGE), accessible at: https://seculoxx.ibge.gov.br/images/seculoxx/economia/financas_publicas/fp05_receitadespesamunicipios.xls. Accessed on May 2, 2020.

and 1890, and a general upward trend onwards. On average, industrialisation became a constantly evolving pattern from that moment onwards, which had not been the case in the centuries before despite the fast pace of the Industrial Revolution in Europe and the US. The initial phases of the Industrial Revolution did not spill over into Brazil thanks to the controlling hands of the monarchy. Thus apparent that the republican times brought along factors that promoted a sharp turn to development by initiating a capitalist mechanism.

Indeed, despite previous neglect, production and free employment would spike. As Jorge Caldeira's research reveals the regions of Amazonas and Para, as case studies, that:

> ...between 1890 and 1900, the population of Amazonas grew 70% and, in Pará, 37%. The value of rubber exports increased six-fold between the end of the 1880s and the end of the century...the six-fold increase in income in the Brazilian currency had immense effects on the growth of the domestic market. In 1897, Amazonas exported 37 thousand *contos de réis* and imported 15 thousand. In Pará, exports amounted to 116 thousand *contos*, and imports did not reach one-third of that value: 33 thousand *contos*. The trade allowed for the accumulation of internal capital, translated into the installation of a robust banking system, with paid-up capital of 22 thousand *contos*. (Author's translation of Caldeira, 2017, p. 353)

The population rise in those two states indicates that the local economic activity quickly reached labour scarcity and ended up attracting migrants from other Brazilian regions and countries. This labour scarcity had resulted in an average yearly net income growth of 3.1% for 21 years (Costa, 2012, p. 63). The development can only be explained through the new set of social, political, and economic factors in place, namely free and scarce labour, the growth of workers' wages, reinvestment of profits into further production, the advancement of labourer technical skills through state investments in education, improved infrastructure, and the application of export earnings into industrial production.

The quick developmental experience in the Amazon region was unfortunately short-lived, as it depended mostly on the resources arising from the rubber export cycle, as mentioned in Chapter 2. Local capitalists and governments alike failed in one crucial matter: they did not have a coordinated plan to diversify and strengthen the local economy to a point where it could survive the end of the cycle. State policy is essential to mobilise assets from transient profits from economic cycles towards long-term development programmes, such as the foundation of new industries and safety nets to protect workers' wages to keep internal markets running sustainably. Revenues from economic booms are useful to fund continuing development plans but depending on it alone is reckless.

The End of Slavery

There is a long history of debates whether slavery has been necessary for the booming of capitalist societies. This passage will not revive all the arguments from the different sides of the spectrum, nor will it go in theoretical details, but in the case of Brazil, the answer is yes and no. If the object of analysis is the formal economy, as sponsored by the State, then without doubt slavery was profitable for the few businesspersons involved in the production of exports relevant to the Portuguese/Brazilian Crown. Frequently, historians, economists, and experts have overemphasised the Brazilian economy as being that represented by the single-crop sectors supporting the monarchy's mercantilist venture. There is a general disregard of the informal economy of the countryside, which went unrecognised by the State but whose size was not negligible. According to current estimates, the informal economy seemed to have been more significant than the formal one throughout. Those many uncounted producers and traders, sometimes working for their subsistence and other times for capital accumulation, never employed slave labour. Instead, since the sixteenth century, they had applied traditional, although extra-official, forms of work agreements that guaranteed the liveability of workers and the sustainability of the regional economic systems.

For this B-side of the Brazilian economy, the more than five million slaves trafficked into the country never brought any advantage. Slavery was important for a fragment of the country's growth, benefitting only a small group of rentiers. One could argue that slavery was not conducive to development, as all capital gains arising from this mode of labour was concentrated in the hands of state-elite rentiers, who obstructed the development of mass incomes and consumer markets. This means that slavery served well those rentiers installed by the state elite and not the independent, productive sectors, which proved the source of future development.

It is crucial to briefly discuss the topic of slavery to show that the disadvantages of such a barbaric system affect not only the enslaved people but also society in its entirety. "Slave labour tends to pull down the wages of free labour in the same area, thus lessening the disposable incomes of free families. At the same time, slaves are not able to play a full role in their local economy in that they have little or no purchasing power, and so they subsist on the barest necessities" (Datta and Bales, 2013, p. 210).

Forced labour as a hindrance to growth is well known and documented. Enslaved people are deprived of essential services such as education, which makes it impossible for them to fulfil their creative and productive potential. In another slavery-based economy, the US, results were the same: labour exploitation was a tremendous obstacle to growth and development (Conrad, 1967).[4] Notably, the Southern US *per capita* income only began to catch up with that of the north following the abolishment of slavery. In comparison, most of the high-income, wealthy countries of the nineteenth century were those adopting free-labour only regimes. Unsurprisingly, the ten countries currently with the highest prevalence of coerced labour, according to the latest Global Slavery Index, are also among the poorest in the world: North Korea, Eritrea, Burundi, the Central African Republic, Afghanistan, Mauritania, South Sudan, Pakistan, Cambodia, and Iran (Global Slavery Index, 2018).

In 1888, one year before the founding of the Republic, Brazil removed that major obstacle to prosperity. Jorge Caldeira interestingly describes this new era:

> the abolition put an end to this slow (economic development) time, relenting to the values of the *Anciên Régime*, with an air of eternity fixed on the monopoly powers of the sovereign (the king), reflected in the economy by the cashless transactions allowed by the monopoly based on slave production. After the liberation of the slaves, the old masters became stricken, needy for money as their former slaves or any merchant. They suffered in the new time. Even with their main political base succumbing to the lack of money, the leaders of the party's economic policymaking were very reluctant (to accept the new times). They found it hard to believe that the need for money was subject to something as prosaic as supply and demand. They feared that by increasing the amount of paper money in circulation, they were falsifying the real promise of the currency's stable value, diminishing the gold value of paper notes by the inevitable crash of

[4] Meta-study conducted by a panel of experts from the City University of New York, Cornell University, and Universities of Rochester, Columbia, and Harvard, Dartmouth College and the Massachusetts Institute of Technology.

> the exchange rate that would follow - and destroying the sanctity of the Monarch's personal power (to control the economic mechanisms and to choose who profits). (Author's translation of Caldeira, 2017, pp. 287–288)

This excerpt illustrates well that, for the first time, rentiers had to compete for profit and survival in an open market. Guaranteed returns were no longer a given, and the rush to catch up in the new context forced many of the elites to invest in industries and to reinvest their profits in technologies and know-how, sowing the seeds for capitalism in Brazil.

Since 1850, capitalist countries interested in creating a broader consumer market in Brazil for their exports, allied with the French *Lumières* and progressive movements within the country, strived to compel the Brazilian Monarch to limit or halt the trade and recruitment of slaves. As a compensation for the loss of labour, there was already an ongoing process to attract immigrants and expedite the access to land for farmers willing to work on their own land. In that year, the government enacted the Land Bill, which established that land ownership would be available via purchase only, ending direct state concessions. The average Brazilian could not afford property, so the Bill intended to keep the land in the hands of the same elite but also to occasional foreign investors bringing capital and their workforce into the country. In 1888, however, the break with the slave system was definitive. Upon losing most of the country's workforce overnight, and unwilling to encourage employers to recruit freed slaves for pay, the federal government moved to ramp up the influx of labour migrants, forming a programme whereby the national budget would fund the European farmers'[5] inbound journey to Brazil along with their accommodation costs until they had found a job.

Until 1888, vast portions of land far from the coastal areas had remained predominantly unexplored. Centuries of indifference, lack of capital, and difficulties of access through dense forest coverage, coupled with limited capacity to transport goods across enormous distances, had kept investors away. Now, the government had decided to open economic frontiers and incentivise new productive ventures. The policies for such an endeavour were a success temporarily. Between 1889 and 1913,

[5] People from African and Asian nations were discouraged to come. The programme was clear in mentioning specifically white European experienced farmers as the only ones eligible for financial aid. In the beginning, it was also a requirement to be a Catholic to benefit from stipends, although this criterion fell early on.

2,606,525 people immigrated to Brazil,[6] most of whom went to Sao Paulo to work in the coffee plantations and the nascent industry of the state capital. By 1901, 90% of the industrial workers of Sao Paulo city were non-Brazilian born.[7] Furthermore, workers from several Brazilian rural areas migrated to cities, like Sao Paulo, in pursuit of higher wages, which on average caused the per capita income to shoot up together with the domestic consumer market and GDP. This positive effect was only possible due to the workers' ability to choose their professional activity. In other words, higher levels of labour empowerment are necessarily related to growth and development.

It is crucial, however, not to romanticise the new situation in Brazil, as the government had maintained remnants of its former authoritarian labour laws. For example, employers had legal mechanisms to force migrant workers to fulfil their job contracts, even if the working conditions were unfair to the worker. The rights to refuse the job position or task and walk away were not guaranteed. Moreover, while former slaves found themselves free from the actual shackles of forced labour, still no laws or policies were put in place to rescue those people from underemployment, poverty, social exclusion, and a life in ghettos (and later *favelas*).

The official end of slavery was, nonetheless, an undeniably crucial step not to be relativised. It caused or contributed to many advantages: (i) a wage-based work relationship that secured the liveability of most workers; (ii) the expansion of an internal consumer market; (iii) higher productivity levels due to workers' improved health and general well-being; (iv) diversification of the economic activities, including industries; (v) the attraction of immigrants bringing a myriad of technical skills and professional experiences previously missing; (vi) a reduction of the state-supported rentiers' economic influence and an enhanced, free and competitive domestic market; (vii) the development of regions away from the coastal strip; and (viii) the from illiberal mercantilism towards liberal capitalism.

[6] IBGE, séries estatísticas. Accessed on 6 May 2020, accessible at: https://seriesestatisticas.ibge.gov.br/series.aspx?no=1&op=2&vcodigo=POP2&t=migracoes-externas-total-imigrantes-brasil.

[7] IBGE, território brasileiro e povoamento. Accessed on 6 May 2020, accessible at: https://brasil500anos.ibge.gov.br/territorio-brasileiro-e-povoamento/italianos/os-imigrantes-nas-cidades.html.

The Arrival of Capitalism

At the end of the nineteenth century, the rhythm of transformations was frenetic but still not enough to generate a solidly different system. Coffee exports from Sao Paulo were so profitable that most investments accumulation concentrated there, through a mass domestic consumer market did not appear overnight. This meant that neither main the industrial nor the agricultural sectors at that point possessed the prowess to sustain the country's wealth on their own. In that context, the first capitalists in Brazil, including foreign transnational companies, looking for a haven to maximise their returns seized control of the well-established export means of production.

Historically, aboriginal, non-capitalist producers possessed the land they cultivated or from which those products were extracted, especially the Amazon rubber tappers. They kept all the occasional profits for themselves. When the capitalist investors first arrived in the country's interior, they brought along companies that converted those traditional producers into their salaried workers (Caldeira, 2017, p. 363). The federal and state governments enacted laws that only recognised possession of land through purchase. Consequently, rubber tappers lost most of their income, which, in turn, led to a sharp productivity loss of 80%. There were no mechanisms in place to protect the workers' income or their working conditions. The new companies did not possess their own plant extraction expertise or techniques and, therefore, depended solely on the local workers' abilities. This dependence and the deficiency in production autonomy inevitably resulted in returns that fell short of the investors' expectations.

Capitalism requires workers whose labour is freely exchanged. Development cannot thrive in an environment where labour is a bounded resource, which only state-enabled rentiers can access, as was the case in Brazil until 1888. Abolishing slavery generated opportunities for entrepreneurs and workers alike, as they each acquired the prospect of accessing a mass consumer market and higher wages. It also posed a significant challenge: workers must be strong enough to put the brakes on the exploitation impetus of capitalists to an extent where the relationship between the two sides does not favour the owners of capital unduly. When the relationship is unhealthy, accumulation risks falling short of investment potential. Nowhere in the world has this relationship been relatively proportionate without the intervention of the state—it is the fulcrum for national coordination and a propitious economy. Placing limits, establishing rights and obligations on both sides, and enacting regulations to make sure the capitalist system can yield benefits for which it has the potential to provide is essential. Workers can benefit from a swelling income while capitalists benefit from the capital accumulation: although each side tends to fight only for their interests, and with a general power imbalance favouring the capitalists, the state can be the democratic impulse for rebalancing. That is when states must intervene with the aim of keeping potential abuses in check and prioritising overall national development as opposed to single-class enrichment—hence, long-term planning, regulation, and redistribution. The state is also the only entity capable of mobilising national resources towards collective, higher goals.

As one example of state inactivity generating developmental losses, historian Robert Levine recounted that after the abolition of slavery in Brazil, sugar prices continued to fall, and the average worker's life became even more precarious. For day labourers, who already felt the shock of the market competition following the entry of recently freed ex-slaves, real wages fell by almost half compared to the mid-century average (Levine, 1980, pp. 59–60). This was in the federal state of Pernambuco in the northeast, whose main economic activity had been sugar from the sugar cane[8] since the beginning of the sugar economic cycle around the sixteenth century. Pernambuco's economy depended on sugar, and the local governments never challenged the power of its producers. In this context, the state lacked the political autonomy, capacity or even political will to develop a programme to diversify and plan for an eventual end of the cycle. Otherwise, the local economy was in the hands of the sugar-producing capitalists, who invested in that state only while the sugar business was viable. Once the international market could no longer absorb all the sugar produced, the capitalists left the state. The first consequence was the abrupt creation of a massive labour surplus, which necessarily precedes marginality and poverty.

Brazil is "too large to be pulled out of middle-income status by big wins in particular industries. While the four small NIC (newly industrialised country) economies could be completely transformed by the success

[8] Sugar can also be extracted from other vegetables. The sugar from the beetroot produced in the Caribbean, for example, was the largest competitor to the Brazilian sugar from the sugar cane and caused its downfall in the mid-sixteenth century.

of important export industries—such as shipbuilding (Korea) or semiconductors (Taiwan)—the BRICs are too big for that. They need domestic development, not just export success" (Elsenhans and Babones, 2017, p. 7). Countries of Brazil's diversity can use its cycles towards its overarching developmental goals, but to depend on such cycles is detrimental. In general, large countries like Brazil need a diversified industrial sector coupled with dynamic technical expertise, instead of relying on capitalism based on cycles of international single-product demand.

After the abolition of slavery, entrepreneurs and governments alike had no experience on how to manage the economy without the exploitation of labour. Hence, in an attempt to replicate how the markets worked in times of slavery, but adjusted to the new reality, the state and capitalists outsourced their labour needs to migrants. On the one hand, the federal government facilitated land ownership and access to the labour market for immigrants. On the other hand, there were no guarantees of property acquisition or even jobs upon arrival in the country. Migrants were free workers, but the burden of success was entirely on them. They were ultimately responsible for bringing in their labour to work the land, they were expected to be equally or more productive than the slaves, apply their capital to buy land and produce, and to bring and transfer their agricultural techniques. In sum, the *milieu* imposed on the immigrant a veiled exploitative situation, in which the State or the capitalist unavoidably extracted benefits from the foreigner.

Considering that the migrants constituted the new primary workforce in the country and acknowledging the maintenance of a considerable power imbalance between worker and capitalist, average wages remained low throughout the country, preventing Brazil from creating mass consumer markets necessary for riding the growth wave into more vigorous development. The cumulative income growth was just 8.2% between 1890 and 1913. In the same period, Argentina's GDP per capita would reach US$3,797, equivalent to 4.68 times that of Brazil. For comparison, the size of the Brazilian worker's average income was greater in Chile by 3.27, Mexico 2.13, and Colombia 1.58 (Maddison, 2006). The domestic consumer market had expanded but still fallen short of its potential with the state and capitalists still focussed on exports without internal market expansion. Additional business sectors and entrepreneurs could have encountered a more conducive environment to start and thrive had the government concentrated less on the oligarchic cycle-based, single-product economic activities, and in its place, promoted early, full employment to boost the domestic market due to labour empowerment.

However, the signature of early capitalism in Brazil was its relationship with the coffee plantations. At the beginning of the twentieth century, the international coffee market weakened, with lower demand in rich countries. To make matters worse, the coffee crops indicated that 1906 would see a massive harvest. Abundant supply with low demand led to a colossal fall in price and revenue, and with coffee being Brazil's primary economic activity, the damage was considerable. In despair, the coffee growers, who also were also the state elites, pressurised the government to deploy the State apparatus in their favour, risking a break of the economic and political status quo. Thus, the federal government launched a programme using taxpayer money to buy unsold coffee and stock it to a) keep the accumulation of the coffee growers steady and b) artificially maintain the price high in the international market. The state of Sao Paulo, the largest coffee producer, went one step further and institutionalised the price-protection practices as permanent instead of as an ad hoc need-based policy. The Coffee Institute of Sao Paulo was established to continually keep the coffee business economically viable. Recurrently, the coffee silos under the upkeep of the state would become so full as to render maintenance costs unsustainable that they would buy the plant only to burn it. Instead, taxpayer's money should have been used for industrialisation diversification and expansion and purposes, but rentism caused a reinforcement of existing privileges through the wasteful upholding of the coffee price.

This fact above demonstrates, once more, that the advent of the republic cannot be considered as a real revolution as it did not address latent inequalities. Referring to Chapter 2, the sovereignty of coffee plantations is a case of maintenance of the pre-capitalist status quo, authored by the ever-active presence of state-backed rentiers. Not that this scenario was unpredictable. Let us recall that the military *coup d'état* that demoted the Monarch ran within the agrarian elite's agenda. To succeed, the new regime needed to satisfy the rising progressive republicans and the conservative *latitudinarians*[9] simultaneously. Such duality caused a nonlinear,

[9] *Latifundio* owners, namely the inherited owners of large land holdings.

non-homogeneous progress towards modernity. Therefore, counterintuitively, the coffee valorisation programme has resulted in some essential development effects.

Coffee Valorisation Plan

The decade of World War I was vital. Until then, the Industrial Revolution had been progressing virtually uninterruptedly for over a century in the West. Industrialised nations had accumulated more wealth in this period than ever before and flooded the world with their manufactured goods. The Great War prompted an abrupt disruption in that cycle. Brazil was not among the rich few of the time yet nor was it the theatre of war, which brought a set of indirect, double-edged consequences.

For one, the dwindling demand for coffee in the rich world was an immediate catastrophe for the Brazilian rent class. It seemed like the coffee cycle was ending, but it had become a business of such enormity that there could be no swift replacement for it. All evidence suggested that the country was destined to shatter. The warring states, also the wealthiest ones, had turned their industrial capacities to producing items required for warfare. Therefore, agriculture-based countries like Brazil rapidly lost access to the consumer goods the wealthy nations suddenly stopped producing. This environment opened space for Brazilian capitalists to fill the demand void in the internal market.

Consequently, the federal government launched in 1906 a programme aiming at protecting the profits of the coffee growers by purchasing any excess of the product. At the other end, the obvious unsustainability of the coffee plantations in the long run, allied with the new opportunities for profiting with industrialised consumer goods, led many of the rentiers to take a sharp turn and become regular competing capitalists. The coffee rentiers had simply exhausted their extraction capacity. This signified a revolution at the end of an era, perhaps even more so than independence or the republic because the very fabric of multi-century aristocratic structures, the status quo, was crumbling before the state class. Responding to this new era, farmers began investing their profits in imported machinery and skilled immigrants, mostly from Europe but also other regions such as Lebanon and Japan. Just as Elsenhans and Babones surmise, "When private capitalists are able to reinvest rents productively, it may be unfair in relation to competitors, but it does not harm the economy. When private capitalists are incentivised to use rents unproductively, they must be prevented from acquiring them in the first place" (Elsenhans and Babones, 2017, p. 38).

Caldeira notes that it was not a revolution brought in from abroad, but one built from inside. At the most basic level, Brazil's global role remained the same: exporter of coffee and other agricultural raw materials. Concerning the global insertion of the Brazilian economy, there was no structural change between the previous period and now. The landmark change in pattern was the Coffee Valorisation Plan, which was not a milestone for exports, but the country's internal development. Even though it continued to be a coffee producer, the Valorisation Plan altered Brazil's history by making the country for the first time, its own economic architect for the first time (Caldeira, 2017, p. 485).

Five main elements were present, concomitantly, to enable a sturdier development beyond economic growth in Brazil in the early twentieth century: (a) higher levels of employment and workers' wages, following a migratory movement from rural to urban areas; (b) enhancement of technical and productive capacities of workers, mostly through European immigration of relatively more skilled labour; (c) higher level of technological transfer from the industrialised nations, via import of machinery and equipment; (d) shifting of resources from non-competitive to competitive sectors; and (e) diversification of the economy and an expanding consumer base, especially the flourishing of large urban areas. "During the valorisation of the coffee, the Brazilian economy experienced for the first time a real growth rate per capita higher than that of the US. The rate was probably greater than 2% per year. Based on any of the price indicators, it can be concluded that the economy grew rapidly" (Pelaez and Suzigan, 1981, p. 152), even in the aftermath of a world war. The plan spurred results so good that it managed to attract international investments in a time of global crisis, to the point where the national government, then broke, became solvent again (Caldeira, 2017, p. 485) in an extraordinarily short time. Brazil was finally growing at a faster rate than the Western powerhouses and, unprecedentedly, its residents were experiencing a comparable improvement in livelihoods.

There was, however, a sixth less spoken of factor at play. It was already mentioned that in the twentieth century the various regions became relatively more integrated and trade between them started pulling up each other's economies. This new locomotive-convoy system, led by the Southeast States, deserves some extra attention.

Domestic Convoy System

Repeatedly, data has shown that rich countries/regions can affect their neighbours' economies significantly and positively. In a meta-study of quantitative analyses of 20 years (1970 to 1990) around the world, Vamvakidis (1998) found robust statistical evidence that "the economies of countries near large and open economies grow faster. In addition, the level of development of neighbouring economies, especially when they are open, has significant positive spillover effects. By contrast, the size and level of development of closed neighbouring economies have little or no impact on domestic growth" (Vamvakidis, 1998). This suggests that economic integration, especially trade, between less and more developed regions, cause developmental advantages to the former group. Similarly, the study demonstrates how a convoy model for development is not only practical but often essential. In Brazil, that constant was not different, as the economic prowess of coastal areas, such as Rio de Janeiro and Sao Paulo, spilled over even to the farthest Brazilian federal states as soon as they began interaction.

Earlier in Brazilian history, interaction between the Brazilian states was weak. The Brazilian emperors fought and crushed many rebellions and independence movements. The rulers managed to keep a tremendously large territory with extremely different societies under one single State. None of that, however, sufficed to create a unified nation. Stark regional disparities were preserved as the kingdom never crafted a national plan to integrate them. Those territories and peoples kept by force under the Crown served a physiological need to continue plying the royal family with resources, for-export products, cheap labour, and soldiers. In the republican era, those subjugated territories were upgraded to federal states, but they still felt foreign to one other within the national theatre. The difference during the Republic was an enhanced autonomy, where the states did not solely obey the elites from Rio de Janeiro. That had organically altered how those states interacted in the economic realm. They commenced forming a structure with ever-increasing interdependence; one where exporting was rendered irrelevant to most producers of the interior of the country. Caldeira, citing Ramos and Franco et al., narrates it as the following:

> *Each region, according to its economic significance, is supplied by the product of the others, while at the same time finding many more consumers for its products in those regions. The Rio Grande beef jerky is transported weekly to the extreme North, which in turn sends back the goods that Riograndans lack. Pernambuco and other northern states provide three-quarters of the sugar consumed in Santos, almost all of the rest goes to Rio de Janeiro; and both Santos and Rio de Janeiro respond by providing what they produce to the surrounding regions.' These internal exchanges of rural production have brought prosperity to urban areas: 'Coastal cities receive exportable products from the countryside as they intermediate the distribution of other regions' products to yet more regions. As such, they are tributaries of the crops, as members of the same family or builders of the same building. Ask a trader in Rio Grande, Paraná or São Paulo why he thrives or withers. He will invariably answer: because coffee, beef jerky, maté-tea, tobacco or sugar sells or not in other regions.* (Author's translation of Caldeira, 2017, pp. 488–489)

Nothing affected more the life of the ordinary Brazilian citizen of the early twentieth century than the development brought by the newly structured state-to-state convoy model. Rentiers did not cease to exist and accumulate, nor did they lose their power, but were no longer alone. Conversely, many producers from the non-coastal areas accessed new markets for their products elsewhere, creating an organic accumulation and diversification, stronger redistribution of wealth and the interiorisation of productive investments, consequently a new path for a broader development. The biggest lesson of the time was that development can spill over as investment and deliberate domestic pro-growth policies spread across borders (international or domestic alike).

Disillusionment

Despite the numerous changes at the beginning of that century, some elite forces still managed to push the country back towards the traditional status quo, in which concentration of capital and a weak internal market persisted by design. The continued lack of "democratisation of income and wealth, policies to promote full employment, and (fundamentally) the redirection of the benefits of economic growth away from elites in favour of ordinary consumers" (Elsenhans and Babones, 2017, p. 4) is the historic formula for underdevelopment.

Certainly, a sudden integration of the regions of the country occurred, and that was essential to a new phase of development (1889–1929).

However, there were no durable national policies to sustain that process. Most railroads in the country still only connected the countryside to the seaports with the aim to transport export goods, instead of linking region to region towards facilitating domestic trade, diffusing economic exchange and developing internal markets. As an example of how insufficient regional integration and transportation was, transporting cotton in 1909 from the state of Pernambuco to Rio de Janeiro was almost as expensive (17.8 cents/lb) as getting it shipped from Liverpool (19.5 cents/lb), a distance nearly four times greater (Franco and Correa do Lago, 2011, p. 32). This trade inefficiency restricted the rich federal states' appetite to consume products from the peripheral ones, undermining the convoy system and wealth redistribution within the country.

And, certainly, the end of slavery and the arrival of immigrants dramatically lifted domestic markets, enlarged the pool of professional skills available in the workforce and gave rise to new, small entrepreneurs. But the state inaction to develop social inclusion programmes targeting former slaves pushed black Brazilians to the margins of society, eventually into ghettos and favelas. That exclusion of such a large population group impeded the harnessing of productive and economic potentials. Marginalisation in Brazil equated to reinforcing income concentration in the hands of the traditional rentiers.

As one knows, capitalists lose when people in the country are not able to consume, but this was not the case with rentiers who still accumulated from exports and did not depend on domestic consumption. That is especially true in countries that do not charge taxes on anyone's earnings, as was the case in Brazil at the time. Additionally, the artificially high prices of coffee in the international market provoked a devaluation of the national currency and an appreciation of coffee growers' revenues, who sold their beans in the much-appreciated pound sterling. In turn, rentiers profited and too much capital concentrated in their hands. The domestic market attracted fewer resources, which hindered accumulation and investment on goods production (industrialisation), hence stalling development prematurely. Evidence of this partial success of the Brazilian development history is the fact that Brazil had just 54% of the average GDP per capita of the average of Latin America. In 1913, the Brazilian per capita income was less than 1/6 that of Argentina; less than 1/6 of the US; and about 2/3 that of Portugal (Franco and Correa do Lago, 2011, p. 32).

Brazilian prosperity required more productive investments, social inclusion, labour empowerment, an expanded consumer market, and deeper national integration. All of that was a threat and could lead to the ruin of the traditional Brazilian elites. However, it remained unlikely to expect that such factors would all fall into place and co-exist in balance between owners of capital and labour overtime. The State needed to have the will and means to make that possible—it had neither. Resources needed to be channelled towards national development aiming at productive and competitive accumulation. And that unified, national strategy is what we will analyse in Chapter 4.

Bibliography

Caldeira, J. (2017). *História da Riqueza no Brasil – Cinco Séculos de Pessoas, Costumes e Governos*. Rio de Janeiro: Sextante.

Conrad, A. (1967). Slavery as an Obstacle to Economic Growth in the United States: A Panel Discussion. In: *The Journal of Economic History*, Accessible at: www.jstor.org/stable/2116262.

Costa, F. A. (2012). *Formação rural extrativista na Amazônia: os desafios do desenvolvimento capitalista (1720–1970)*. Belem: Núcleo de Altos Estudos Amazônicos.

Datta, M. N. and Bales, K. (2013). Slavery Is Bad for Business: Analyzing the Impact of Slavery on National Economies. In: *The Brown Journal of World Affairs* 19, no. 2 (Spring/Summer).

Elsenhans, H. and Babones, S. (2017). *BRICS or Bust? Escaping the Middle-Income Trap*. Stanford: Stanford University Press.

Franco, G. H. B. and Correa do Lago, L. A. (2011). A Economia da República Velha, 1889–1930. In: *Texto para discussão*, no. 588. Rio de Janeiro: Pontifícia Universidade Católica do Rio de Janeiro.

Global Slavery Index. (2018). Accessible at: www.globalslaveryindex.org/2018/data/country-data/brazil/.

IBGE, Séries Estatísticas. Accessible at: https://seriesestatisticas.ibge.gov.br/series.aspx?no=1&op=2&vcodigo=POP2&t=migracoes-externas-total-imigrantes-brasil.

IBGE, Território Brasileiro e Povoamento. Accessible at: https://brasil500anos.ibge.gov.br/territorio-brasileiro-e-povoamento/italianos/os-imigrantes-nascidades.html.

Instituto Brasileiro de Geografia e Estatística. (1990). *Estatísticas históricas do Brasil*. Rio de Janeiro: IBGE.

Levine, R. (1980). *A velha usina – Pernambuco na federação brasileira, 1889–1937*. Rio de Janeiro: Paz e Terra.

Maddison, A. (2006). *The World Economy*. Paris: OECD.
Pelaez, C. M. and Suzigan, W. (1981). *História monetária do Brasil*. Brasília: UnB.
Vamvakidis, A. (1998). Regional Integration and Economic Growth. In: *World Bank Economic Review* 12, no. 2: 251–270.

CHAPTER 4

Brazilians, the Architects of Brazil?

Edgar Federzoni dos Santos and Neil Wilcock

It is usual for the Brazilian economics scholarship to label the period from independence until World War II as the *Brazilian economic formation*. Only after then have the studies of the *Brazilian economy* begun. As shown in Chapters 2 and 3, the government's system and policies before then used to privilege colonial patterns' continuity or did little to break with such practices fully. No medium- or long-term national-wide economic plans had, until the mid-twentieth century, ever been delivered to foster any self-constructed development.

Following the collapse of the coffee business, President Getúlio Vargas took power after leading a revolution in 1930, which had overthrown the elected President Washington Luís and, with that, the "República Velha" (or the Old Republic from 1889 to 1930) was brought to an end. República Velha was marked by the rotation of presidents from Sao

E. Federzoni dos Santos (✉) · N. Wilcock
Leipzig University, Leipzig, Germany

N. Wilcock
e-mail: neil.wilcock.07@aberdeen.ac.uk

E. Federzoni dos Santos
University of Vienna, Vienna, Austria

N. Wilcock and E. Federzoni dos Santos (eds.), *Not Paying the Rent*,
https://doi.org/10.1007/978-3-030-78861-2_4

Paulo and Minas Gerais's states, the largest producers of the most essential goods for the country of that time: coffee and milk. Those producers constituted the natural state elite, governing the country themselves, in a rent-based economy continually centuries-old traditions.

Vargas instituted a new style alongside profound shifts in the understanding of the role of the State. The "Estado Novo" (or the New State, Vargas's administration from 1937 to 1945) had created a national plan that enlarged the state's reach dramatically in society and economy. Firstly, the state was reshaped to perform increasingly complex functions in all sectors of the economy. Second, the governmental economic policy had become more ambitious, centralising, and nationalistic, which in its broadest sense constitutes the so-called Nacional-Desenvolvimentismo (or Developmental Nationalism). As a conscious political choice, the determination to promote and expand the national industry reflected the interests of the urban masses who demanded employment and a higher income, and of the national bourgeoisie who demanded a market for their businesses. The national plan's aims were to modernise, be more independent from international markets, and build an economic sovereign country, essentially a fast industrialisation process (Silva, 2003, p. 40). Vargas promulgated several laws protecting labour rights, fiscal incentives to industry segments, and imports of supplies for them. Nevertheless, the possible new paths for Brazilian politics and economy were still rooted in the capital that the elite of coffee growers held. However, this secular reality would switch radically during and, mainly, after World War II.

In this context, this third chapter will explore the era in which Brazil developed its most ambitious and home-grown strategy to develop. It will discuss whether Brazilians finally managed to architect their national plan.

Brazilian Economic Modernisation and Catching-Up Processes

The US and the UK had been supporting the Brazilian political and economic restructuring since the early 1900s. These countries enjoyed a new phase of capitalism and needed capable, available markets for their products abroad. However, since the immediate post-war, the North American interests in supporting economic development initiatives in Brazil, including industrial development, had changed completely. The priorities of that country were centred in Europe and later in Asia (two continents destroyed by war), leaving Brazil behind. In 1946, the US position of further financing of Latin America from their end depended on those southern governments' ability to create favourable conditions for foreign investments (Silva, 2003, p. 42). The rich North pushed the Southern nations to deploy their resources to develop domestic markets to exploit the latter's markets with minimum spending and maximum profit.

Brazil was the only Latin American country to fight in World Wars I and II, contributing with material resources and troops. Thus, the Brazilian State expected to receive economic and political compensations for its efforts in the aftermath of the Allies' victory. Such compensations never came after either war, which aroused stark dissatisfaction in the Brazilian government, the economic elites, and intellectuals. Opinion-makers converged to the perception that Brazil was being exploited and increasingly dependent on the international system it had helped create after World War II. A strong sentiment of anti-colonisation, unfair distribution of global power, and an international division of labour took over public opinion more strongly than ever before.

"It is not enough for some to define others as objects. It is also necessary for those who are objectified thus to reproduce, to live up to, their presumed 'responsibilities' as objects of a colonial global order" (Muppidi, 2004, p. 282). The general feeling was that the US could choose whether, when, and to what extent Brazil could have economic benefits. Technology and capital supporting development in Brazil had three primary geographical sources since the 1900s: US, UK, and Germany. After World War II, these pillars had been reduced to one: the US.

Furthermore, Brazil had not reacted against the American neglect after World War I and performed the same outlay level and political support to the US for World War II. The Brazilian aid to the Allies, interpreted as a matter of goodwill towards the West during the First War, now started to be seen as an obligation for the Second War. Elaine Scarry states:

> Our behaviour toward objects at the exceptional moment when they hurt us must be seen within the context of our normal relations with them…the chair routinely relieves the problems of weight. Should the object prove insufficiently mimetic of awareness, insufficiently capable of accommodating the problem of weight…the object will be discarded or set aside. (Scarry, 1985, pp. 295–296)

The Brazilian government found itself pushed and motivated to define an ambitious plan for industrialisation, development, and modernisation and, consequently in this context, reach higher levels of independence. In sum, the most significant goal was to catch up to the wealthiest nations and generate autonomy from them. So began the most extensive state-directed, long-term development plan ever made until then. Brazil was not alone. Along with it, many other Latin American and Asian countries also felt disadvantaged and exploited, as they were not rewarded for their efforts. The technological supremacy of Americans and Europeans, their advanced phase in the industrial revolution, and their superior productivity rendered the previously called Third World Countries no match to compete in the international market. The reaction to these comparative disadvantages was the surge of nationalistic policies and the public defence of inward-driven economic growth through vigorous national control.

In South Korea, the influential economist Ha-Joon Chang summed up the logics behind development by saying that all major wealthy countries, including the UK, used interventionist economic strategies to encourage industrialisation and safeguard their national industries before they had achieved the stage of evolution at which they were able to compete in the world market. Only after that competitive stage had those industrial nations adopted a free market discourse, seeking to reach two chief objectives: (a) to open the third world countries' markets for their products and (b) to prevent those third world countries from adopting the same developmental strategies, through internal market protection and state control, that resulted in the now-developed countries to be at the level they are (Chang, 2002). With history in mind, the developing countries concluded that the path towards development and autonomy should eliminate imports from rich countries, replacing them with self-sufficiency as much as possible. In Brazil, this mentality represented the exact opposite of the economic policies carried out until that point. The attentions were drawn to the external to the detriment of the internal markets.

Thereby, the foundations of the Import Substitution Industrialisation (ISI) were historically and theoretically placed. Apart from a simple industrial growth, "Import substitution refers to a set of ideas about why mass poverty has prevailed and continues to prevail in many countries while other countries have grown rich, and about a general approach to the elimination of that poverty" (Bruton, 1998, p. 904). In other words, ISI attempted to respond and, in turn, solve the problem of why some countries develop and others do not. Import Substitution seemed to represent the bulwark of developing countries and their de facto self-determination. The enthusiasts of ISI aimed at finding paradigmatic strategies to take their countries out of the backwardness and dependency.

ISI was the flagship economic policy in Brazil (and Latin America) between the 1930s and the 1980s. It focused on manufacturing domestically as much as possible those goods the country traditionally imported. For that, the government adopted highly protectionist measures anchored in fiscal and tax disadvantages to imports. Paradoxically, ISI promoted some imports, as foreign production goods, equipment, tools, machinery flooded the Brazilian economy. At the same time, incentives to attract foreign money flourished. These items enabled the installation of a basic industry, given that Brazil did not possess internal technology, expertise, and resources.

Notably, ISI reduced Brazil's participation in global trade to ashes as the country turned inwards. This new reality heavily penalised the traditional agrarian rentiers dependent on exports and gave a tremendous boost to a new bourgeois, urban elite. Quickly, industrial elites emerged between the 1950s and 1960s. The national industry was overall inefficient and technologically obsolete, which forced the government to maintain substantial subsidies to protect in-land production, coupled with heavy taxation on imports to artificially maintain the competitiveness of the national industries. Additionally, inadequate infrastructure and an unskilled workforce added to underwhelming levels of productivity with high production costs. In other words, the sustainability of surplus from industrial activities depended deeply on political intervention in the economy, ironically forming a new class of state-backed rentiers.

During Vargas's administration, the traditional agriculture and cattle raising (that constituted some 90% of Brazilian GDP until that moment) sectors were rapidly jeopardised by sudden incentive cuts. Masses of peasants lost their jobs in the countryside, and there was neither time nor enough investments to capacitate them in industrial productions. As a result, the market overflow of unskilled, under salaried labour and no technological autonomy greatly limited the fulfilment of many agrarian regions' economic potential. That happened because "economic development is a process of moving from a set of assets based on primary products, exploited by unskilled labour, to a set of assets based on knowledge, exploited by skilled labour" (Vries, 2013, p. 101). Brazil's economic transition did not happen for some time yet.

Despite that, by 1980, the Brazilian GDP had leapt 1400% compared to 1930s figures. The fast industrialisation put Brazil into its economic golden ages. Even the several crises across the period, including World War II, did not stop the general upward trend. It appeared as if the country had finally become less vulnerable to external factors due to its new national industries. This, however, was an illusion derived from the distortions that the state-directed development policies had created.

Brazil State-Directed Development

A near unanimous constants in economics scholarship is that development is good. Liberal economics literature deems development as the chief objective of every nation. Development, mainly when heavily sponsored by the State, is a rational choice involving political priorities. As such, development strategies often deliberately opt to promote economic activities asymmetrically. Ergo, the pursuit of development can also be seen as a historically flexible concept whose outcomes vary according to whom it intends to benefit.

"The economic development can no longer be natural (…) in other words, the deliberate purpose of guiding facts to the fulfilment of the fundamental design of economic development (are not natural)" (Bianchi, 2006, p. 34). This sentence is from a 1952 ECLAC (Economic Commission for Latin America and the Caribbean) convention that focused on developing Latin American nations. Under this spirit, states throughout the subcontinent triggered inwardly driven policies that would allow them to import less and accumulate capital to lessen dependency from the Global North. Eventually, the autonomy should lead those Latin American countries to a stage of development closer to that of the industrialised nations.

In Brazil, the currency lost its value, import tariffs on consumer goods increased, and production fell. The BNDE (National Economic Development Bank, acronym in Portuguese) was founded to invest primarily in industries; attract foreign capital; and implement a centralised national funding programme, which increased the Federal Government's powers over society and the economy. Thus, the project "Brazil, the Powerhouse" was officially launched. Weiss and Hobson, while discussing late developers, cited the well-renowned author Alexander Gerschenkron in his book 'Economic Backwardness in Historical Perspective' (1962), who argued that late developers such as Russia and Germany in the nineteenth century required strong state intervention to catch up with the early developers. He said "the greater the degree of backwardness, the greater the degree of state intervention" (Weiss and Hobson, 1995, p. 93). In this context, Brazil was ruled for almost 55 years by dictatorial governments during the ISI policies' implementation. National (and nationalist) economic plans bore fruits that increased the authoritarian governments' legitimacy in power. Those plans pleased the national bourgeoisie, created jobs, and appealed to a powerful nation's ideation. This process had created a virtuous cycle in which ISI and government fed one another where growth and political stability should meet.

The rate of imports decreased following the ISI reforms, but the capital circulating in the economy was mainly of foreign origin, especially foreign banks. Therefore, overall imports have not reduced. Somewhat, they changed in nature: from importing goods to importing capital. Moreover, until the 1990s, no substantial investments had been made in technology and innovation. Consequently, the knowledge required for development and industrialisation had also still had to be imported (Lima, 2011; Suzigan, 1988; Machado, 1999). Despite the described contradictions, the growth brought about in the ISI era is not negligible.

After President Getulio Vargas left office in 1951, Juscelino Kubitschek went on with the modernisation process. In 1956 he decreed the "Plano de Metas" (Plan of Targets), establishing for the first time an annual goal for industrial growth. He regulated the relations between private, foreign and state-owned capitals; increased the state's share of direct investments in basic industries of steel, mining and petrochemicals and infrastructure in telecommunications, transport and energy). As a result, consumer goods imports reduced starkly, for the most part being replaced by domestic production (Suzigan, 1988). The great slogan of the Kubitschek administration was "50 years in 5", alluding to the intention to make Brazil develop in 5 years what would have taken it, without the *Plano de Metas*, 50 years.

However, "the later a country industrializes in chronological history, the greater the probability that its major manufacturing firms will be foreign-owned" (Amsden, 2001, p. 286). This is due to that "The distance from the world technological frontier and the degree of government intervention, therefore, do not necessarily move in unison in a latecomer. Instead, as the distance from the frontier rises, what probably does increase is the role of the foreign firm" (Amsden, 2001, p. 286). *Plano de Metas* did not promote the overarching development expected throughout all classes, layers of society, or regions. Instead, there was an enormous expansion of certain sectors and specific industrial branches, such as carmakers, with meagre development in most of the others. Volkswagen and General Motors founded their plants in Brazil over these years, after the federal government had constructed hundreds of kilometres of highways connecting important cities to generate demand for automobiles.

The list of consumer products leading the industrialisation process of that era made it clear that the market relied on a small group of high-income consumers. Chapter 3 showed that the masses' average income had not increased significantly in the first half of the century, which denotes that the holders of the highest incomes were still the old agrarian rentiers and the new industrial, urban industrial bourgeoisie, and the individuals who represented both groups often overlapped. In other words, the very motor of the modern Brazilian development process, despite a clean break from the *physiocratic* past, remained strongly attached to the status quo discussed in Chapter 2. Regime after regime, the central tenet for sustainable capitalist progress was still underdeveloped: mass internal consumer market. For a country to succeed as a capitalist country, it must develop a well-enumerated and enfranchised working class from the onset of its development process. The later that scenario is established, the less likely is growth to last. Brazil did not foment that scenario. Elsenhans and Babones reiterate:

> …the ceiling for middle-income countries is caused by the inequalities that are typically generated early in the development process itself. An insufficient expansion of mass consumption shifts middle-income economies toward an emphasis on luxury goods, while profits are disproportionately captured by elites. High-income countries with strong civil societies are prevented from falling down the global income hierarchy by politics that favour mass consumption. (Elsenhans and Babones, 2017, p. 8)

Once the pie has grown and shared among only a small number of people, it becomes challenging to redistribute it later. The new elites will hold on to their wealth and power and avoid the pulverisation of their possessions for democratic allocation. Hence, the pie's sharing must occur as early as possible, still in the seminal phase of development. Failing to do so will champion growth but jeopardise long-term development and generate class struggles in the future, which involves overcoming rentiers.

Therefore, it is crucial to recognise Keynes' revelation that workers' compensation is not a passive factor but contributor to development.

Between 1963 and 1967, the economy based on import substitution of luxurious goods demonstrated weaknesses and slowed down significantly. The deterioration of the balance of payments, the falling profits, high inflation rate, and masses of workers striking for better work conditions regularly led Brazil to an economic halt. According to Saulo de Castro Lima paraphrasing Paul Singer, "The notable expansion of our (Brazilian) exports in the last ten years, is not a result of our technological superiority" [as occurred in Japan and Germany]..."but the abundance of our natural resources and low cost of our manpower" (Lima, 2011, p. 36). With these difficulties, the populist alliance in power since 1961 did not enjoy much support, and in 1964, a military coup empowered the most dictatorial government in the Republican era. After three years of modernising reforms, Brazil adopted a schizophrenic behaviour by keeping a liberal discourse towards the economy yet controlling every aspect of social life through politics.

In 1967, President Costa e Silva proposed the "Programa Estratégico de Desenvolvimento" (Strategic Program for Development—II PND). This programme aimed to reduce inflation rates, maintain jobs at the cost of Spartan salary policies, attract foreign capital, and state investments in basic industry. Under this programme, the country resumed growth, and the dictatorial government grew in popularity. Saulo Lima explains "...all confidence in the great destiny of Brazil in the early 1970s is represented in the II PND, which would be the way to complete the condition of the country as a powerhouse, taking up the idea of a nation as a project to be built, which ridgepole will now have finally completed its paving" (Lessa, 1988, p. 53).

During the dictatorship, the country's motto was "Brasil Potência" (Brazil, the Powerhouse). Economic plans came year after year, and the pattern had been consolidated of economic power mixed with State power in the international system. Ultimately, economic success became an end in itself and unified political and economic priorities. Economic nationalist discourses set the tone to offset the adverse effects of intermittent recessions, political discontent, and inflation rates that averaged 40% per year in the 1970s and 330% in the 1980s. By the 1970s, the development plans had changed and begun promoting exports as a principle for two main reasons. Firstly, the multinational companies that installed their plants in Brazil and produced manufactured goods wanted to use Brazil as an exporting platform due to the country's low cost of labour (Silva, 2003). Secondly, Brazil had the immense need to attract external resources to continue financing its rising governmental expending. However, after eight aggressive modernising plans, the end of the Bretton Woods system in 1971 and the OPEC oil crisis of 1979, the Brazilian economy's situation deteriorated. External financing was scarce; debt of the balance of payments had gone to a downward spiral that would last over a decade; and the country could not afford to import so much technology and oil for its industry anymore.

Despite all the efforts, development was incomplete and over-dimensioned in some productive sectors unable to break the fate of economic cycles. Inequality was rampant, creating market distortions that doomed sustainable growth. Brazil has never overcome those shortcomings as South Korea and Taiwan have in the same period. Indisputably, ISI bore fruits for the economy. It enabled Brazil to change forever its condition of a non-attitude taker. Nonetheless, full-employment capitalism still lived in the shadows of a state-directed, rent-enabling economy.

Recurring Missed Opportunities

The second half of the twentieth century sent mixed signals of what Brazil's development should be. The goal seemed to be to expand the GDP, even if the elites appropriated its spoils. For one, the country experienced a technological and investments boom. For another, technology and investments were foreign-owned, which boasted the Brazilian dependency on wealthy nations. Likewise, some states were enriched in unheard-of ways, especially in the centre-south, while many other states were excluded from the process, enhancing inequalities. Some industrial sectors consolidated their productive capacity and competitiveness but to the detriment of many others that did not receive governmental attention. Consumption improved on the one hand but was coupled with record-breaking inflation rates, which limited further advancement of consumption, on the other hand.

Furthermore, countries that steer their economic efforts towards satisfying and relying on elites or rentiers commonly suffer from high capital flight levels. These economic groups concentrate most of the profits generated in the economy, allowing them to amass large fortunes practically without democratic accountability. Individuals with a large sum of resources will most likely engage in speculation, borrow against interest, and indulge in niche overseas products. In other words, those fortunes are commonly not put to work at home or otherwise, in productive activities. Thus, a significant portion of the wealth created in the Brazilian ventures is lost before it reaches the population. Many Brazilian super-rich "make their money in sectors that are closely linked to government and thus highly reliant on political favour" (Elsenhans and Babones, 2017, p. 23). This process is fatal to capitalism, which feeds from reinvestments and ever-larger scale production, competitive efficiency, and surplus extracted as competitive profit. ISI boosted government-favoured sectors by supporting a non-competitive national industry anchored in luxurious consumer goods run by rentier oligarchs.

The take-off from this period is typically twofold. For one, development reliant on a few productive sectors and on the purchasing power of a small group of people might be enough to ignite economic growth. However, growth based on these two factors will impede the broader society's access to income and undermine growth itself in the long run. It is to Brazil's eternal discredit that it has not made use of its capacity to trigger mass incomes and mass internal markets which its size and diversity it affords. For another, no country can develop and keep most of its people impoverished at the same time. Poverty is much more poisonous to capitalism than it is to rent.

Conversely, the sure-fire strategy to foment equitable development is to eliminate rentiers and labour marginality. Both factors are intertwined. "Rents will not be eliminated until high levels of employment in the modernising sector of the economy are achieved to such an extent that labour scarcity manifests itself even in the less dynamic sectors of the economy, like traditional agriculture and traditional services" (Elsenhans and Babones, 2017, p. 49). For that, state-directed development must find a balance between incentives to industries and policies to implement redistribution of wealth and economic power.

Bibliography

Amsden, A. (2001). *The Rise of the Rest: Challenges to the West from Late-Industrializing Economies*. Oxford: Oxford University Press.

Bianchi, A. M. (2006). The Planned Development of Latin America: A Rhetorical Analysis of Three Documents from the 1950s. In: S. de Paula and Gary A. Dymski (Eds.), *Reimagining Growth: Towards a Renewal of Development*

Theory. R. Robertson (Ed.), *Globalization, Poverty and Inequality*. London: Bloomsbury, pp. 27–51.

Bruton, H. J. (1998). A Reconsideration of Import Substitution. In: *Journal of Economic Literature* 36, no. 2 (June).

Chang, H.-J. (2002). *Kicking Away the Ladder: Development Strategy in Historical Perspective*. London: Anthem Press.

Elsenhans, H. and Babones, S. (2017). *BRICS or Bust? Escaping the Middle-Income Trap*. Stanford: Stanford University Press.

Lessa, A. C. (1988). A diplomacia universalista do Brasil: a construção do sistema contemporâneo de relações bilaterais. In: *Revista Brasileira Política Internacional* 41, esp. n. 40 years.

Lima, S. C. (2011). Da substituição de importações ao Brasil potência: Concepções do desenvolvimento 1964–1979. In: *Aurora* 4, no. 1.

Machado, L. T. (1999). A teoria da dependência na América Latina. In: *Estudos Av* 13, no. 35.

Muppidi, H. (2004). Colonial and Postcolonial Global Governance. In: M. Barnett and R. Duvall (Eds.), *Power in Global Governance—Cambridge Studies in International Relations*. Cambridge: Cambridge University Press.

Scarry, E. (1985). *The Body in Pain: The Making and Unmaking of the World*. Oxford University Press.

Silva, H. C. M. (2003). Deterioração dos termos de Intercâmbio, substituição de importações, industrialização e substituição de exportações: a política de comércio exterior brasileira de 1945 a 1979. In: *Revista Brasileira de Política Internacional* 46, no. 1 (Brasília January/June).

Suzigan, W. (1988). Estado e industrialização no Brasil. In: *Brazilian Journal of Political Economy* 8, no. 4.

Vries, P. (2013). *Escaping Poverty: The Origins of Modern Economic Growth*. Vienna: Vienna University/V&R Unipress.

Weiss, L. and Hobson, J. M. (1995). *States and Economic Development: A Comparative Historical Analysis*. Cambridge: Polity Press.

CHAPTER 5

A Neanderthal in Spacesuit

Edgar Federzoni dos Santos and Neil Wilcock

The previous three chapters cover the general economic model of Brazil. The elitist foundation persisted over time, only temporarily threatened by some political movements, and remains intact until today. Since the end of the military rule, only between 2003 and 2015 was there another attempt at structural reforms, especially in terms of poverty alleviation, pro-equality policies, and general economic competitiveness. Despite all efforts thus far, the richest have still tended to rebound from any endeavours to remove them from their power positions.

As of 1985, the annual GDP was just short of 223 billion US dollars (converted to current values). By 2019, it had reached 1.84 trillion US dollars, peaking in 2011 at 2.616 trillion. Despite the 825% jump, the production output's added gross value failed to change the inequality panorama and curtail the state class. As a manifestation of that, the

E. Federzoni dos Santos (✉) · N. Wilcock
Leipzig University, Leipzig, Germany

N. Wilcock
e-mail: neil.wilcock.07@aberdeen.ac.uk

E. Federzoni dos Santos
University of Vienna, Vienna, Austria

N. Wilcock and E. Federzoni dos Santos (eds.), *Not Paying the Rent*,
https://doi.org/10.1007/978-3-030-78861-2_5

average Brazil Gini index between 1985 and 2017 was 56.89, with a minimum score of 51.3 in 2015, representing a decrease of just 18.2% in 32 years. Brazil never left the bottom tier of the ten most unequal societies worldwide, even during fast-growing economic eras. This shows that most of the country's population did not experience an improvement in their quality of life nearly as close to the rate of economic growth. The Gini points of 2017 were 53.3, virtually equal to those of 1985, 55.6. The economic reforms implemented in the first decade of the 2000s caused an index spike but served only to offset the losses of the previous years, not to set a new bar. Besides, when accounting for inequalities, UNDP calculated in 2019[1] that the Brazilian *real* Human Development Index (HDI) was 0.570. This *real* HDI (or inequality-adjusted HDI, the IHDI) is 25.5% lower than the raw HDI. In other words, the HDI accounts for the potential human development of a country if inequality did not exist. In contrast, IHDI provides a snapshot considering the actual context with its social-economic distortions. That result puts Brazil at the end of the medium development countries list, in the same league of much poorer nations such as Paraguay and Guyana, and behind non-market economies, such as Turkmenistan.

Development programmes have come and gone in Brazil, but wealth redistribution and equitable development never genuinely thrives. Indeed, elites are not necessarily the same as they used to be in colonial times (even if some *latifundio* owners are still currently part of the same dynasties as centuries ago), but those who have lost their position were replaced with others just as, or more, powerful ones. That is because large absolute wealth coupled with constant relative wealth concentration are conducive to more elites that are affluent and, in Brazil, more resilient rentiers. These dominant groups imbued the country's developmental narrative with the false understanding that development equated to continual growth, which would only be achieved through a never-ending productivity expansion, technological advancement, exports, and state subsidies.

The almost obsessive pursuit of development through productivity is one major factor for the bleak scenario arrived at above. While a certain level of productivity can be accepted as a pre-condition for development, it must not be an end-goal. It cannot alone trigger nor sustain the

[1] http://hdr.undp.org/sites/all/themes/hdr_theme/country-notes/BRA.pdf.

development process. Too low labour productivity will lead to marginalisation, but higher productivity within structurally unequal societies can strengthen inequalities. If a small group of people are allowed a more significant portion of the total production revenues, then an intensified production effectiveness will make that group's capacity for profits even greater, broadening the income gap. In Brazil, the 10% wealthiest own 43% of the national GDP. This amounts to say that roughly half of the spoils of any productivity gains will not reach the larger consumer markets and just be siphoned off by a minority.

Furthermore, holders of huge fortunes do not tend to spend in the real economy. Chances are resources from those fortunes will end up in investment banks, luxury goods imported from abroad, and speculative ventures. In highly competitive economies, capitalists must allocate a relevant portion of their earnings for productive reinvestments and innovation to stay competitive—that is not valid in rent-laden economies.

Speculators believe they will create a greater return in the financial markets than in the real economy because there is a lack of demand in it, and this belief further deflates that lack of demands. What is in place is demand management by governments being replaced by uncontrolled bubbles and a bust-based market view of profitability.

Exports constitute another possible slippery slope to rent economics. Exporting is the first way for the accumulation of international currency in countries endeavouring to catch up. However, domestic markets' pathways to development run dry whenever the productive sectors point their turrets mostly towards the global market. Entrepreneurs and governments uninterested in investing in the internal market will overlook wage policies, wealth redistribution, labour rights, and being too dependent on foreign factors for success.

Productivity scaling-up and outward trade were successful strategies to bring about fundamental change and development in smaller nations, such as the Four Asian Tigers. However, Brazil would require deeper state reforms as a pre-requisite for such strategies to work. Yet, it has the advantage of a huge internal market for its long-term growth. The direct application of superficial growth policies performed well in discourse, convincing governments (and voters) believe they were doing the right thing, by following examples from wealthier countries. Administration after administration celebrated and fed their supporters' appetite by showing GDP increments as the end-goal everyone expects. Governments are constantly under pressure to focus their actions on delivering economic growth above all things as it attracts votes. Governments and voters have been convinced that economic growth equates progress and justifies politician's power to whom can achieve it. Even voters who will not benefit as much adhere to that electoral behaviour.

Brazil reached the ten largest world economies persuaded the nation that modernity had finally arrived. From there, the country was to focus on competing in the international arena to become a global superpower, fulfilling nationalists' frequently trumpeted prophecy to be Brazil's fate. That new-large-economy reality served as a shelter to hide the old elitist and rent status quo still running the show, unchallenged and unable to reconcile its growth in GDP with a multi-generational underclass. Brazil was but a Neanderthal in a spacesuit.

Adjustments to Keep Growth Coming

In the second half of the twentieth century, Brazil transited from an agrarian, pre-modern nation to an industrial, urban country. Contrary to all orthodox expectations, such a transformation was far from a revolution for the people. Inequality worsened in the twentieth century, in the fastest-growing period for the country. The military government and its multiple development programmes brought about an economic miracle in GDP expansion and industrialisation, but it failed to make these results serve the broader society's needs. In that period, wealth concentration was exacerbated together with fast environmental degradation (Dweck and Rossi, 2019, p. 98). During the dictatorship, low levels of transparency were also conducive to establishing several endemic corruption schemes that oozed through democratic times and caused political and economic turmoil decades later.

By the 1970s, Import Substitution Industrialization had been showing several signs of weakness. Throughout the 1980s, that process aggravated and showed its exhausted capacity to keep the economy expanding at desired rates. Hyperinflation, moratorium, and economic stagnation proved to Brazilian political and entrepreneurial elites that the neo-mercantilist approach, which earlier protected the domestic business sector's interests, was now acting against them. The 1990s made ISI moribund due to the prevalence of neoliberalism, acceleration of globalisation, and growth of regional trade blocs that rendered economic protectionism counterproductive. Notwithstanding, that same decade experienced a surge in *nouveaux riches*, a by-product of more than 40 years of industrialisation, permeated by ISI policies, that undeniably contributed to Brazil's overall generation of wealth. Those new elites would have now, however, to replace the very system that created them. It is essential to highlight that Brazil had a strong elite attached to and reliant on the state during the dictatorship period through international protectionism. After the democratisation, the state lost its centralising political capacity, and the economic elites outgrew the state in power and determining to a large extent political outcomes by its financial power.

According to Marcos Aurelio Guedes de Oliveira, this new elite initiated, through political pressure, some of the Brazilian foreign policies that would be the flagship of Fernando Collor de Mello's presidency (1990–1992):

> These new classes have found ways to feed their interests through actions and ideas that indicate the formation of a counter-hegemonic project for Brazil. For them, the main issue and the first step to overcome backwardness is to reduce the country's comparative disadvantages when compared to other developed regions of the global capitalist system. (Oliveira, 2010, p. 125)

The tactics by the new elites to try once more to overcome the economic backwardness included two main pillars. First, Brazil must open its economy to the global markets and improve bilateral diplomatic and trade relations with the global powerhouses (the US and Europe). Advocates of this thought understood that only these rich regions could provide the inputs necessary to re-establish and sustain growth. They defended that Brazil had invested too much in the past trying to secure agreements with not so significant countries (i.e. the Middle East, Central America, Africa, and Asia) aiming to diversify its main partners. However, the economic returns could never match the profits that the European or North American markets offered (Oliveira, 2010). In the same vein, policymakers at the Brazilian Ministry of Foreign Affairs, whom nothing or little had to do with the entrepreneurial elites, also agreed to the necessity to develop privileged relations with the superpowers. They had a standard view that Brazil was seen internationally as a peripheral country, regardless of four decades of attempts to shed that status. Hence, an alignment with the US would be the fastest and safest avenue in the direction of insertion in the new world order (Pecequilo, 2008, p. 137).

Second, examples of integration processes from the Global North showed how established powers could cement their regional prominence by forming free trade areas (Almeida, 2009, p. 11). The US started negotiations in 1988 with Canada and Mexico to create the North American Free Trade Agreement (NAFTA), which entered into force in 1994. The technological and productive American supremacy became even more evident when NAFTA's trade balance proved to be hugely more lucrative to the US within the bloc, despite seasonal oscillations. Free trade seemed to heighten the profits of the richer countries' established productive sectors in their region, and Brazil was the richest of its vicinity. Around the same time the Treaty of the European Union was signed in 1992, forming the second largest world economy. Brazil took inspiration from NAFTA and the EU to harness its potential as the hegemon in South America (Burges, 2008, p. 75) by proposing the creation of a soon-to-be free trade area: the Mercosur. Over time, Mercosur proved to be commercially beneficial primarily to Brazil.[2]

By its foundation, in 1991, the total transaction volume among the bloc's members was 4.5 billion USD at its inception; by 2019, those countries sold and bought 309.5 billion USD, with a peak of 359.6 billion USD in 2011. Intraregional trade expanded almost 8000% in 30 years, which was significantly faster than the 524% escalation of the global trade in the same period. Brazil always represented at least 70% of those transaction volumes. Of the Brazilian exports to the other bloc countries, currently between 70 to 80% are manufactured and production goods (machinery and equipment). Mercosur served as a solace to the new industrial elites (emerged between the 1950s and 1970s) when ISI protectionism began to fail. The comparative disadvantages of the national industry became strongly evident in the 1980s and 1990s.

Brazil still enjoyed large relative competitiveness in many sectors compared to the other countries of the bloc. Despite that, European and American transnational companies took advantage of that and used Brazil as an exporting platform to South American countries. They could produce with cheap labour, relatively good infrastructure and export their output with lower tariffs within Mercosur as they could from their central plants. On top of those factors, the transnational companies had enough

[2] Mercosur was originally founded by Brazil, Argentina, Paraguay, and Uruguay. In 1996, Chile and Bolivia became associated members. In 2004, Venezuela was admitted as a full member but was suspended in 2016 due to its undemocratic regime.

economic power and lobby to extract tax relief and subventions from the Brazilian federal and local governments. The leading example of that is carmakers. Nowadays, around 80% of the cars exported from Brazil go to Argentina, and about one-third of the overall Brazilian exports portfolio were cars, tractors, and spare parts. On the other hand, just one-fifth of the products exported by competitive micro and small companies go to the other Mercosur countries.

This shows that much of the spoils from made-in-Brazil goods consistently concentrate in the hands of state-favoured sectors, be in mercantilist, neo-mercantilist, or neoliberal eras. It becomes visible that many of the economic policy changes were but meaningless to overall, fair development and represented more exercises of self-adjustments for the elites to uphold their positions of privilege.

Deindustrialisation and Growth

More recently, Brazil has gone through an unravelling process of its industry. In 1970, the industrial sector accounted for 21.4% of the GDP and by the end of the 1980s reached 46%. Just one decade later, the manufacturing industry plummeted to 25% of the GDP, intensifying its relative losses even more in the mid-2000s to reach a rock-bottom rate of 21% in 2019. The causes for such a flop are multifactorial: the abandonment of national development plans since the 1990s; a lack of capacity to innovate and develop technology; barriers imposed by an intricate tax system; poor infrastructure; domestic political and economic crises; a lack of incentives and targeted policies; an over-appreciated currency making it more difficult to export and easier to import.

Nevertheless, a critical factor for deindustrialisation since 2003 was the commodities boom in the international market. The Chinese industry's exponential acceleration forged a two-edged sword that had cut through the Brazilian manufacturing capabilities. On the one side, it was virtually impossible to compete with Chinese prices due to the economy's sheer productivity and low wages, plus the Chinese government were less concerned at what price they were being sold at as long as they were being produced. On the other hand, the Chinese demanded more and more raw materials as inputs for their manufacturing and food items. Brazil, as an agricultural powerhouse, was in an "advantageous" position to supply those demands. The new rich in Brazil, together with the old elites, rode the more effortless wave towards easy returns and halted investments in industries, which would require complex, structural reforms to compete with Chinese products in the first place. Instead, investments and governmental subsidies gravitated around the extractive and agricultural sectors, the commodities whose international prices soared due to that sudden, gargantuan demand.

Despite Brazil's effective deindustrialisation, its economy grew 44.4% between 2003 and 2019. Perhaps the rise could have been more significant had industries received more investments. However, this demonstrates that industrialisation alone is not a *conditio sine qua non* for economic growth in contemporary middle-income countries. Rather, deindustrialisation leads to salary deterioration, urban diaspora, and slower advancement of technology coupled with a lower need for high technical skills from the workforce. In sum, it is a backlash for economic and human development and slumps on the domestic consumer markets. All of this takes place at the same time as *latifundiarios*, the traditional rentiers, multiplied their sales in raw materials.

A certain level of deindustrialisation is typical in rich countries. High-income populations reach a turning point when they start spending less on consumer goods and more on services, such as travels, leisure activities, personal care, among others. They also consume more imported products. All of that curtails the domestic industry. Far from being a problem, these countries do not regress nor lose their developed status because of some deindustrialisation. The service sector swells and commonly can preserve an ample middle class and a dynamic internal market. In Brazil, however, deindustrialisation struck before the country had been able to join the high-income economies. The deindustrialisation happened too soon, halting labour from further specialisation opportunities, salaries raising, competitiveness blossoming, innovation accelerating, production increasing, and productive investments from mounting. Consequently, it jeopardised economic and social development.

A development strategy must aim, instead, at economic growth as a means to social transformation. A thorough wealth and political power redistribution could lead to stable prosperity, not bound so much on external factors and short cycles of economic growth followed by subsequent crashes. For that, it is imperious to adapt the productive structures to afford most of the population with the opportunity to be similarly productive and lead a dignifying life; a structure where investment and technical expertise are the chief conditions to success, instead of political favours. In sum, "structuring collective life, ensuring quality employment and universal access to health, education and culture and other basic social services must be the ultimate objectives of economic policy" (Dweck and Rossi, 2019, p. 98).

Remedying the Rentiers?

> The coexistence of both profits and rents in underdeveloped economies does not constitute a particular variety of capitalism. It is instead a characteristic of an essentially non-capitalist economy, because the existence of rents implies that the access to economic surpluses depends primarily on nonmarket mechanisms. In such environments, profit-based capitalism is too weak to cohere the whole society and has not only to tolerate but even to require the vitality of a non-capitalist sector. The more the non-capitalist sector is free from having to follow the criterion of maximising its own profit, the freer it is to subsidise and enable the capitalist sector. The capitalist sector may and will remove this sector when the problem of overcoming underdevelopment and the establishment of full-fledged capitalism is made possible. With booming demand, capitalist entrepreneurs are able to build strong enough coalitions for imposing a functioning capitalist system against the existing non-capitalist structures. (Elsenhans and Babones, 2017, p. 38)

The point of emphasis in these four chapters is that capitalism and development will be severely constricted whenever rent is present. It is impossible to envisage a conciliation between undemocratically controlled rent and a competitive economy because resources are finite, and they compete for and deplete each other's resources. Above all, rentiers will always count on the political theatre to win the tug of war against regular market competitors.

Conceptually, competitive capitalism is essentially self-regulated, as competition promotes a continuous circulation of capital between sectors and economic activities. This circulation creates and recreates the social division of labour by deepening the productive structure's specialisation and separating social strata. In a monopoly or rent-extractive activities, the intra-business expansion causes the circulation of capital to strengthen among associated oligopolies of banks, state classes and industries, implying the creation of large conglomerates corporations within the same block of money, which starves the investments and accumulation outside of said groups (Nozaki, 2019, pp. 63–64).

Even the most modern, innovative, and well-crafted development strategies will fail if infra-reforms are not in place to disenfranchise rent. It is analogous to potent software run on incompatible or obsolete hardware. This fact is most often goes unacknowledged in policy-making or thrown into a second plan. Governments focus on popular, appealing strategies that usually act only in society's superstructure, not its infrastructure. For one, governments do that because such strategies catalyse political support. For another, by working only on the surface of the problem, politicians do not confront the elites who fund or uphold the very political system from which they arose within and now benefit. It would be a self-destructive behaviour, in the Brazilian case, for public office incumbents to discharge their powers to undermine the inner workings of the same groups that gave rise to them. As well, some politicians are not well versed in economics or economic thinking. Please make no mistake: not every politician is good or bad, or even conscientious of their actions' implications. Predominantly, incompetence superimposes evil in politics. For these officials, the bare minimum and simple action might configure as a success if immediate goals are accomplished. There is a fundamental lack of understanding and interest concerning the deeper causes, nature or consequences of societal issues.

One must recognise that the state is fundamental for changing that scenario finally. It ought to be capable of enacting nation-wide policies regulating the markets for the collective good and incentivising productive investments as a priority. Austerity in Brazil is nothing but unnecessary and detrimental. The logical course of action is re-prioritising and re-allocating investments, not spending less. As we have seen, Brazil's expansion of mass consumption has led to superior opportunities for rent extraction by Brazilian companies (Elsenhans and Babones, 2017). With rent thriving, investments plummet. If the government also stops investing, due to austerity, competitiveness suffers; it potentiates rent-based activities, limits poverty reduction, and undermines development. Then, to tackle these major problems would only be more insurmountable.

Disenfranchising Rentiers

The single most important and urgent matter and the only action that can genuinely solve Brazil's development problem is disenfranchising rentiers. This battle will be the toughest one as rent capillarity in local, regional, state, and national politics in Brazil is all-pervading. The bond between government and rent dates back from the very formation of the State:

> *This association is materialized in a Hobbesian scheme in which wars stimulate the creation of taxes, which finance them. Currencies appear as a way of delimiting the territorial horizon of tax collection, and, finally, the circulation of a unit of value standardization ends up engendering exchange and trade. Therefore, the precedence of power over wealth is one of the theoretical principles for interpreting capitalism. Thus, the knot that binds the owners of power to the owners of money seems to reveal itself with particular clarity, precisely in the sphere of high finance. In other words, in that dimension in which state and capital rights are confused in the process of monetary management, precisely because the currency fulfils both public functions and companies.* (Author's translation of Nozaki, 2019, p. 57)

Step 1 to break the state/rent ties is to lift the official policies that facilitate ever-generating profits without matching investments. As rentiers already count with a wealth of benefits that place them miles ahead of market competitors, an initial force is required: overtaxing rentiers' export goods. Taxes should be put at an even higher level whenever there is a short boom in prices for rentiers' products in the international market or when demand for those products is maintained due to monopsonies or oligopsonies. There is a caveat, however: If the country has no productive structure or idle capacity to produce other items and replace the rentiers' exports, and if the government is too reliant on exports revenues and foreign currency, then this country might run into severe financial issues in a very short time. Overtaxing rentiers' products must come after or concomitant with an extensive programme for incentives to productive investments in other sectors, or at least in a few selected strategic industries that have the potential to develop faster and replace the dependency from the traditional exports.

Step 2 is to resolve unfair productive opportunity distribution. The majority of the strongest and deeply rooted Brazilian rentiers are *latifundiarios*. They own massive strips of land that no one else ever had access to or a chance to cultivate. Some of these *latifundios* belong to the same families for centuries, and many are kept untapped purposefully. Agrarian reform is mandatory in Brazil. In this current scenario, both the land and potential agriculturalists are being banned from generating wealth. Such a reform was crucial to consolidate capitalism in Japan, South Korea, and Taiwan as it enabled rapid industrialisation. Land was expropriated from powerful landowners and transferred to its occupants. Production and productivity improved as a result of technical advances. Brazil cannot develop in any meaningful way without agrarian reform. The fact it is not high on the agenda points to the continued political power of the *latifundios*.

China, for example, only managed to develop their superior export performance we see today because of the agrarian reform with land redistribution. The countries that succeeded in developing following such a bold move form an extensive list. Japan in the 1980s and, more recently, South Korea and Taiwan, took the same route. After the reforms, they experienced an expansion in their export capacity associated with growing labour absorption for production and, hence, creating a solid internal market with social security and fair wealth distribution. Access to productive means had emptied rentiers' powers in favour of workers, who depended less on oligarchs and began producing as per the mechanisms of a free, competitive market (Elsenhans and Babones, 2017).

Step 3 is that the state should coordinate and channel productive investments associated with labour rights. State intervention is essential because, in a rent-driven country, society and capitalism agents are too weak to counter-balance rentiers. Contrary to economic orthodoxy, the government needs to regulate the markets to a high degree and increase demand for consumer goods from the working class. This way, the state will be sending the message that producing is profitable, triggering a race for more investments and technological advancements to compete for consumers. "Market competition is the best mechanism yet developed for dispersing power and thus forcing people to innovate if they want to make money" (Elsenhans and Babones, 2017, p. 35).

Step 4 is to put an end to privileges of any kind. There is no room for privileges in a democratic, republican state functioning under the rule of law. Conceding favours and special rules to privileged individuals or groups allows them to have too many de facto unconstitutional powers over society. These powers are used to undermine development efforts and fundamental change in the name of the maintenance of a status quo that benefits only themselves. An end to privileges includes banning lobby groups from legislative houses, which often enact pieces that facilitate the transfer of public resources into private hands to the detriment of collective services and investments. It also requires the taxation of large fortunes and the lifting of special under-taxation of luxury goods. Finally, it is urgent to enact laws to impose a maximum wage. These measures would create an extra push for wealth redistribution, followed by heightened opportunities for the masses' consumer goods production.

Nevertheless, the path towards economic development is not a one-way street that can be travelled only by discouraging rent. On the other side of the road, the rest of society should also see favourable policies for their empowerment. We have already seen historical evidence for that, which was the episode of slavery abolition in Brazil. The end of the legal exploitation of the workforce in Brazil did not lead to an automatic integration and assimilation of the former slaves into society economy or politics. The state did not plan for that insertion, leaving the then-recently free black population impoverished and excluded in ghettoes. In other words, disenfranchising the powerful does not automatically lead to the enfranchisement of the marginalised. This enfranchisement has to be planned, intentional, and sustained.

Enfranchising Labour

We have established that the improvement of living conditions within capitalism depends upon the construction of a wage society. In other words, more people must have access to better jobs and salaries. Although productivity is vital to raising the standard of living in an underdeveloped economy, the mere fact that labour is more productive does not ensure that capital will be distributed more fairly (Calixtre, 2019, p. 45). In this context, the two most important actions are, firstly, we must create an economic and social policy that assures that everyone has enough means for a dignifying living. All levels of government must work in tandem to:

a. Provide a safety net and the minimum necessary for a dignifying life, especially to the unemployed and the homeless.
b. Stop the forced labour and labour exploitation and increase the inspection to ensure these activities do not happen.
c. Enact stronger labour regulations to mandate a minimum wage to all workers and enforce it.
d. Eliminate unproductive jobs.
e. Invest more in training and ever-advancing the technical skills of the workers.

Second, after ensuring minimum living standards, labour should be enfranchised through two primary principles. The first focuses on expanding the mass consumption market resulting from the incorporation of working families into it. The second focuses on the government's public and private investment in infrastructure. Combined, the expansion of the domestic market provided through this incorporation of workers and investments in infrastructure contributes to economic growth and development. The higher demand, stimulated by the consumer market size and investments in infrastructure reduces systemic costs as it promotes an economic upscale. This is a virtuous cycle, wherein the expansion of the market and wage increases benefit each other. In such an environment, government revenues surge, which allows for further investments in rising demand and production. This mechanism generates a virtuous cycle in which the workers' salaries are pivotal (Dweck and Rossi, 2019, p. 99).

Rent extraction damages national revenues and savings by the withdrawal of capital from the open market, resulting in lower economic agents' capacity to invest or re-invest, whereas social investment has a positive effect on both the reduction of inequality and economic development, and the creation of jobs. In 2010, the Brazilian Institute of Applied Economic Research reported that, for example, an increase of 1% of GDP in education and health expenditure generates GDP growth of 1.85 and 1.70%, respectively. Social investment also decreases income inequality: an increase of 1% of GDP in public health expenditures and the *Bolsa Família* programme reduces inequality by 1.50 and 2.20%, respectively, as calculated by the Gini index. Social spending should not be viewed as a strain on public accounts in this context. It can be an essential mechanism for sustainable development, combined with other economic policy instruments, and can guarantee the expansion of the state financing sources (Dweck and Rossi, 2019, p. 106).

All of these initiatives aim at three key outcomes: allowing more people to produce more; enabling more people to consume more; ensuring that workers achieve bargaining power before capital owners. Better employment and wages are intended to provide the masses with superior living standards and ensure that workers have access to the resources they have created. Economic growth becomes more meaningful, sustainable, and conducive to overall development at all levels when this happens. Therefore, catching-up economies like Brazil have to create structures that preserve comparatively equitable income distribution while also providing prospects for innovation and entrepreneurship. Empowering labour in the market is the vital technical developments and economic growth are turned into lasting gains (Elsenhans and Babones, 2017).

Production Diversification

When a few individuals, maybe a small community of oligarchs, dominate the economy, investments and government choices only naturally gravitate around those classes, perpetuating inequalities, rent, imperfections in growth, and a subpar development.

A possible solution for countries with a history of rent is a rational choice to steer away from this condition by using the rent extraction as a springboard to a new scenario. “Using” is a keyword in this context because countries can use rent during a transient phase of transformation instead of depending on it continually. These nations could take advantage of profits from the sectors that already have their goods competitive at reasonably high prices on the international market. This capital, then, goes to build new manufacturing lines that would be commercially viable in the future. Thinking in a nationally concerted manner is more critical than benefitting any single company or sector, regardless of that sector’s weight in the economy. Development is an objective whose outputs satisfy the collectivity. The policy inputs to achieve development must also stem from the collectivity instead of individuals or small groups.

South Korea’s textile industry found itself in a rather crowded domestic market. Therefore, its government proceeded to increase the costs for importing and locally producing textile machinery. As a result, previously not as competitive or not as cost-effective sectors as the textile industry gained momentum to grow. As a result, the South Korean government sparked diversification as the capital started to flow into other economic branches. The previously weak branches were mostly so because they had not received investments before. This way, they had a chance to stand out (Elsenhans and Babones, 2017, p. 48). Frequently, promising and strategic industries do not receive enough investments that would allow them to fulfil their potential because capital is leaking into other sectors for non-market reasons. Elsenhans and Babones conclude that:

> Similar instruments to upgrade production include local content rules, export taxes, and obligations for training workers. They all apply the same type of mechanism: “artificially” (i.e., state-imposed) increased costs

> in branches of industry that can bear such costs in order to appropriate rents in the form of taxes for subsidising diversification to other industries. (Elsenhans and Babones, 2017, p. 48)

In contrast, a lack of production diversity could well constrain the positive development effects of an internal market expansion. Domestic consumer markets' importance and their contribution towards progress are hindered when there is not enough supply on the other side to accompany demand. If the demand is higher than the capacity to cater for it, then imports will increase, causing inflation to rise and domestic markets not to expand. That was the scenario in Brazil during the early 2000s. And an internal demand requiring external supply can trigger industrialisation abroad. That was the case of Brazil deindustrialising to China.

Some forms of state-imposed policies that help foster production diversification are often beneficial to fair competition, a hallmark of a healthy capitalist system. In rent economies, equal competition is a problem because rentiers are not subject to the same rules as regular entrepreneurs. Fair competition intensifies equality of opportunities and economic success among investors and workers alike. It motivates market agents to innovate and develop technical skills, knowing that they may well profit more from an ever-improving culture.

For that purpose, one standard policy adopted worldwide is subsidies. However, investments in education, technology and science result in more effective and sustainable benefits. All five BRICS countries have introduced policies to establish national innovation structures through university networks, regional expertise, and national private or state-owned businesses. These structures have evolved in ways that have been heavily affected by each country's unique institutional arrangements. Even so, the overarching aim of these initiatives is still to develop domestic enterprises' capacity to succeed internationally on their own. Throughout this, China, Brazil, and India were so successful that some of their firms could access international markets, including developing world markets, though with overt government subsidies (Elsenhans and Babones, 2017, p. 43). Brazil's EMBRAER is an example of a highly technological company in a country with a much lower technical level that has conquered buyers from around the world, competing head to head with companies from more advanced economies. The model must not be constricted to a few industries. Aligning production diversification with technical advancement in the majority of them is essential for the success of development.

In sum, for production diversification and general competitiveness, technical progress is the ultimate solution. It decreases the work needed for existing goods to be produced and new products to be developed. Increasing workers' wages and swelling costs for unskilled and semi-skilled labour also encourages technical progress, as businesses will prefer to use technology to save on labour. If technological advancement leads to productivity increases, production costs will decline, and firms will attempt to ramp up their sales by cutting prices. Production and jobs will go hand-in-hand. As a spillover effect, in countries with low unemployment, overall technical progress will lead salaries to rise even in technologically underdeveloped sectors due to the suppression of marginality (Elsenhans and Babones, 2017, p. 56).

International Markets

If the policy adopted by the developing economy is usefully instrumentalised, openness to international capital can be beneficial. An inflow of investment from abroad is not in itself an automatic engine for accelerated industrialisation. For example, China's foreign direct investment portfolio accounts for roughly 10% of GDP, virtually unchanged for more than 15 years, while India has stood at about the same level since 2010 (Elsenhans and Babones, 2017, p. 92). In the meantime, their industrialisation and modernisation have continued to intensify rapidly, but foreign direct investment has not. It is an indication that these countries could use such assets for their growth, but they go beyond such a source of capital to develop. National, long-term development goals should be given priority over international and financial markets. Foreign currency revenue from exports is the ultimate national imperative in rent-based economies when the state supports its elites for profit. In that case, society is reduced to a mere supporting role. Therefore, to reposition society to the forefront is to see foreign investments and export revenues as a means, not aims.

Conversely, as economies grow, countries should not withdraw surplus capital from the economy to reallocate it to financial projects or speculative ventures abroad. Extra resources contribute to temptation and give governments greater flexibility to apply them to non-productive activities. Like a person who has become wealthy and is beginning to spend more and more on services and luxury items than on consumer goods, countries engaged in neo-mercantilist ventures of non-productive accumulation contribute less to their own and their neighbours' growth and development in the long run.

This phenomenon is taking place in the BRICS. Mauritius' financial hub accounts for one-fourth of Indian foreign capital stock. Including Singapore, the share of capital in tax havens is up to one-third. Financial centres such as Cyprus, Luxembourg and the Virgin Islands account for one-fifth of South Africa's international assets and two-thirds of the Russian capital. BRICS countries tend to have a large proportion of international capital invested in financial speculation, not production, infrastructure, or innovation (Elsenhans and Babones, 2017, p. 96).

Instead of funding the necessary start-ups, green technologies, social enterprises, capital is incentivised to go "where they can find the greatest secrecy, the most lax regulations and freedom from the rulers of civilised society" (Shaxson, 2011, p. 78). While we went through the reckoning of the 2008 Global Crash due to such financial products, their equivalents are reappearing in what are called collateralised debt obligation.

Final Remarks

> The debate on the ideal model to initiate structural transformations starting from accumulation should advance the sustainability of the cycle of transformations beyond the superficial progress in income, poverty and inequality. In other words, attention should be focused on consolidating the structural changes necessary for a definitive break with the past, not only on how to initiate this progress. The problem is that insisting on structural changes necessarily leads to macroeconomic imbalances caused by shifts in resource distribution. Unfortunately, conventional economic theory is tediously repetitive in prescribing the system's stability, which, in the case of underdeveloped countries, means the stability of inequalities between capital and labour and underdevelopment. The economic tradition prefers to sacrifice the dynamic turbulence provided by development for the stability of the privileges maintained by backwardness. (Author's translation of Calixtre, 2019, p. 45)

Whenever the structural status quo is not broken, any GDP advancements, productivity, and other goals will never suffice to generate actual, sustained development. The advancements mentioned above are tools used by the pre-modern system agents to persuade society that development has occurred when it has not—and people know it. Some of the sacred Western, orthodox economic advice served to perpetuate an outdated structure masked as new and transformative, e.g. perfect market hypothesis. Economic stability is a prominent example of such kind of advice. In the economy, there is a relentless battle between sustaining the safe yet perverse status quo or risking a potential instability arising from a clean break, in Brazil's case its rentist origins. Brazil's status quo managed to preserve massive regional and social inequality since colonisation and slavery while pinning to the ground the country's huge development potential. The status quo has reproduced the historical priorities rooted in social conservatism, rent-based investment decision-making, and the perpetual replication of ultra-concentrated wealth under the false appearance of macroeconomic steadiness (Calixtre, 2019, p. 45).

Thus, the country can only win the development challenges through the pulverisation of economic and political power; by redistributing it through mass incomes and consumer markets and imposing limits on any new acquisition of power by any society's agents. The state must no longer be permeable to foreign and mercantile interests and should not cater to private oligopolies. What Brazilian history shows is not the creation of a powerful, broad, and anti-market State, but, on the contrary, a State with systemic gaps sealed over by a cheaply bought body *politik*. It is a State inefficient in organising the land, capital, and policies. Yet, that State seeks to direct the modernisation, development, industrialisation, and urbanisation processes of the country (Nozaki, 2019, p. 69). Due to the State's weakness, elites acquire the ability for their agendas to interfere and hijack government action to thwart easily implemented social policies that would transform millions of lives.

In practical terms, the government must rationalise its decision-making by acknowledging the deeper Brazilian issues and resolving them at its core, which will permeate any development strategies in the future. Without distractions, the legal framework and policy must mitigate the most prolonged standing and concrete problems, discussed at over the past four chapters. As well as embracing and managing the possibly disruptive and risk-taking practices that a genuine national transformation entails, the State must plan its actions only according to public purposes (Dweck and Rossi, 2019, pp. 107–108).

Bibliography

Almeida, P. R. (2009). O Brasil e as relações internacionais no pós-Guerra Fria. In: N. I. Ladwig and R. S. da Costa (Orgs.), *Vinte anos após a queda do muro de Berlim: um debate interdisciplinar*. Palhoça: Editora da Unisul.

Burges, S. W. (2008). Consensual Hegemony: Theorizing Brazilian Foreign Policy After the Cold War. In: *International Relations* 22, no. 1.

Calixtre, A. B. (2019). Sociedade salarial e resiliência: reflexões sobre a economia política da mudança estrutural. In: M. V. Chiliatto Leite (Org.), *Alternativas para o desenvolvimento brasileiro: novos horizontes para a mudança estrutural com igualdade* (LC/TS.2019/27). Santiago: Comissão Econômica para a América Latina e o Caribe (CEPAL).

Dweck, E. and Rossi, P. (2019). Políticas sociais, distribuição, crescimento e mudança estrutural. In: M. V. C. Leite (Org.), *Alternativas para o desenvolvimento brasileiro: novos horizontes para a mudança estrutural com igualdade* (LC/TS.2019/27). Santiago: Comissão Econômica para a América Latina e o Caribe (CEPAL).

Elsenhans, H. and Babones, S. (2017). *BRICS or Bust? Escaping the Middle-Income Trap*. Stanford: Stanford University Press.

Fonseca, P. D. (1992). Vargas: o capitalismo em Construção. In: *Análise Econômica* 10, no. 18: 143–145.

Nozaki, W. (2019). Estado e desenvolvimento no Brasil: estrutura de poder, dinâmica política e instabilidade institucional. In: M. V. Chiliatto Leite (Org.), *Alternativas para o desenvolvimento brasileiro: novos horizontes para a mudança estrutural com igualdade* (LC/TS.2019/27). Santiago: Comissão Econômica para a América Latina e o Caribe (CEPAL).

Oliveira, M. A. G. (2010). Sources of Brazil's Counter-Hegemony. In: *Revista Brasileira de Política Internacional* 53, no. 2.

Pecequilo, C. S. (2008). A política externa do Brasil no século XXI: Os eixos combinados de cooperação horizontal e vertical. In: *Revista Brasileira de Política Externa* 51, no. 2.

Shaxson, N. (2011). *Treasure Islands: Uncovering the Damage of Offshore Banking and Tax Havens*. New York City: Palgrave Macmillan.

Wirth, J. D. (1971). *The Politics of Brazilian Development, 1930–1954*. Stanford: Stanford University Press.

CHAPTER 6

Institutional Complementarity, Not Rent, Is the Recipe of Brazil's Economic Failures

Fabricio H. Chagas-Bastos

Development problems and their proposed solutions have filled libraries. More ink has been spilt than we can ever hope to make use of from the knowledge produced. Framing a precise and specific set of causes over long periods to explain why a country (or in more strict terms, an economy) has not accumulated wealth and technological development are hard tasks—although it has been done (e.g. Grinin et al., 2020). It is similarly complex to pinpoint a single causes that explain development difficulties.

Hence, I will bypass from the outset the arguments presented in Chapters 2–5. Although presenting a rich background of the reasons for Brazil's difficulties over history to achieve desired developmental levels, I will not cast the same broad net to cover the arguments and facts presented. Moreover, it has been proven by a voluminous literature on institutional economics that couching the reasons of underdevelopment on such long historical roots has not survived the scrutiny of time.

F. H. Chagas-Bastos (✉)
University of Copenhagen, Copenhagen, Denmark

N. Wilcock and E. Federzoni dos Santos (eds.), *Not Paying the Rent*,
https://doi.org/10.1007/978-3-030-78861-2_6

I will concentrate on Federzoni's arguments on Brazil's lagging development. On the one hand, the two pieces of my argument first reject the idea of a possible "convoy model" as an explanation and policy source. According to Federzoni's argument, Brazilian development was moved by a metaphorical locomotive that leads to developmental spill-over from more to less developed regions. The idea of a "pull up" between regional economies seems in reverse—a peruse of the data from Brazil's Northeast can show that it was more a "pull down" from the rich regions to the poorest ones than the other way around. On the other, I diverge from the heterodox and particular view of Brazilian development, where rentiers are the critical problem in Brazil. Instead, the purposeful institutional disarray lies at the core of the country's developmental failures.

I lend the first part of my argument from Taylor (2020, p. 12), as he puts it

> *All of these phenomena —failure to refurbish the developmental state, failure to reach a new neoliberal equilibrium, and the hyperactivity of reform—have the same source. The institutions of the Brazilian political economy drive toward a common equilibrium that is hard to break, not least because of institutional complementarities across five institutional arenas that jointly explain the country's trajectory since 1985: the resilience of developmentalism as an idea with effects on both policy choices and institutions in the macroeconomic realm; the concentration and segmentation of firm life in the microeconomic realm, DHME*[1]*; the consensual politics inherent to the coalitional presidential system, which undermine the checks and balances that are frequently assumed to be central to presidential systems; the resulting weakness of the control mechanisms needed to effectively govern the developmental state; and an autonomous bureaucracy that is able to undertake reforms that ensure the developmental state's continued viability but also contribute to its growth-constraining effect by reinforcing the incentive structures set in place by the other institutions.*

In short, Taylor argues that institutional strategies to reach equilibrium in one domain may be shaped by the incentives coming from another. One should bear in mind that particular institutional trajectories are

[1] Developmental Hierarchical Market Economy, a concept crafted by Taylor. See Taylor, M. (2020). The Developmental Hierarchical Market Economy. In: *Decadent Developmentalism: The Political Economy of Democratic Brazil* (pp. 90–118). Cambridge: Cambridge University Press. https://doi.org/10.1017/9781108900072.004.

constrained by past choices and constrained by the past trajectories of other, complementary institutions. This institutional complementary in Brazil led to a vicious cycle that does not limit capital rentiers—it would be too narrow-minded and heterodox to couch a multicausal explanation to a single point in the curve.

Here we meet the second part of my argument: dependency. Stavenhagen (1972) advanced Cardoso and Faletto's propositions pinpointing that the same international dependent dynamics were reproduced domestically. The sizeable empirical evidence coming from regional development disparities in several countries and, for instance, from the Latin American countries' failure to integrate with each other show that the asymmetrical dynamics of dependency happen (and have happened) across and within countries. As a *post-hoc* model, the convoy model holds its explanatory power on the analysis of the difficulties faced by late development economies without looking at the power and institutional dynamics as I proposed here.

My argument can be summarised as the long-standing problem with Brazilian development resides on precarious institutional arrangements that allow individuals and/or corporations to take advantage of the system and use them to reproduce privilege and inequality across domains—not exclusively the rentier sectors of the economy. As Taylor (2020, p. 10) puts it, "[i]f Brazil has failed to make the developmental state effective, it has also failed to go down an alternate, more market-oriented path often referred to as the 'neoliberal' path". If the problem were the rentier class's longevity pulling down and thwarting development, neoliberalism had triumphantly won in Brazil. That is not the case.

Challenging Problems, Complex Solutions

I will not take the four policy conclusions in Chapter 5 as remedies for the development ills of Brazil, and offer my take. As stated (p. 84) "[t]he single most important and urgent matter and the only action that can genuinely solve Brazil's development problem are disenfranchising rentiers. This battle will be the toughest one as rent capillarity in local, regional, state and national politics in Brazil is all-pervading. The bond between government and rent dates back from the very formation of the State". He follows as (p. 85):

Step 1 to break the state/rent ties is to lift the official policies that facilitate ever-generating profits without matching investments. As rentiers already count with a wealth of benefits that place them miles ahead of market competitors, an initial force is required: overtaxing rentiers' export goods. Taxes should be put at an even higher level whenever there is a short boom in prices for rentiers' products in the international market or when demand for those products is maintained due to monopsonies or oligopsonies. There is a caveat, however: If the country has no productive structure or idle capacity to produce other items and replace the rentiers' exports, and if the government is too reliant on exports revenues and foreign currency, then this country might run into severe financial issues in a very short time. Overtaxing rentiers' products must come after or concomitant with an extensive programme for incentives to productive investments in other sectors, or at least in a few selected strategic industries that have the potential to develop faster and replace the dependency from the traditional exports.

The productive side of the argument cannot hold, as Brazil has a variegated productive capacity. Similarly, the over-taxation argument has proven weak. For instance, Presidents Lula da Silva and Dilma Rousseff applied for almost a decade fiscal incentives (tax cuts) to specific sectors of the economy. There was not, and there will not be, any guarantees that companies favoured by such incentives will use their surpluses to increment productive capacities, hiring or other investment-like measures. In the same vein, literature shows that taxation will not produce relocation of the capital to productive investments in less developed countries. Rather, the better away ahead is in a general tax reform that puts all productive sectors on an equal footing, instead of embracing the cherry-picking game of specific-sector's incentives or punishments. Brazil has accustomed itself to such a capital flight: when the Brazilian political landscape gets unstable, capital moves to the US or EU treasury (safe) bonds.

Step 2 is to resolve unfair productive opportunity distribution. The majority of the strongest and deeply rooted Brazilian rentiers are latifundiarios. They own massive strips of land that no one else ever had access to or a chance to cultivate. Some of these latifundios belong to the same families for centuries, and many are kept untapped purposefully. Agrarian reform is mandatory in Brazil. In this current scenario, both the land and potential agriculturalists are being banned from generating wealth.

The four-chapter series *Arrabalde* recently written by João Moreira Salles to *Piauí* refutes Step 2. Salles (2020, 2021) shows how land property rights in the Amazon over the military rule were confusedly shared between local, state, and federal governments in a spaghetti-bowl of institutions created but ultimately dissolved over time.

Brazilian state institutions deliberately reinforce the disarray of land property registrations, not limited to rentiers, but to a vast range of people. Additionally, groups take advantage of such state's disorganisation to grab land illegally. Often, instead of receiving any punishment for their illegal acts, they are even recompensed with disproportionate economic advantages as the authorities turn a blind eye.

Even over the neoliberal period, between 1994 and 2002, agrarian reform has been progressing; it was deepened between 2003 and 2016, but a serious and sustained agrarian reform can only exist when incentives to institutional change are robust enough to tackle such challenges. The foremost difficulty is to reduce the incentives given to those who can benefit from such illegal land grabbing.

> *Step 3 is that the state should coordinate and channel productive investments associated with labour rights. State intervention is essential because, in a rent-driven country, society and capitalism agents are too weak to counterbalance rentiers. Contrary to economic orthodoxy, the government needs to regulate the markets to a high degree and increase demand for consumer goods from the working class. This way, the state will be sending the message that producing is profitable, triggering a race for more investments and technological advancements to compete for consumers.*

Recent history shows that institutional complementarity can enhance institutional disarray. The gargantuan corruption scandal involving the political system and the oil company Petrobras revealed from 2014 onwards evidence that taking from the state is profitable but incurs many legal risks. Only states can fulfil an economic, social, and moral obligation to provide social meaning to labour. However, as Taylor reminds us, with weak control mechanisms to govern the developmental state effectively and an autonomous bureaucracy able to ensure policy continuity, state-led economic projects can lead to anti-cyclical changes—given that behaviour reinforces behaviour. Moreover, the regional dispute for budget allocation in Congress and state governors in Brazil often leads to conflict between subnational entities and reinforce asymmetrical development characteristics, as per Stavenhagen's argument.

The idea of a state orienting the economy is not a preposterous one. It was believed to be the only way forward, however, to liberal economists who embraced ultra-liberal theories and guided the economic policies in the governments of Michel Temer and Jair Bolsonaro. The main one is the idea of "expansionary contraction", which gave support to fiscal austerity programmes and public expenditure control. It describes a virtuous circuit triggered by the pursuit of fiscal balance. Severe public spending cuts were seen as necessary and would result in the resumption of business and investor confidence, as well as economic activity recovery. The return of investments would promote the generation of jobs and the expansion of the market. The meagre growth of the Brazilian economy since 2014 shows that the plan has fallen short of the expectations. However, more than a decade of low growth in much of the Western world has cast doubt on the effectiveness of "expansionist contraction" models. Its supporters, led by Alberto Alesina, a Harvard political economist, had already published on the virtuous circuit imagined as the effect of fiscal austerity programmes.

The abrupt halt in international economic growth between 2007 and 2008 led to a reduction in Brazil's export revenues and the damage to the country's increasingly important export sector. Two factors that chiefly worked to project the Brazilian economy regionally and globally along the 2000s were not in play anymore. Firstly, the high prices for most Latin American export commodities oscillated sharply, putting pressure on a dangerously mounting public deficit—as for 2019, for instance, the Brazilian federal deficit corresponds to BRL 139 billion (around $35.29 billion). Second, the financial liquidity provided by global interest rates were meagre for much of the period started to disappear. The effect on Brazilian firms was critical. Some of the "national champions"—in particular animal protein companies—were allowed to borrow money in strong currencies abroad to extend their export-oriented activities at home, and the rapid devaluation of Brazilian Real combined with the increase of international interest rates drove some companies to bankruptcy. Both were associated with the country's economic presidential diplomacy under Lula that allowed Brazilian companies to expand their operations in South America, Africa, China, and even the US (Chagas-Bastos & Franzoni, 2019). Much in the same way, given the sustained reduction in growth rates in the Chinese market and its associated stalled recovery in European, the commodity-export driven path of growth seen in Brazil in the early 2000s was presumably expected to find its limits, which was realised in 2015 and 2016.

> *Step 4 is to put an end to privileges of any kind. There is no room for privileges in a democratic, republican state functioning under the rule of law. Conceding favours and special rules to privileged individuals or groups allows them to have too many de facto unconstitutional powers over society. These powers are used to undermine development efforts and fundamental change in the name of the maintenance of a status quo that benefits only themselves. An end to privileges includes banning lobby groups from legislative houses, which often enact pieces that facilitate the transfer of public resources into private hands to the detriment of collective services and investments. It also requires the taxation of large fortunes and the lifting of special undertaxation of luxury goods. Finally, it is urgent to enact laws to impose a maximum wage. These measures would create an extra push for wealth redistribution, followed by heightened opportunities for the masses' consumer goods production.*

Tackling the same problem, Sanchez-Ancochea (2020) notes that "[a]cross Latin America, the wealthy have faced limited incentives to invest in new sectors —they make healthy profits regardless— and have been unwilling to pay enough taxes to fund public social spending. Inequality has been one of the drivers of weak institutions and the emergence of anti-system politics". Taylor (2020, p. 14) notes that "[b]ecause the rule constrains behaviour, and behaviour reinforces the rule, there is considerable room for continuity", so institutional complementarity feeds into precarious arrangements and provides incentives to the continuation of weak institutions. At the same time, "a change in behavior can change the rule: failure to apply the rule, failure to comply with the rule, or failure to recognise the rule, for example, might all lead to change". Therein lies the challenge: to promote institutional change without allowing breaches in democratic and republican structures. The fortune spin can go both ways: if virtuous, it can lead to development and growth; if negative, it can undoubtedly make the economic and political landscapes go back decades.

Final Remarks

Brazil has been living in a political and economic crisis state since 2013. The slowdown of international commodity markets followed by a steady decline of industrial activities showed that unresolved social problems were still present—even though Brazil experienced a decade of growth and poverty reduction over the 2000s. In 2013, massive demonstrations took the streets across the country (with a remarkable 1 million people march in Rio, in June 2013). Since then, the political system fractured and fragmented. The following years were no calmer.

I mapped out in this chapter some critical responses to Federzoni's proposal to undock Brazil's development path. As Federzoni describes, Brazil has taught the world over years how to miss opportunities to move from one developmental stage to the other. But development cannot rely on resurrecting old ghosts that have proven not to work. The past chapters form an essential framework to understand how institutional development has accumulated over history. The journalist Millôr Fernandes used to joke that ideas come to Brazil to retire (late communist ideas, ill-equipped, ultra-liberal recipes, among others). Unfortunately, the country seems to be plagued with decrepit mindsets…and institutions.

Bibliography

Carvalho, L. (2018). *Valsa Brasileira*. São Paulo: Todavia.

Chagas-Bastos, F. H. and Franzoni, M. (2019). Frustrated Emergence? Brazil and Mexico's Coming of Age. In: *Rising Powers Quarterly* 3, no. 4, 33–59.

Grinin, L., Grinin, A. and Korotayev, A. (2020). A Quantitative Analysis of Worldwide Long-Term Technology Growth: From 40,000 BCE to the Early 22nd Century. In: *Technological Forecasting and Social Change* 155, 119955.

Moreira Salles, J. (2020a). Arrabalde—Parte I_A floresta difícil. In: *piauí* 170: 40–51.

Moreira Salles, J. (2020b). Arrabalde—Parte II_Sete bois em linha. In: *piauí* 171: 40–50.

Moreira Salles, J. (2021a). Arrabalde—Parte III_A fronteira é um país estrangeiro. In: *piauí* 172: 46–57.

Moreira Salles, J. (2021b). Arrabalde—Parte IV_A reviravolta. In: *piauí* 173: 46–52.

Moreira Salles, J. (2021c). Arrabalde—Parte V_O reencontro. In: *piauí* 174: 42–52.

Moreira Salles, J. (2021d). Arrabalde—Parte VI_O que queremos? In: *piauí* 175: 12–16.

Safatle, C., Borges, J. and Oliveira, R. (2016). *Anatomia de um desastre: Os bastidores da crise econômica que mergulhou o país na pior recessão da história.* São Paulo: Portfolio-Penguin.

Sanchez-Ancochea, D. (2020). *The Costs of Inequality in Latin America: Lessons and Warnings for the Rest of the World.* London: I.B. Tauris.

Stavenhagen, R. (1972). Siete tesis equivocadas sobre América Latina. In: R. Stavenhagen, *Sociología y Subdesarrollo.* Mexico: Editorial Nuestro Tiempo.

Taylor, M. (2020). *Decadent Developmentalism: The Political Economy of Democratic Brazil.* Cambridge: Cambridge University Press.

Part II

CHAPTER 7

Defending International Organisations in a Liberal International Order: Case Study of the World Health Organization

Neil Wilcock and Edgar Federzoni dos Santos

Leftist discourse holds up capitalism as leading the world to widespread poverty and social turmoil. While increasing inequality and the rise of a precarious labour class, it is not capitalism but rather the forces away from full employment capitalism towards rent which are leading to those failures. Instead of seeking to abolish capitalism, rather the aim should be to realise capitalism's potential emancipation, prosperity and peace.

State policies in one country to that end have been considered in the previous chapter, and this chapter will serve as an introduction to how

N. Wilcock (✉) · E. Federzoni dos Santos
Leipzig University, Leipzig, Germany
e-mail: neil.wilcock.07@aberdeen.ac.uk

E. Federzoni dos Santos
University of Vienna, Vienna, Austria

N. Wilcock and E. Federzoni dos Santos (eds.), *Not Paying the Rent*,
https://doi.org/10.1007/978-3-030-78861-2_7

international organisations[1] and the international community in which they operate can serve that drive towards full employment capitalism. Important policy areas are explored through the respective international organisations that can foster development, namely labour policies at the International Labour Organization (ILO, this chapter), trade policies at the United Nations Conference on Trade and Development (UNCTAD, Chapter 8) and health policies at the World Health Organization (WHO, below). International organisations, such as the ILO, UNCTAD and the WHO, can rally forces outside the major state powers from developing countries such as civil society and social movements for pro-development policies.

Lasting development policies that address structural (causes) rather than ameliorative (symptoms) conditions need to remove labour marginality and replace existing rent relations by open markets which are characterised by a dynamic expansion of mass demand. This chapter will firstly expand on the need for upholding an international order in delivering those structural policies, and secondly, through the case study of the WHO, give an example of the pressure in/on an international organisation in doing so.

International organisations progress through a "crooked trajectory", meaning setbacks coincide with inroads in the layered world of international cooperation. Given its topicality and accessibility, the World Health Organization in the pandemic will be explored to show one such "crooked trajectory" of an international organisation whereby victories and defeats inevitably coincide. A closer look at economic development-focused policies will be explored in the following chapters: chapter 7 hypothesises the ILO coordinating a stones-for-cash scheme which would effectively create a labour market where there was previously no labour demand, and as a result trigger mass consumption; and Chapter 8 retells how the political management of trading relations used to be recognised through the UNCTAD and how developing countries should again collaborate to pressurise for non-reciprocal trading to stimulate their internal markets. Firstly, let us turn to the internal order in which these organisations operate in and its relevance for achieving development.

[1] The use of "international organisation" here includes intergovernmental organisations. The wider term is used to encompass the wider array of actors in that arena.

A Liberal International Order

Princeton professors G John Ikenberry and Daniel Deudney coined the expression a "liberal international order" in 1999, which became an ideology for the western foreign-policy elites to build on and defend. The idea of such an order was "powerful countries agree[ing] to work together, in their mutual interests, through global institutions…in which principles like open trade and international law are firmly established" (Rachman, 2020). Despite the complexities of the international organisations which make up that "liberal international order", the continued political management of increasingly global challenges, and the transition towards a multi-polar world, requires such ingrained multilateralism.

The political economic arguments made in case study of Brazil are relevant to creating that liberal international order as the national and international intersect profoundly. Ikenberry, in his follow-up book "A World Safe for Democracy: Liberal Internationalism and the Crisis of the Global Order" (2020), argues liberal internationalism only prospers in alliance with a domestic counterpart, linking democracy promotion at home with constructive participation in multilateralism abroad. Therefore, the hope for a liberal international order in the future relies in the first instance on domestic democratic accountability and prosperity. Gideon Rachman expands (2020) in his review of the latest Ikenberry book:

> [Woodrow] Wilson believed that democracies could only protect their domestic freedoms, if they paid attention to the broader international environment. A world in which tyranny is advancing is unlikely to be hospitable environment for liberalism – either at home or abroad.

As US President Woodrow Wilson (1913–1921) foresaw when establishing the League of Nations (forerunner to the United Nations), a completely uneven and fragmented domestic sphere will lead to the demise of the liberal order internationally. The threat to the current liberal international order emanates from a version of globalisation which is undermining living standards and social safety-nets in the West. Unless the threats from that rent-based capitalism are overcome domestically by presently capitalist countries, an illiberal international order will inevitably emerge with international organisations incapable of enacting emancipatory policies.

In the twenty years since coining the expression "liberal international order", the world has experienced the pulling back from international cooperation by the major powers US and China, and continued resistance by Russia, alongside the emergence of new challenges from the surge in migration to the coronavirus, not to mention the existential threat of climate change. Nevertheless, Ikenberry (2020) believes that the liberal international order has always followed a "crooked trajectory". A "crooked trajectory" means that while the spirit and rules of international organisations have suffered setbacks ranging from major powers actively scuppering their efficiency to running roughshod over due process in international conduct,[2] simultaneously inroads have been made in international cooperation in the likes of the law, the sharing of intelligence, climate change agreements, addressing world hunger and disaster relief. Increasingly (and gratefully), the world is resolving its conflicts through "jaw-jaw" rather than "war-war".

International organisations like the World Bank, the World Trade Organization, the International Monetary Fund, the UN agencies including the World Health Organization exist for the provision of addressing common cross-border challenges and collective needs. Without such an infrastructure, the necessary and pragmatic effort to defend freedom, prosperity, and peace would be without the necessary institutional support for turning agreements into reality. Rather, it would fall onto bilateral agreements between major powers.

The challenge to the liberal international order comes under three broad categories: the nationalist right (Turkey's Recip Erdogan, Hungarian's Viktor Orban), illiberal countries and the "anti-imperial" left. The latter critique ranges from global Keynesians (the view of these authors) who see the issue as a "global demand gap" which needs to be overcome to anarchists that want the dilution of the nation-state and free associations between all people's without the violence of the state. While notions of global governance without nations are theoretically conceivable, democracy nationally and internationally remains inconceivable without nations in the first place. Elsenhans (Wilcock and Scholz, 2016, p. 138) marks a difference between the role of international organisations for left-wing versus right-wing policies:

[2] A striking example being the US and UK failure invasion of Iraq in 2003 which was in breach of the United Nations Principle of Non-Intervention.

> *[T]he left is well advised to promote what the right is doing to gain new institutional powers, like the strengthening of the European Central Bank and the European Investment Bank, because even if it doesn't look so evident now, all these new levers can be used for redistribution in the future. Look at the situation today, we do not have a European institution powerful enough to install a banking union with global bank monitoring even if the left wanted such an arrangement. The right may create such levers now but afterwards the left could impose different solutions through these new found powers of the institutions.*

The implications for the left are that it should seek to bolster, not bypass, the institutions required to implement development policies. It renders far-left objections to institution-building self-defeating, which a cursory view of their far-fetched proposals confirms. The fact that institutions, whether that's the two banking institutions mentioned above, or the World Bank, IMF, etc., are incepted under neoliberal leadership need not determine its political direction in perpetuity. Take the IMF's response to COVID-19 in 2020, over 100 countries[3] have already approached the IMF for short-term emergency assistance (IMF, 2021) and provided "grant-based debt relief in tranches so that debt relief can be immediately available to all eligible countries hit by the Covid-19 pandemic". The more progressive terms of the debt relief contrast with IMF past policies which gave access to funds to countries on the condition of privatising essential state services. The obstacles to achieving a global Keynesian agenda are multiple, however, borne by necessity to uphold economies activity in the pandemic it was proven (often by right-wing governments) that such policies can be adopted nationally and with the support of international organisations.

The effectiveness of institutions is crucial to the execution of any development model based on agreements. It is for that reason that one of the Sustainable Development Goals is Peace, Justice and Sustainable Institutions (SDG 16[4]). Just as only through institutions can the other SDGs like clean water and sanitation (SDG 6), no poverty (SDG 1), climate

[3] Which is incidentally over double the number that called on the fund in the immediate aftermath of the 2008 financial crisis.

[4] Effective institutions "ensure responsive, inclusive, participatory and representative decision-making at all levels. [Such institutions will] Broaden and strengthen the participation of developing countries in the institutions of global governance" (SDG 16 definition).

action (SDG 13) be achieved, so too can a global Keynesian agenda fixated on closing "global demand gap" can only be realised within a liberal international order.

Therefore, developed and developing countries alike must not retreat to an exceptionalism, or even worse nativism, that bypasses international bodies in their foreign policies. For that reason, it is all the more galling to see those on the left celebrate the UK's exit from the European Union oblivious that without those levers of government it will be even more difficult to implement their desired economic and social policies.[5] Rather, evolutionary strategies are needed to promote economic growth and tackle immanent disparities in a fairer globalisation while ensuring democratic principles. Otherwise, raw power bypassing negotiation with potential rivals will become the dreaded norm.

"Crooked Trajectory" of an International Organisation: Example of the World Health Organization During the Covid-19 Pandemic

The World Health Organization's origins lie in a cluster of organisations (IMF, World Bank, United Nations system) that emerged in the post-war period to coordinate global responses and policies to cross-border topics. The WHO has been the international organisation in the spotlight in 2020/21 given the COVID-19 pandemic,[6] and for that reason, it is timely to explore it as an example of the "crooked trajectory" of an international organisation as it carries out its lofty mandate to "direct and coordinate international health". While the WHO has been under intense scrutiny during the pandemic, the ineluctable position it finds itself reflects a reality for international organisations and presents useful parallels on how we might better understand such organisations' role to fairly judge them.

[5] It is for this reason that Brexit is as much the legacy of the left-wing Jeremy Corbyn (Leader 2015–2020) and the Labour Party as it is right-wing Boris Johnson and the Conservative Party.

[6] In a move to deflect from his bungled handling of the pandemic ahead of a re-election campaign, President Trump withdrew the US from the WHO, thereby thrusting the global health body into the crosshairs of international geopolitics. President Biden has since recommitted the US to WHO membership.

Firstly, international organisations are only as effective as their constituent members (termed “Member States”) allow them to be by granting them adequate funding and providing reliable and timely statistics to carry out their mandates, with a strength which relies mostly on their convening power and veil of neutrality. For example, the WHO’s handling of the COVID-19 pandemic was severely compromised by China, the origin of the virus, not providing the organisation with the accurate, timely and full information thereby jeopardising its response.

Criticisms of international organisations often start with the wrong preconception that they have substantial global leverage. Many of the nigh on 200 governments are autocratic with no free media or effective opposition; therefore, the compulsion from outside government to aim for the facts let alone obtain them is absent. In other cases, states lack the capabilities to measure statistics accurately or at all. Many of the criticisms of the WHO centre on their deference to Beijing and reluctance to set the record straight after they had received spurious information. However, this is par for the course for international organisations which have limited powers of recourse to the states that effectively keep them in business.

International organisations are at the mercy of the data they receive which only tells a nation-centric story and leads to a skewed picture. “The WHO receives its case numbers from governments around the world. It cannot verify these numbers and it cannot oblige governments to provide accurate numbers…[the numbers] are contaminated with politics”, explained Michael Meyer-Resende (quoted in Pratt, 2020), executive director of the rights group Democracy Reporting International, in response to the scrutiny surrounding the WHO. When confronted by illiberal countries that are not used to producing facts accurately domestically, it cannot miraculously be transformed when entering the international sphere.

Depending on whom you ask at any given moment in time, the international organisation in question is almost invariably seen as either the hero or villain, be it the WHO in a global health crisis or the UN High Commissioner for Refugees (UNHCR) in the refugee crisis or International Atomic Energy Agency (IAEA) in a nuclear emergency. Such organisations exist in a kind of damned if you do, damned if you don’t perpetuity. Their broad mission of serving the world’s needs while simultaneously dealing with the realpolitik of how an organisation is funded is a constant tightrope act.

Given the varying donor priorities from the Chinese Government to philanthropic foundations to the European Commission, it becomes evident that the organisations exist more in a geopolitical maze than in an "international safe-space". With regard to the WHO, Steven Hoffman, a professor of global health, law, and political science at York University in Canada, said, "The organisation struggles with that duality…On one hand it's expected to be a world-class public health agency, but at the same time it's expected to manage the complicated global politics that emerge on health issues" (ibid.).

International organisations also suffer from false perceptions about their scope and resources. While international organisations can advocate particular approaches, they are not responsible for individual policies adopted by national governments. Their power rarely exceeds convening governments, being the secreatriat of common agreements and offering technical assistance upon request from governments.

While the missteps of the WHO have become apparent, the international organisations still keep the world informed, mobilise the best available resources of people when required, and through their convening power bring countries intent on verbal war around to consider a united response to common challenges. The fact international organisations like the WHO exist means the pooling of the best experts on global health, providing technical assistance to states when they need it most, and direct funding to areas of high vulnerability; which without them they would be completely inaccessible, particularly to poorer countries.

Such inequality of access, due to a lack of strength in international organisations, is apparent in the roll-out of vaccine. The UN Secretary General Antonio Guterres admitted it was "vaccine nationalism moving with full speed" (quoted in Pratt, 2021). Campaigners have warned that nine out of ten people in the poorest countries could miss out on the vaccination in 2021 because of hoarding of the doses in the rich nations (ibid.). In anticipation of the forthcoming inequality, the WHO launched in April 2020 project COVAX for the equitable distribution of COVID-19 vaccines. Even if COVAX reaches its two billion dose goal, it will "only be enough to vaccinate 20% of people in low-income countries". As an example, the implications are obvious: the lack of a concerted international cooperation through the WHO and wider UN bodies, particularly by the developed countries, has meant the roll-out of vaccines is uneven and risks exacerbating inequalities and global tensions. Parallels can be drawn with the roll-out of a vaccine for polio in the 1950s and 1960s which led to the disease's eradication in most developed countries; however, it took until August 2020 for the WHO to declare Africa free of wild polio.

The WHO during COVID-19 has provided us with valuable lessons if we are to defend international organisations in the future. Firstly, defending international organisations will be increasingly difficult if countries cannot see mutual interests aligned while working together. If anything, this calls for enhanced capabilities to deliver on their mandates not less. Secondly, the symbolic and convening power of international organisations such as the WHO, UNCTAD, and the ILO, to be the only bodies capable of bringing all Member States together and its leading voice, should not be underplayed by its entrusted representatives. Rhetoric is an element of power, particularly so, when resources are in short supply—the WHO's failure of leadership in this respect was undeniable during the pandemic. Finally, for better or worse, Member States tend to look at international engagements on a respective value-for-money basis. However, there is a strong "bang for your buck" case to be made for participating in international organisations given their global influence.

Conclusion

This chapter has made the case that multilateral cooperation is necessary beyond the national policy lens if we are to uphold a "liberal international order", and thereafter, a global Keynesian agenda which addresses the global demand gap. Challenges and threats are becoming increasingly interlinked between countries and continents and added to that the trends to a multipolar world heighten the importance of means for effective international cooperation. International organisations with unique global mandates still lead the debate and policy responses in tackling global underdevelopment. Only through concerted international cooperation can risks exacerbating inequalities and global tensions be averted in a defence of freedom and prosperity.

The compromised nature of international organisations leaves them open to easy criticism, which was explored in the case of the WHO during the coronavirus pandemic. However, amid the din of anguish more than protest, the rallying of support through increased funding for the WHO by Member States proved that its values and worth actually rose rather than fell in the face of unprecedented scrutiny. The temptation is to see setbacks as reversals rather than as part of a "crooked trajectory" enhancing the spirit and rules of international organisations. With the irreversible trend towards globalisation, that spirit embodied in international organisations will be need to take forward an agenda which seeks to overcome inequalities among and within nations.

Bibliography

Ikenberry, G. J. (2020). *A World Safe for Democracy: Liberal Internationalism and the Crises of Global Order*. New Haven: Yale University Press.

IMF Website. (2021). The IMF's Response to COVID-19 [Viewed 1 April 2021], Accessible at: https://www.imf.org/en/About/FAQ/imf-response-to-covid-19.

Pratt, D. (2020). Caught in the Crossfire—The World Health Organisation. In: *Sunday Herald* (19 April), Accessible at: https://www.heraldscotland.com/news/18389727.david-pratt-caught-crossfire---world-health-organisation/.

Pratt, D. (2021). The World: A Vaccine for the Haves … and Another for the Have-Nots. In: *Sunday Herald* (3 January), Accessible at: https://www.heraldscotland.com/news/18982833.david-pratt-world-vaccine-haves-another-have-nots/.

Rachman, G. (2020). A World Safe for Democracy by G John Ikenberry—Free Thinking. In: *Financial Times* (17 December), Accessible at: https://www.ft.com/content/9259df30-4c0b-4f7f-aab7-cee195507b53.

Wilcock, N. and Scholz, C. (2016). *Hartmut Elsenhans and a Critique of Capitalism: Conversations on Theory and Policy Implications*. London: Palgrave Macmillan.

CHAPTER 8

Rating the Liberalism of International Versus World Society: Global Health as a Case in Point

Salvatore Babones

If there really is such a thing as the liberal international order, then intergovernmental organisations are central to it. It is now little-remembered that Deudney and Ikenberry (1999) theorised the international liberal order as primarily a "Western" liberal order, tying together the liberal democracies of North America, Western Europe, and Japan. Their article was a critique of "the preoccupation of many liberals with building global institutions with universal scope, such as the United Nations" (p. 196), stressing the importance of purely "Western" institutions like NATO, the European Union, and the US-Japan alliance. They did not mention, but one might add, organisations like the OECD, the G7, and the more recent "Quad" grouping of Indo-Pacific democracies.

Wilcock and Dos Santos (this volume) follow many other scholars in stretching the international liberal order to include broadly global intergovernmental organisations like the International Monetary Fund, the International Labour Organization, and (with special attention) the World

S. Babones (✉)
University of Sydney, Sydney, NSW, Australia
e-mail: s@salvatorebabones.com

N. Wilcock and E. Federzoni dos Santos (eds.), *Not Paying the Rent*,
https://doi.org/10.1007/978-3-030-78861-2_8

Health Organization (WHO). They correctly concede that these United Nations specialised agencies have as members nearly every country in the world, and that many of these countries (though perhaps not as many as they imply) are governed by decidedly illiberal regimes. They follow Elsenhans (Wilcock and Scholz, 2016, p. 138) in suggesting that this should not temper one's enthusiasm for building up the power of these organisations, since they can only be turned into tools for good once they are sufficiently robust to serve as tools at all.

Wilcock and Dos Santos effectively rebut the obvious rejoinder that such organisations could just as well be turned into tools for bad. There is, however, a more subtle reason to doubt the efficacy of intergovernmental organisations as tools for liberal internationalist policy reform. Simply put, intergovernmental organisations pursue the interests of their members, and their members are governments, not people. They are fundamentally international society organisations, not world society organisations. As Buzan (2004) explains, international society is a second-order society of the world's states, while world society is the (hypothetical and still emerging) first-order society of individuals living throughout the world. While Wilcock and Dos Santos (and, by extension, Elsenhans) look to international society to provide tools for "enacting emancipatory policies", there seems little reason to believe that these organisations could ever be transformed into tools for overturning the interests of the very states that form their membership. Even if they could be wielded as such tools, the question remains: who would wield them?

World society institutions, by contrast, are at least inherently capable of being wielded—by special interest groups, by political movements, or even by individual countries or coalitions of countries—as tools for emancipation. These organisations include global non-governmental organisations (NGOs) that have as their members individuals, corporations, or even other NGOs, but also social movements, university networks, standards-setting bodies, open-source collectives, and a range of other institutional forms, including even quasi-autonomous government-sponsored organisations. In the domain of public health, world society institutions include from umbrella groups like the Global Vaccine Alliance, charities like the Bill & Melinda Gates Foundation, traditional NGOs like Medecins Sans Frontieres, university-based organisations like the Earth Institute, government-sponsored laboratories like the Institut Pasteur, and many other institutions of various forms.

Such organisations offer a more direct, less potentially corrupt conduit for the promotion of global health than working through intergovernmental organisations like the WHO. To use the WHO as an example, it is an organisation that China has systematically attempted to control for at least fifteen years, and perhaps longer (Babones, 2020b). Although Wilcox and Dos Santos acknowledge that the WHO was unable to accurately report the scale of China's initial coronavirus outbreak, reasonably attributing this to non-cooperation on the part of China as a member state, they fail to mention China's disastrous influence over the WHO's public health advice. Throughout the early months of the pandemic, the WHO, following China's policy line, consistently advised against the imposition of travel restrictions to stem the spread of the virus (Babones, 2020a, p. 16). Instead of serving as a tool for imposing good policies on recalcitrantly illiberal countries, the WHO in this instance served as a tool for insinuating bad policies on gullibly liberal countries.

When in May, 2019, US President Donald Trump took the administration of American funding for global public health initiatives away from the WHO and put it in the hands of reputable NGOs, he was (presumably unknowingly) favouring world society institutions over international society organisations. Despite the widespread outcry of people who self-identify as liberal internationalists, this shift was likely to advance the consolidation of the international liberal order. President Joe Biden's decision to reverse Trump's action immediately upon taking office in 2021 moves the highly compromised WHO back towards the centre of global public health policy implementation. As a political gesture, Biden's embrace of the WHO is certainly intended to signal an embrace of liberal internationalism. It is important for analysts, however, not to confuse intentions with actual effects.

One way to underline the futility of hoping to use the WHO as a vehicle for promoting the liberal international order is to consider the biography of its secretary-general, Dr. Tedros Adhanom Ghebreyesus. Dr. Tedros began his career as a guerilla in the Tigray People's Liberation Front (TPLF), an ethnic minority rebel group that overthrew Ethiopia's Soviet-supported regime in 1991. After rising to membership in the TPLF's politburo, Dr. Tedros studied for and was awarded a PhD in community health from the University of Nottingham in 2000. Dr. Tedros then returned to Ethiopia to become first health minister (2005–2012) and then foreign minister (2012–2016) in a series of Ethiopian People's Revolutionary Democratic Front (EPRDF) governments that never won less than 90 per cent of the seats in Ethiopia's parliament. The Tigrayan-dominated EPRDF remained in power until a realignment in 2018–2019 saw the TPLF lose control of the government, upon which the party resumed armed rebellion.

By that time, Dr. Tedros was safe in Geneva, having been elected director-general of the WHO in 2016. By early 2021, most of his Tigrayan former cabinet colleagues were either in jail or in exile. Barring changes in the political situation in Ethiopia, it is unlikely that Dr. Tedros will be able to return to the country upon completing his term(s) in office at the WTO.

The TPLF-led government that ruled Ethiopia from 1991 to 2019, in which Dr. Tedros rose to become foreign minister, was closely aligned with China, positioning Ethiopia as China's main investment base for Africa (Ziso, 2020). It is widely understood in the international relations community that China promoted Dr. Tedros' candidacy to head the WHO, although no direct evidence of this can be presented, since such diplomacy is conducted behind closed doors. What can be said with certainty is that China was Ethiopia's chief international benefactor during the period when Dr. Tedros, as foreign minister, was responsible for managing Ethiopia's relationship with China. After the TPLF was finally ejected from the governing coalition on December 1, 2019, Dr. Tedros became even more reliant on China, since his own party went to war with the government of his home country. Thus at the very time that the coronavirus was beginning to spread, the director-general of the WHO became dependent on China not only for political support, but perhaps even for his post-WHO personal security.

Of course, the director-general is only one officer of the WHO, and no doubt many dedicated professionals work within the organisation at lower levels. Yet even before the coronavirus crisis, the WHO was under fire for repeated irregularities in its outsized travel expenditures, with the organisation spending more on staff travel than on fighting major diseases like AIDS and Ebola (Cheng, 2019). As in other intergovernmental organisations, rumours abound of staff members being appointed on the basis of nepotistic connections to members of highly corrupt regimes, rather than representing "the best experts on global health", as Wilcock and Dos Santos would have it. Of course, such irregularities are difficult to substantiate, but they seem much more likely to compromise the integrity of intergovernmental organisations like the WHO, where appointments are made on a political basis, than of world society institutions that recruit staff on professional and fundamentally commercial basis.

There is always the risk that Western biases, neo-colonialism, and even racism can creep into criticisms of broadly international organisations like the WHO. Thus it is important to consider that the same structural considerations that tend to compromise these organisations also apply to the strictly Western liberal international organisations considered by Deudney and Ikenberry (1999): their leaders are appointed through overt political horse-trading among powerful member states and their staff members can be seconded from national bureaucracies as rewards for favours performed. The arguments presented here that intergovernmental organisations are unlikely to serve as future tools for human emancipation are unrelated to Wilcock and Dos Santos' concessions about the unsavoury nature of some of their member states. It is based on the very structure of the international society of states, as opposed to the world society of individuals.

World society institutions may not always fulfil the hopes of liberal internationalists for movement towards (to quote Wilcock and Dos Santos) "freedom, prosperity, and peace", but they often have both the potential and the ambition to do so. They are (for the most part) voluntary associations motivated by the idealism of their individual members, and when they fall short of those ideals, the potential exists for their members to hold them accountable, or to create new organisations to replace them. If an intergovernmental organisation like the WHO is found to be deficient or corrupt, it is politically very difficult for the countries of the world to reform it, and almost impossible for them to disband it. World society institutions, by contract, continually rise and fall, generating competitive pressure for performance. Individual institutions may occasionally disappoint, but as long as human idealism continues to motivate people to improve the world, world society institutions be useful instruments for them to wield in their efforts.

Bibliography

Babones, S. (2020a). COVID-19 and the Perils of Expert-Driven Policy. In: *Quadrant* 64, nos. 7–8: 15–21.

Babones, S. (2020b). Yes, Blame WHO for Its Disastrous Coronavirus Response. In: *Foreign Policy* (17 May), https://foreignpolicy.com/2020/05/27/who-health-china-coronavirus-tedros/.

Buzan, B. (2004). *From International to World Society? English School Theory and the Social Structure of Globalisation*. Cambridge: Cambridge University Press.
Cheng, M. (2019). Correction: WHO Travel Story. In: *Associated Press* (22 May), https://apnews.com/article/7c645221c40d450b863b695085b4a03b.
Deudney, D. and Ikenberry, J. G. (1999). The Nature and Sources of Liberal International Order. In: *Review of International Studies* 25, no. 2: 179–196.
Wilcock, N. and Scholz, C. (2016). *Hartmut Elsenhans and a Critique of Capitalism: Conversations on Theory and Policy Implications*. Basingstoke: Palgrave Macmillan.
Ziso, E. (2020). The Political Economy of the Chinese Model in Ethiopia. In: *Politics & Policy* 48, no. 5: 908–931.

CHAPTER 9

Development Through International Trade: UN Conference on Trade and Development

Neil Wilcock and Edgar Federzoni dos Santos

International trade is considered the main method by which a country can develop its economic status vis-à-vis other countries. David Ricardo's theories on comparative advantage (1817) show that specialisation of production followed by free exchange of goods can allow both participating countries to obtain their desired goods at reduced costs. Practically, however, present day countries of the Global South are not developing through trade, free or otherwise. It is developing countries' specialisation in raw materials controlled by rentism that is blocking development and eschewing any theoretical gains from comparative advantage.

Poor terms of trade blight the developing world with its reliance on raw materials with little value-added production and in the process

N. Wilcock (✉) · E. Federzoni dos Santos
Leipzig University, Leipzig, Germany
e-mail: neil.wilcock.07@aberdeen.ac.uk

E. Federzoni dos Santos
University of Vienna, Vienna, Austria

N. Wilcock and E. Federzoni dos Santos (eds.), *Not Paying the Rent*,
https://doi.org/10.1007/978-3-030-78861-2_9

solidify rentiers control of the lucrative raw material assets. Measuring terms of trade—the ratio of export prices to import prices—shows a huge deficit for developing countries that are locked into low added-value productions. The Prebisch–Singer thesis forecasted that "over long periods of time the terms of trade is turning against the developing countries…[they are] forced to produce and export ever-increasing quantities of their primary products to finance the imports of manufactured goods from developed countries" (Marrewijk et al., 2007). Developing countries, especially in Africa, are locked into the primary commodity export sector characterised by deteriorating terms of trade and volatility of prices without the necessary diversifying or upgrading of productions.[1]

There are occasions when commodity prices might rise faster than those of manufactured goods. In such times, producing and exporting less can increase bargaining power and earn more as was the case with Brazilian soy beans in the early 2000s and OPEC Group during the 1970s. Krugman and Obstfeld (2000) confirmed that the group of advanced countries experienced rare terms of trade deterioration during the first oil crisis (1973–1974) and the second (1979–1980). The OPEC Group created a unity within suppliers in their select primary good (oil) and its ability to control the market (price). While the OPEC countries were motivated by penalising nations that provided military aid to Israel in the 1973 Yom Kippur War, it proved a valuable lesson that the terms of trade are politically controlled. Therefore, if trading rules are geared towards upholding poor terms of trade which retards development, the political battle needs to be won to create transformative rules which target overcoming underdevelopment.

The OPEC rentier states used the hike in oil prices to solidify their rentier positions and further self-enrichment, because they were under no compulsion to reinvest the additional surplus they had gained. The governments were not operating within a market competition with labour sharing in the gains. However, different political priorities could have led to the beginnings of diversifying their product base and triggering open markets—a transition required to become a high-income country as was discussed in Chapter 1.

This chapter will explore the two levels of governance, the international and the national, that require transformation if trade is to be

[1] Bleaney and Greenaway's (2001) empirical analysis from 1980 to 1995 showed a negative relationship between specialisation in primary products and GDP, and that diversification of exports led to a reduction in terms of trade volatility.

development-focused. Firstly, we will explore the international governance of trade, particularly an historical example of how developing countries have successfully altered the terms of trade and its relevance for development today.

International Opportunities for Development Through Trade: UNCTAD's History of Non-reciprocal Trade Agreements

The most central and powerful international organisations tasked with the fight against poverty and regulating world trade are the World Bank, the IMF and the World Trade Organization. However, they come with a chequered history of undermining the national sovereignty of recipient countries and enacting political tolls for Western nations and multinational corporations.[2] Therefore, we will concentrate on the transformative potential of a more democratic and less ideological international organisation (including the willingness to consider structurally-determined outcomes) in the United Nations Conference on Trade and Development (UNCTAD).

UNCTAD operates by the principle of one member one vote, unlike the above organisations, and with an explicit purpose to "support developing countries to access the benefits of a globalised economy more fairly and effectively and equip them to deal with the potential drawbacks of greater economic integration" (UNCTAD, 2020). While UNCTAD does not have executive power and its resolutions are recommendations for the UN General Assembly, history proves as we will now revisit that this does not render it impotent. From its origins, UNCTAD has been an incubator for heterodox economic ideas that challenge the structural conditions reproducing underdevelopment that the more powerful organisations refuse to acknowledge let alone act upon.

Political momentum through an organisation is needed to overcome the non-equal relations of trade which have been resulting in long-term unfavourable outcomes for the already least well-off countries. Such dissatisfaction of developing countries with their role in the world

[2] Lending money has been one of the strongest political weapons for control of the past two centuries, whereby the most powerful literally borrow money to lend. Unsurprisingly, no country pays their external debts wholly, just the service on those debts.

economy in the 1950s and 1960s coalesced itself in the Group of 77[3] which set up a permanent international organisation concentrating on their interests—UNCTAD. UNCTAD held its first conference in 1964 as the result of this South-South coordination to internationally recognise, then remedy, damaging terms of trade.

The governments of the Global South in their deteriorating terms of trade knew they had the resources the developed countries needed and through their collective bargaining power sought to promote local import-substituting industrialisation.[4] The deteriorating terms of trade[5] coupled with "tariff escalation"—the phenomena where developed countries would levy low tariffs for the imports of primary products but later in the production process impose high tariffs for the processed goods being sold back to the developing countries—brought the Group of 77 through UNCTAD to endorse the need for non-reciprocal terms of trade to overcome economic and political disadvantages.

UNCTAD tackled the inequality in trade between developed and developing countries through initiating unilateral preferences on market entries. The second UNCTAD conference of 1968 led to the Generalized System of Preferences (GSP) whereby OECD countries applied non-reciprocal preferential tariffs to imports of (primary) products from developing countries—namely free access to developed markets for developing countries but tariffs and quotas applied in reverse—with the aim of providing an impulse to growth through trade for the less developed countries.[6] The GSP enacted some policies to address the debilitating terms of trade and tariff escalation developing countries faced.

[3] "The Group of 77 is the largest intergovernmental organization of developing countries in the United Nations, which provides the means for the countries of the South to articulate and promote their collective economic interests and enhance their joint negotiating capacity on all major international economic issues within the United Nations system, and promote South-South cooperation for development" (G77, 2021). The number of founding countries was 77, its membership now stands at 135.

[4] "Import-substituting industrialisation targets the protection and incubation of newly formed domestic industries to fully develop sectors so the goods produced are competitive with *imported* goods" (Investopedia, 2021a).

[5] When the price of a nation's exports decreases relative to the price of its imports.

[6] Simultaneously, the World Trade Organization's (WTO) trading agreements in the 1960s and 1970s also addressed non-reciprocal trade preferences with the aim of integrating the Global South in an economic development paradigm.

The calls for new trading rules grew in momentum to a high point with the adoption of the 1975 Lomé Conventions "offer[ing] duty-free access to the European market for most ACP [African, Caribbean and Pacific Group of States] exports, without obliging the ACP countries to provide similar preferential treatment to European exports: in other words, they were non-reciprocal arrangements" (Ravenhill, 2008, p. 190). It allowed the group of African countries to (1) sell in European markets at prices much higher than those prevailing elsewhere, (2) give direct financial transfers to the ACP, and (3) grant special arrangements on specific products crucial in their production chain.[7] As a result of the Lomé Convention, the share of non-fuel primary commodities in ACP exports fell from an average of 77% of total exports in 1975 to 69% in 1988 while ACP exports of manufactured goods increased from an average of 10% in 1975 to 14% in 1988 (Mahler, 1994). It demonstrated the economic changes needed for development through trade: moving up in the added-value production chain, diversification from single production lines, and investments in strategic productions.

This type of preferential trading arrangement reflected a context in which, through political pressures exerted by UNCTAD, industrialised countries recognised the demands of the less developed for bespoke trading relations. Through the rush to regionalism beginning in the 1960s, in the aftermath of former colonies gaining independence, UNCTAD sought to promote local import-substituting industrialisation to enhance the bargaining power of participants vis-à-vis external actors. It coincided with the height of demands from the UNCTAD, the Group of 77 and the Non-Aligned Movement for the creation of a New International Economic Order (NIEO) that aimed at overturning *structural inequalities* through regional representation.

By the 1980s, the NIEO fell afoul of being incompatible with WTO rules and the EU abandoned its non-reciprocal trading agreement, despite the principle of reciprocity being treated explicitly as an exception for developing countries in the General Agreement on Tariffs and Trade (GATT), the forerunner to the World Bank. John Ravenhill (2008,

[7] For a good analysis of the macro-effects of the Lomé Conventions, see "Lomé IV: Dynamic or Static Improvement on the Previous Conventions?—The Sub-Saharan Africa Perspective", JO Odek, *The Comparative and International Law Journal of Southern Africa* 27, no. 2 (July 1994): 164–198.

p. 191) describes the point at which non-reciprocal terms of trade, like the Lomé Conventions, collapsed:

> In finding that the EU's banana regime contravened several of its provisions, the WTO rejected European arguments that the trade arrangements with the ACP were legitimized by WTO rules on RTAs [Regional Trade Agreements] and on special treatment for less developed economies. The WTO found that the Lomé Convention did not conform to its rules for regional trade arrangements because the ACP countries were not required to remove their tariffs on European imports (under the requirements of Article XXIV, *all parties to a regional economic agreement must liberalise 'substantially all trade' between them*) [Italics added]. More importantly than the specifics of the banana dispute itself are the implications of the WTO's judgement for rules governing the relations between industrialized and less developed economies.

By the 1970s the rush to regionalism was fraying at the edges and the tide turned after the debt crisis of 1982. The US pushed for the abandonment of non-reciprocal trading relations to be replaced by trade liberalisation as US President Ronald Reagan rejected its anti-import and pro-interventionist frameworks. The US had become frustrated at the slow progress in global trade liberalisation and their exclusions from the RTAs, particularly those generated by the European Common Agricultural Policy. The NIEO had broken down as individual countries were played off against one another destroying the unity of supply required to maintain market control (and price). The Global South had lost their negotiating power they had asserted through the UNCTAD and "a presumption in favour of all the lateral reductions in trade barriers, whether they be multi, uni, tri, plurilateral" (ibid., p. 189, quote from Larry Summers, Clinton's under-secretary of the Treasury). The momentum switched from increasing South-to-South cooperation to South-to-South competition as the developed world sought bilateral relations over collective agreements.

UNCTAD and the African, Caribbean and Pacific Group of States that make up the Group of 77 have failed to collectively influence policies to any comparable extent since the 1960s and 1970s. To illustrate the need for a reformulation of current trading rules, contrast the development gains from the Lomé Conventions for the ACP countries to the meek ones extracted from Chinese trading and investment relations in African states today. The Chinese business proposals are met by

African rentiers without a state or regional or continent-wide development strategy through trade. Agreements forged in the spirit of Lomé Convention would be a defence against ad hoc and individual short-term business opportunities that unequally favour Chinese development plans. While it may not be intellectually or politically fashionable to resurrect past policies, recognising the international trading patterns between the developed and developing worlds as perpetuating the huge disparities in economic outcomes as structurally determined is as necessary as ever if trade is to be in all participating countries' benefit.

Having explored the opportunities to development through trade in the international sphere, we will now turn our attention to domestic policies which would encourage development through trade and current obstacles to their success.

Domestic Policies for Development Through Trade

State classes in the developing world currently impede policies that could economically diversify or create labour-intensive productions. State-backed rentier classes profit from monocultures for export under no incentive to change trading patterns, as that could lead to losses in their specific sectors. For example, the minerals industry in an African state will not be in a disadvantaged relation to other countries' higher productivities and technological advancement as long as there is a lucrative market for their minerals.

Echoing the arguments of Chapter 1, functioning capitalism with a labour force empowered through diversified productions is the best route to prosperity, with rent as the biggest threat to development. Rent weakens labour as because the surplus from resources and productions accrues to the connected (rentiers) relying on political guarantees rather than market outcomes. In functioning capitalism, when the labour force that takes a proportionate share of wage in economic growth (wages rise in line with productivity increases), demand is maintained through the mass markets needed for development. Rent collected, invariably from the most profitable country resource due to that resource having the most political influence, should be used to subsidise employment programmes and technological advancement. It would have the effect of diversifying into new production lines which are not yet competitive upon which labour can be prioritised.

A domestic policy which could curtail rent and promote development is a form of protectionism which was banned but its banning was never enforced by the WTO (then GATT), namely “voluntary” export restraint (VER). It is when a country agrees to limit its exports to another country. Japan in the 1980s limited the number of cars exported to the US through a VER for the sake of the US’s trade balance and to protect its car market. While this was triggered by pressure from the importing country, the US, in fact it helped Japan become less reliant on one product and diversify through investment in new production lines, for example electronics, which expanded domestic markets.

The most lucrative assets in the developing world from the Gulf States to the Caucasus’ to Latin America are invariably owned in hierarchical rent relations not democratic capitalist ones. Therefore, any tax on their exports will impact rent. For the same effect as a VER, albeit from different motivations, a country could tax its most lucrative exports as a redistribution tool and effective tax on rent relations. Owners of production may threaten to reduce supply if they were taxed but more likely they will resort to increasing production to maintain profits from their exports, which will lead to yet more tax collected and workers employed in the process.

The most common policy of promoting trade is exchange rate devaluation. Simultaneously, devaluation as well as boosting exports is a form of import control, which can promote internal markets when sufficiently supported. As imports become more expensive, people actively try to substitute them and start producing certain goods that strengthening the domestic market by inducing three effects: Exports increase, the country becomes more attractive for foreign producers, and the domestic production of goods increases.

A temporarily undervalued currency keeps real wages high in domestic currency while simultaneously keeping the actual costs of labour low in foreign currency. While the international cost of wages can be anything from 1/20th to 1/50th of the developed world’s wage cost, real wages—adjusted for the local cost of living—are much closer. So a “Chinese factory worker earning only one-fifth the salary of a US factory worker may live at something like one half the standard of living” (Elsenhans and Babones, 2017, p. 82). Therefore, a US worker is not in competition with a Chinese worker at a fraction of 1/20th.

As a Country A’s economy grows, it is able to expand its internal markets which maintains demand for its own economic health. Still poorer countries will use that devaluation-driven growth in demand from Country A for their own development in tow as Country A's currency appreciates (referred to as the "convoy model", explored in Chapter 1). The strategy of devaluation below purchasing power parity will not be followed by all developing countries simultaneously and the exchange rate should rise as growth occurs into value-added productions.

"The possibility of developing through exports depends on maximising multiplier effects from the export branches which are best realised if the additional demand created via employment in the export sectors increases demand for local industries" (Wilcock and Scholz, 2016, p. 71). Devaluation is also a pro-poor approach as it increases employment if exports are increased in labour-intensive production processes, which should be the priority.

The policies of VAR, taxing exports, and exchange rate devaluation would be used temporarily and not simultaneously by developing countries. The key is to use such "soft protectionist" policies strategically in certain sectors and time-bound to achieve their goals of generating the markets upon which labour can freely avail itself. Indefinite protectionism generates rent practises of its own as industries internalise uncompetitive practises that can rely on guaranteed government support. The aim is for the industries to become competitive on the world market which requires industries to have become productive.

Prosperity is not a zero-sum game and should not equate to the pursuit of becoming a powerhouse. Rather, the economic growth of developing and emerging countries should be celebrated as it has helped subsidise Western ways of life through expanding markets and keeping up demand.[8] The economically most powerful countries have more chance, not less, to *accumulate and prosper* with the growth of developing countries. The developed countries with the highest Human Development Index (Norway, Switzerland, Iceland, Denmark, Singapore, Australia, New Zealand) are far away from the economic centres of the world. Being one of the world's centres of economic power does not guarantee prosperity for those living within it, examples being the low standard of living of the average worker in London or New York despite them living in world economic centres.

[8] The economic growth of China in the past decades has effectively imported low inflation into the West.

As was hinted to as the beginning of this section, the political problem to overcome in any trade-centred development plan is that rentiers and government are mostly one and the same. The risk of state intervention of the type advocated above being abused for further entrenchment of power inequalities is valid. To reduce state-backed rentiers requires *political will* and a two-levelled approach more effectively to exert that political will: from below by the masses of dispossessed demanding a labour share in production such that they are no longer excluded from surplus gains and from above in the international sphere through South-to-South cooperation through fora such as UNCTAD.

Not all state intervention is the same, and chances to succeed are surely raised with a development model actually capable of delivering prosperity. It would intensify the political will to see those policies enacted nationally (as happened in the case of South Korea in the 1980s) and internationally (as happened with UNCTAD in the 1960s/1970s). A recent example of political will leading to a change in orthodox policy came in the form of Japanese leadership of the World Bank after the dawn of the East Asian economic growth in the 1990s. Japan challenged the World Bank and its core ideas about the role of the state in the strategy for economic development, aimed at moving beyond the constraints of dependency in a US-centred world economic system that was being espoused by the likes of the World Bank and the IMF at the time:

> Japan's original goal was simply to fend off efforts by the international financial institutions and the U.S. Treasury to impose free-market policies in Asia. With this ploy, Japan began slowly to alter the agenda. By the end of the decade, Washington barely winced as Japan unveiled a succession of programs designed to shore up Asian economies without requiring American-style economics. (Terry, 2000, p. 275)

The potential inspiration for a development model that worked domestically followed by changes in the international sphere exists in the case with East Asian Miracle and the subsequent effects that had on World Bank policies in the 1990s.[9]

[9] The then newly-industrialising countries (NICs) of Hong Kong, Singapore, South Korea, and Taiwan successfully used tariffs, import quotas, and non-tariff trade barriers as part of strategic trade policies in the 1980s and 1990s.

Conclusion

Africa's population is expected to increase by roughly 50% by 2035, growing from 1.2 billion people in 2017 to over 1.8 billion (UNDP, 2015). African states amid that growth would do well to remember that their common development needs will be best served by a collective strength through international fora. UNCTAD with its more democratic grounding than the World Bank and IMF can act as a collective force for unorthodox, albeit not new, development focused policies like "voluntary" export restraint, taxing exports, and exchange rate devaluation.

There is a need to regain recognition in global trading practises for the structural conditions of inequality since their formal recognition through UNCTAD, and their disappearance since. The recognition of structural conditions will bring into focus the various stages of economic growth required for development. The 1975 Lomé Conventions non-reciprocal trading relations are an example of trade policies on an international scale which recognised the debilitating terms of trade and the need for political management of the terms of trade for a reversal of unequal outcomes.

There are policy options available to encourage development through trade if countries have the foresight and discipline to sacrifice short-term profits for the few. The most difficult obstacle confronting all such policies is that new labour opportunities come at the expense of rentiers in favour of new productions. And while overcoming economic hurdles is difficult, the political barriers are the necessary first step which will make or break their realisation. UNCTAD presents an avenue to win arguments needed to transform international trade and create the political will to take on the rentiers' currently inhibiting development.

Bibliography

Bleaney, M. and Greenaway, D. (2001). The Impact of Terms of Trade and Real Exchange Rate Volatility on Investment and Growth in Sub-Saharan Africa. In: *Journal of Development Economics* 65: 491–500.

Elsenhans, H. (2021, forthcoming). *Capitalism, Development, Empowerment of Labour: A Heterodox Political Economy*. London: Routledge.

Elsenhans, H. and Babones, S. (2017). *BRICS or Bust? Escaping the Middle-Income Trap*. Stanford: Stanford University Press.

Investopedia. (2021a). Import Substitution Industrialization [Viewed 15 March 2021], Accessible at: https://www.investopedia.com/terms/i/importsubstitutionindustrialization.asp.

Investopedia. (2021b). Purchasing Power Parity [Viewed 1 April 2021], Accessible at: https://www.investopedia.com/updates/purchasing-power-parity-ppp/.

Krugman, P. and Obstfeld, M. (2000). *International Economics: Theory and Policy*, 5th edn. New York: Addison-Wesley.

Mahler, V. (1994). The Lomé Convention: Assessing a North-South Institutional Relationship. In: *Review of International Political Economy* 1, no. 2: 233–256. Retrieved February 3, 2021. Accessible at: http://www.jstor.org/stable/4177101.

Marrewijk, C., Ottens, D. and Schueller, S. (2007). *International Economics: Theory, Application and Policy*. Oxford: Oxford University Press.

Mitchell, T. and Manson, K. (2021). China Sees EU Investment Deal as Diplomatic Coup After US Battles. In: *Financial Times* (1 January), Accessible at: https://www.ft.com/content/64ef5592-25b4-48c4-a70b-b42071951941.

Odek, J. (1994). Lomé IV: Dynamic or Static Improvement on the Previous Conventions?—The Sub-Saharan Africa Perspective. In: *The Comparative and International Law Journal of Southern Africa* 27, no. 2: 164–198. Retrieved April 13, 2021 Accessible at: http://www.jstor.org/stable/23905699.

Ravenhill, J. (2008). *Global Political Economy*, 2nd edn. Oxford: Oxford University Press.

Terry, E. (2000). The World Bank and Japan. In: *Asian Perspective* 24, no. 4: 273–298. Retrieved March 2, 2021, Accessible at: http://www.jstor.org/stable/42705316.

UNCTAD. (2020). *About UNCTAD* (21 December 2020), Accessible at: https://unctad.org/about.

UNDP. (2015). Source: *IFs v 7.26, Historical Data from US Census Bureau via CIA and United Nations Population Division* (quoted in Bello-Schünemann, J. (2017). Africa's Population Boom: Burden or Opportunity? In: *Institute for Security Studies* (15 May), Accessible at: https://issafrica.org/amp/iss-today/africas-population-boom-burden-or-opportunity).

Wilcock, N. and Scholz, C. (2016). *Hartmut Elsenhans and a Critique of Capitalism: Conversations on Theory and Policy Implications*. London: Palgrave Macmillan.

CHAPTER 10

Global Trade: The Return of Protectionism and Isolationism

Vinicius Neves dos Santos

The COVID-19 pandemic has accelerated a movement that began during the 2008/2009 financial crash: an ever-growing erosion of the structures governing international trade and economy created after World War II to bring order to a new emerging world. The collapse of the economy ten years ago traumatised the working classes of the developed countries in such an intricate and permanent way that it led to an inevitable return of populism in the political arena and protectionism in trade and investment.

The "me first" approach in international trade causes a pernicious and sometimes uncontrollable domino effect, in which cooperation becomes more and more difficult, even in those situations in which cooperation is the obvious alternative to achieve the Nash-Equilibrium between two parties. In a political environment poisoned by populism, it is notably easier to push radical ideas to the people who have shown to been let down by the so-called establishment. WTO, IMF, UNCTAD, WHO, and

V. Neves dos Santos (✉)
Federation of Industries of the State of São Paulo, São Paulo, Brazil
e-mail: vinicius.santos@fiesp.com.br

N. Wilcock and E. Federzoni dos Santos (eds.), *Not Paying the Rent*,
https://doi.org/10.1007/978-3-030-78861-2_10

a myriad of other organisations fit the category of "establishment" in this context.

Ultimately, multilateralism took the blame for the issues and distortions seen in the capitalist system. Currently, institutions like the World Trade Organization (WTO), which for decades played a very important role levelling the playing field and bringing the so-desired predictability and stability to the International Trading System, are running the risk of becoming irrelevant. For a country like Brazil, and any other developing country (DC), this is bad omen. At the WTO, small economies are given the opportunity to punch above their weight and fight back against unfair trade practices they suffer from superpowers like the US or China. If the Hobbesian "state of nature" finally prevails over the Rules-Based Trading System, so carefully created by the WTO, the developing world will find itself in more distress than the already troublesome present moment.

The US is the outstanding leader of this historical shifting movement. Nevertheless, it is also a consensus among many experts and policymakers that the WTO and other relevant institutions governing global trade, investment, and economy need urgent revamp. Many of modern issues that affect global trade did not exist when the WTO or UNCTAD were created, and it is a fact that these organisations navigate the waves of new trends at an unacceptably slow pace. E-commerce, sophisticated tax planning strategies and "forum-shopping" practices by the big-techs, automation, among many others are examples of such new trends. Undoubtedly, WTO needs a profound reform to cope with all novelties.

What is ongoing, however, is a systematic attempt to undermine the organisation. There are no viable proposals for systems that could replace the current one, and an abrupt dismantling of the organisation could cause a turmoil capable of leading the global economy into a total paralysis, affecting not only the developing world. Crippling the Appellate Body of the Dispute Settlement Mechanism, as the US has been doing since 2016 is a major blow to the stability of the system as conceived in the Uruguay Round, but that could just prove the tip of the iceberg.

The whole system is based on the premise that the countries will abide by the international rules (*pacta sunt servanda*), and if they do not, the Dispute Settlement Mechanism would eventually allow the affected country to retaliate, forcing the other part to change its behaviour. Taking this piece out of the puzzle means the WTO has lost its teeth, and Member States may just take whatever policies they deem more suitable to their national interest, regardless of international law. A simple extrapolation of this scenario brings us to a chaotic situation and an inevitable and harmful trade war. Needless to say, DCs will carry the heaviest burden of this war.

All these elements put the WTO in a straight route to become a new UNCTAD. In other words, they steered the former to become more of a think-tank than an organisation capable of setting rules and bring order to the International Trading System. The Organization for Economic Co-operation and Development (OECD) has taken the lead as the most important forum for policymaking and governance in fields like trade, taxation, digital economy, among many others. OECD is more flexible and produce non-binding legal instruments (Decisions, Declarations, Recommendations, Guidance, etc.), driven essentially by concrete common interest of its members, in a plurilateral[1] fashion. Curiously, despite being non-binding, the legal instruments OECD puts in place usually enjoy higher levels of implementation than the binding WTO laws. This phenomenon seems to be a strong trend for upcoming years in terms of global governance.

This brings a dilemma for the developing and least-developed countries (LDPs). How to avoid being a mere policy-taker and to become once again a police-maker in the international arena, as they used to be within the UNCTAD in the 1970s and beginning of the 1980s, and more recently in the WTO? The protagonism of OECD will likely rise, and there is certainly no room for the entire developing world in this selective Organisation. There are only six new candidates to accede to the OECD, with an uncertain and long process to follow. As much as the Secretariat would like to expand the number of members and diversify the points of view within the Organisation, the most relevant Member States, especially the US, are adamant on the necessity of admitting only like-minded new members.

Outside the OECD, creating new coalitions in order to leverage the influence of the DCs is less feasible every day and will most certainly not untangle this knot for the DCs. Firstly, because the trend on the international scenario will very likely continue to be a "me first" approach.

[1] Plurilateral agreements are those without a formal negotiation mandate granted by consensus of all the WTO members. This means the accession to the agreement is voluntary and usually only "like-minded" countries participate on the discussions and eventually abide to the rules or norms arising from the negotiations.

And secondly due to the disparities within the developing world, pulling apart potential common interests. The gap between some of the emerging markets and the vast majority of the LDPs has grown remarkably in the last two decades, making any kind of consensus on a common agenda unlikely. For instance, China alone accounted for roughly 13% of world exports in 2018 (US$2.5 trillion, 93% of which manufactured goods), while Brazil, another big emerging market (and member of the BRICS—Brazil, Russia, India, China, and South Africa), has been stuck at around 1% for the past three decades.

It is not feasible either to conceive the BRICS as an alternative for the DCs to participate in the new trade and economy global governance. Firstly, the BRICS are not exactly open to become a multilateral institution and, secondly, due to the discrepancies between its members' economic and military strengths. On the one hand, China's national interests diverges enormously from those of Brazil or South Africa, not to mention the neo-colonialist practises the former has been imposing in its relations with African countries. On the topic of agriculture, for instance, one of the most important economic drivers for Brazil, there are fundamental policy differences with China and India regarding domestic support, subsidies, public stocks, and other mechanisms that distort the international market and jeopardise producers all around the world, including in Africa and Southeast Asia. Russia, on the other hand, has a geopolitical and military agenda that aims at destabilising the Western World as it is, from democracy to the multilateral Organisations. The disruptive approach of Russia is not of interest of the DCs and LDCs, once it will create an inevitably gap of authority in the global governance of economy and trade, a scenario that favours only the most powerful nations.

As the COVID-19 pandemic lingers, more rapidly the forces governing international trade, economy, and geopolitics shift. As time goes by, it becomes clearer that two main forces will prevail over all the others, in a recurrent state of antagonism: US and China. Currently, DCs still can play a double game and act ambiguously. In other words, not declaring full support to any side and benefit from the free flow of goods, services, and capital of both superpowers huge consumer markets. Whether this can last remain to be seen, but evidence shows that, at some point, the world will have to choose to align with one of the two.

That been said, the question remains: what are the alternatives left for DCs to become autonomous decision-makers again and guarantee their viable path to economic and social development? With the limited possibility of cooperation or even a "coalition of the willing", should the DCs and LDCs continue searching for traditional remedies within the WTO or what is left of UNCTAD? Are these fora capable of persuading the superpowers to give away their preferential positions or special treatment to lower-level countries, as per foreseen in the Enabling Clause of the General System of Preferences (GSP) from back in the 1970s? Or, perhaps, the most important question: is it the right thing to do to offer the DCs and LDCs a menu of the same heterodox policies used during the second half of the twentieth century, such as import substitution?

At this point, the typical conflict between liberalism versus interventionism rises. Observing the countries that, in the last three to four decades, effectively managed to overcome the so-called middle class trap,[2] almost all of them share one commonality: an ever-growing ratio of the trade-flow and the GDP. In other words, the successful countries are those open to international trade and with a welcoming environment for entrepreneurship: Hong Kong, Taiwan, South Korea, Chile, Singapore are some of the examples. Nevertheless, there are nations open to free trade that did not achieve the same success, a situation that could be explained by several other issues, including red-tape, corruption, and misallocation of resources in the economy. But it is a safe bet to say that no nation, since the fall of Soviet Empire, has surpassed the "middle class trap" with a closed economy, absent of the global value chains and hostile to the entrepreneurs in general.

Hence, the question lies on the role played by the nation-states as either an enabler or an obstacle for this leapfrog from being a middle-income to a high-income country. For starters, there is no development, of any kind, without an organised National State, with the monopoly of legitimate violence, and, more importantly, with strong and stable institutions that guarantee the free initiative and enable investments. A predictable and trustworthy judicial system is also mandatory. Finally, the National Authority must create the right incentives for the private sector to thrive on the sectors and areas they have a comparative advantage in comparison with the rest of the world. This means, on some occasions, the grant of subsidies, exemptions, and earmarked credit. That is, the

[2] "Middle Class Trap" is a term used to describe the difficult DCs have in surpassing the middle-income status and joining the group of developed countries, with income per capita of around US$30 thousand.

National State plays a fundamental role as an inducer for the development of the economy.

The problems begin with the overregulation, red-tape, and misconceived policies that are either populist or aim at attending private-corporate interests, instead of levelling the playing field for all the competitor in all the economy, national and internationally. The interventionism usually becomes harmful once particular interests come before the overall interest of the general productive sector.

At the end of the day, prioritising elite groups leads to misallocation of resources and the creation of an infant industry that will never thrive in the competitive environment of the global value chains. Moreover, this kind of badly shaped incentive ends up creating an environment of low innovation based on the assumption that there will always be protection against competition, either national or international. Finally, it creates an outdated elite of businessmen and women, that accumulate economic and political power overtime and feedback the well-known structures of inequality in the developing world, probably one of its greatest social and economic challenges.

The challenge is, and will always be, to find the exact dose of incentives so to enable the private sector to freely choose where to allocate their limited resources. If, in addition, that happens in a free-trade environment, resources would flow to the sectors in which the country has comparative advantages, and business will naturally bloom and prosper. Richard Baldwin, professor of international economics at the Graduate Institute of International and Development Studies in Geneva, created the terminology "Juggernaut Effect" to explain that the usage of protectionist policies throughout the years has increased the influence of ineffective and unproductive sectors in the developing countries. Finally, as Robert Putnam's theory of "two-levels games" teaches, theses protectionist forces have a disproportionate strength in the formulation of international trade policies, as of its own interests, instead of the whole nation's interest, leading the nation to adopt a harmful and ineffective posture in the international fora.

On the other hand, those nations, such as South Korea and Taiwan, that focused their economies on the sectors they had comparative advantages have naturally selected the most efficient and up-to-date companies, resulting in a business sector that searches for free trade instead of protectionism. Again, bringing up Putnam's theory, the international trade policies of these countries are much more focused on free-trade agreements, specialisation, and integration into the global value chains. Not coincidently, these are the developed countries as we know today.

It is also not surprising that these developed countries have built a system to protect their interests in the field of economy and trade, such as the WTO, the IMF, and WIPO. UNCTAD was a concession made by these countries to the developing world. Over the years, UCTAD lost its capacity to influence international trade governance, and it nowadays has the shape of a think-tank rather than that of an International Organisation (IO). This is usually the fate of any IO when global leading countries abandon or simply lose interest in their leadership role. Without the compliance of these most powerful nations, all that UNCTAD eventually tries to achieve in favour of the developing countries is sabotaged or just does not have enough punch to bring consistent advantages to those that remain active in the Organisation. That is the case, for example, for many of the "special and differentiated treatments" (STD) UNCTAD successfully managed to introduce in the governing bodies of international trade throughout the years. While the developed world was interested in keeping up with these instruments, they worked relatively well; once the powerful nations' moods shifted from cooperation to confrontation with some of the emerging economies (notably the BRICS), a wave of dismantling and reforms took place, be it the WTO or the GSP programmes offered unilaterally from the developed nations.

This does not mean UNCTAD has become irrelevant. It is still an important source of information and a renowned platform for a fairer international trade. The UNCTAD corollary, though, still is focused on a more protectionist approach against the competition with the developed countries, instead of genuine polices of modernisation of the economy and trade liberalisation. This posture incentivises both tariff and non-tariff barriers on trade in goods and services, and more recently, even capital and data. Summing up, protectionism leads to less international integration and limited access to intermediate goods and technology that allows productivity to grow.

The dynamics of productivity, in fact, are central to understand why protectionism jeopardises economic and social development of societies. Basically, there are two ways of expanding a nation's wealth. The first one is called the "demographic bonus", a situation in which the economy grows simply because more and more young people join the workforce of the country and sustain the GDP growth directly and indirectly through an increase of the aggregate demand and the economy with their fresh salaries. The other way is through an increase in the economy's total factor productivity, which requires constant investment in capital goods, technology and training, something hardly achieved by closed economies.

Trade protectionism has been a bad choice for any nations' development in the long run, in any situation in time. Undeniably, though, the import substitution policy in Latin America as preconised by the Economic Commission for Latin America and the Caribbean (ECLAC) and supported by UNCTAD, helped transforming the region and is the main responsible for the fast industrialisation Brazil experienced from the 1950s to the 1980s. However, any attempt to compare that period with the world in 2020 is simply unrealistic. Most of the imports substituted by local production in the second half of the twentieth century were of very low technological complexity and, moreover, generated a relevant number of low/medium-skilled jobs. Nothing farther from the current scenario. The economy of 2020 is highly complex. The aggregate value of the goods and services has high levels of technology embedded, which cannot be subject to immediate replacement. Especially in countries that do not have a friendly environment for free initiative, free flow of capital, goods, services, and labour. Not to mention the necessity of having a top-notch infrastructure, be it in logistics or information technology. The more closed and protectionist a country is, the more apart from taking advantage of these flows (services, goods, information, capital, etc.) and, more importantly, of highly skilled and well-paid jobs.

Nevertheless, since the 2008/2009 economic crash, the world is experiencing again the taste of national developmentalism followed by a rapid expansion of protectionism and unorthodox measures on economy and trade. So far, the clearer consequences of the COVID-19 pandemic, amid all the fog of uncertainty and bankruptcies, are that it has drastically accelerated the new wave of protectionism and somehow entitled those interventionist voices that had been dormant since the 1980s. Some may say that China's outstanding economic success has finally awakened the Western world to the inevitability of having to use all the National State's power to drive development, regardless of the costs. It sure seems tempting, but any comparison with China is and will always be misleading, given the uniqueness of its 1.4 billion disciplined and government obeying population. Not to mention the lack of transparency of the Chinese management of its monetary policy, and the unfair /illegal moves on trade and intellectual property rights, all of which sum up to make China a non-market economy in many aspects. These Chinese characteristics should not represent desirable benchmarks, despite the success it may have had in China due to the peculiarities of its "state-capitalism".

Contrarily, instead of mimicking China, the world is rather seeking to keep the economy's engine running, in a less cooperative and more self-centred way. Undoubtedly, direct and robust government interventions have prevented both the developed and developing world from suffering much worse consequences. However, perhaps, the ever more spreading idea of a drastic change of the global value chains as established after decades of investments and free flow of capital, technology, and data is just another lure from populist western leaders. It is just not feasible anymore. The path for development will not lay on artificially maintaining jobs that are fated to disappear, or substituting imports for national goods, eventually more expensive and obsolete.

Globalisation was slowing down since the 2008/2009 economic crisis, and the pandemic offered a significant push in this direction. Now the world is experiencing a real retreat in the international flow of capital, goods, services, and people, not to mention the return of protectionism, nationalism, xenophobia among many other forms of isolationism. But globalisation remains inevitable. Simply because it has become the fuel for the world economy (through a constant increase in productivity) to keep on growing. The reflux we will experience in the upcoming years will be temporary, lasting just until the positive results of protectionism and isolationism fade away, which will not take long. For the developing countries, the temptation is even bigger, considering the culture of short-term and the historic of populist leaders relying on unsustainable policies to remain in power.

In conclusion, there are few alternatives for the DCs and LDCs to thrive in international trade and economy from now on. The competition for jobs and best links in the global value chains is becoming fiercer, while States' support for national companies through subsidies, grants and subventions are increasing. Obviously, the capacities of the advanced economies are much bigger than that from the emerging world in this matter, especially on the fiscal side.

It would be expected than that the governing bodies of the International Trading System came up with policies and other kinds of preferences (new old) to level the playing field for the DCs and LDCs. Instruments like the GSP, the enabling clause and the Special and Differential Treatment of the WTO. Again, we bump into the aversion of the great potencies in granting these kinds of preferences to countries like the BRICS, which would turn any initiative like that without effect. Moreover, the questions about the effectiveness of granting preferences to DCs and LDCs remain, while the structural problems of their economies are not solved.

Nevertheless, all crises are also opportunities. The developing world should take advantage of these challenges and properly prepare for the fierce competition they will face from now on, recognising the international system as it is and not as they would want it to be. The new economy that is emerging after the pandemic is characterised by a world highly integrated on data flow, green energy, and ongoing technological disruptions. Understanding how the world after the pandemic will function and taking action to participate in this new economy immediately will be less costly than it will be 10 years from now. Time is for action. I hope that towards the right direction.

CHAPTER 11

Empowering Labour to Save Capitalism and Role of the International Labour Organization

Neil Wilcock and Edgar Federzoni dos Santos

As the first and oldest specialised agency of the United Nations founded in 1919, the International Labour Organization's (ILO) original mandate to "advance social and economic justice through setting international labour standards" is more relevant than ever before given labour's falling share of national incomes.[1] The ILO's conventions on labour standards (or "labour setting"), its technical expertise in achieving them, and its convening power among nations are needed as part of a wider effort to save capitalism from rentism. To do that, this chapter will firstly introduce the role of the ILO, secondly, define labour marginality and

[1] The amount of GDP paid out in wages, salaries, and benefits.

N. Wilcock (✉) · E. Federzoni dos Santos
Leipzig University, Leipzig, Germany
e-mail: neil.wilcock.07@aberdeen.ac.uk

E. Federzoni dos Santos
University of Vienna, Vienna, Austria

N. Wilcock and E. Federzoni dos Santos (eds.), *Not Paying the Rent*,
https://doi.org/10.1007/978-3-030-78861-2_11

why overcoming it is a precondition for development, and finally, sketch a simple stone-for-cash scheme that the ILO could administer which directly overcomes the cause of underdevelopment on a small scale: labour marginality.

The UN, and its antecedent the League of Nations, was created to address the root sources of international conflict by managing systems of labour, productivity, migration, and consumption. Albert Thomas, the first ILO Director-General, from 1919 to 1932, advocated for the eight-hour day, and while it first represented an unenforced and unlegislated ideal, it nonetheless set a benchmark towards which states were obliged to work (Cullather, 2007). The eight-hour day was an example of fixing social standards to throw "into relief the common idea toward which we are all advancing" (ibid., p. 356) and established a common vocabulary for supranational governance. Thomas advocated universal norms as a method of international institution building, in which the ILO would play a leading role.

The ILO as a UN agency is unique in that it was fought for by labour as an economic class[2] and has come to be represented as one of organisation's three major stakeholders alongside states and the private sector. Spaces reserved for non-state actors within international political agencies are more commonly occupied by the professionalised non-governmental organisations, whereas it is filled by labour organisations at the ILO.

The ILO's mission is to "promote rights at work, encourage decent employment opportunities, enhance social protection and strengthen dialogue on work-related issues" (ILO, 2021a). The ILO can only enforce material standards in what is set out in the free agreement of the labour contract. Those standards are agreed upon by its three major stakeholders in Conventions which are then supported in their implementation by ILO through projects and technical assistance. The ILO's original mandate of no slave or forced labour and free labour contracts has evolved expansively since to incorporate decent employment and income and enhancing social welfare protections.

The value of the ILO increasingly lies in being part of agreements between states where they are needed for their technical leadership on labour issues. They act as the eyes and ears against latent abuses,

[2] For example, the Constitution of the ILO was drafted by head of the American Federation of Labour.

protecting the fundamental conventions and rights of "freedom of association and the effective recognition of the right to collective bargaining; the elimination of all forms of forced or compulsory labour; the effective abolition of child labour; and the elimination of discrimination in respect of employment and occupation" (ILO, 2021b).[3]

However, the ILO's present incarnation in technical leadership will not make significant strides considering the scale of the challenge facing labour in the present economy (not to mention the future economy). Not least amid a mainstream economic discourse that views labour empowerment in the form of higher wages, better protections, and a permanent role in corporate decision-making as detrimental to capitalist growth and wider development. Labour's share of national income has fallen in many countries, with a labour surplus dominating developing countries as evidenced by 28 million people in the Middle East and North Africa living below a poverty line of $1.90 a day in 2018, an increase of 250% from 2011 (England, 2021), and the increasingly weakening position of labour in developed countries with casual contracts of low pay and precarious working conditions becoming the norm. For example, the life expectancy in the US has fallen for the first time post-World War II (ibid.).

The strengthening of labour is imperative for developing countries to trigger mass consumption and mass markets, and for developed countries to continue its freedoms economically, socially, politically, and culturally, thereby averting the capture of rentism. The focus of this chapter is the least well-off nations seeking to overcome rentism, labour surplus, and the role of ILO therein. Let us first turn to the role of labour in development.

The Source of Underdevelopment: Labour Marginality

The role of labour in economic development is theorised differently in Marxism, Malthusianism, and neoclassical schools of thought. According

[3] A recent example of the benchmarking on global labour standards is the China-EU Comprehensive Agreement on Investment which was signed in 2021 which will grant the EU enhanced market access in China, in sectors such as health services, chemicals, electric vehicles, and telecoms. The EU described it as a "major breakthrough" (Mitchell and Manson, 2021) to have Beijing sign up to ILO's conventions banning the use of forced labour and the protection of workers' rights of association as part of the deal.

to Marxism, labour is fundamentally exploited as any excess value of production beyond its cost is extracted by the capitalist, while Malthusian thinking held that unemployment was a problem of wrong incentives, and neo-classicalists that wages just need to be low (or high) enough to meet the demand to find an equilibrium labour wage. While Marx made a distinction between value producing labour (concrete labour) and non-value producing labour (abstract labour), none of the three schools of thought accounted for an equilibrium where labour supply meets labour demand below an output needed for labours' survival. In other words, labour cannot find work because there can be no expectation of sufficient return for their employment to justify it. There can be no employment for "labour that produces less than it needs to consume. Such low-productivity labour is essentially unemployable" (Wilcock and Scholz, 2016, p. 31). They are known as "labour marginals" as the value of what is produced in their employment is less than what it will cost to employ them. The marginals are effectively unproductive, and therefore unemployable, through no fault of their own and make up the labour surplus in many countries.

Keynes explained the phenomena as a lack of investment back into the system, which meant people are not given the potential to earn sufficient wages. The people who can invest are under no compulsion to do so, and furthermore there are no guarantees on their returns if they do (in contract, enjoying guaranteed returns through rent). Thus, they inevitably refrain from investing. The owners of wealth that are capable of investing are faced with a population too poor to become mass consumers from their investments because of this same population's disempowerment. Therefore, labour marginality and rentism are different parts of the same problem—namely, that labour surplus exists because the economic surplus is not spent on mass consumer markets through mass incomes that expands employment, but is instead kept in the pockets of rentiers who either save it or spend on unproductive economics activities like expensive foreign products or financial speculation. Now that we have defined marginality, let us look at how it comes about.

Marginality is predominately a problem of the pre-industrialised world. In countries that traditionally suffered from marginality, it was agricultural production that employed the majority of people. Agricultural production is affected by the law of diminishing returns, where increasing labour causes the production per capita to decrease. There comes a point where you have so many labourers with so little land that the additional production from more labour employed becomes lower than what these people need for survival. It is a physical relation between the land and the number of workers. Or in other words, diminishing returns on the land causes marginality. The point at which labour becomes unproductive is called the "threshold of marginality" and beyond it people become dependent on others for their survival.

The marginality concept is powerful because it explains the lack of negotiating power of average to low-skilled workers and why real development relies on empowerment of labour—i.e. a demand for their labour on free and open markets, otherwise they are disempowered and left marginal to society. As Elsenhans (2021, Chap. 8, forthcoming) writes:

> [C]apitalism is successful not because of the moral qualities of those in control of the surplus. It is successful because, under capitalist conditions, increases in production via rising productivity are transferred to the mass of the population because of their scarcity. This scarcity of labour is triggered by increasing (mass) demand... Only the key characteristic of a functioning capitalist economy – scarcity of labour – ensures that the transfer of production increases to labour become the result of market mechanisms. Such a system entails the imposition of competition on the rich and powerful, and the empowerment of labour through its scarcity.

To reiterate, labour marginality exists where markets do not exist for labour to realise its productive potential. In those cases, resources neither human nor natural are available due to their absence altogether or the capture of existing resources in rent arrangements do not allow for labour to avail themselves in their production—i.e. possess negotiating power for their labour on a market. Examples of that case would be present day Niger or Chad which suffer climatic challenges for production and lack of productive resources. However, most instances of marginality exist whereby resources are tied up in non-market structures which keeps labour weakened by its concentration on single assets and lack of diversification, for example Algeria or Ukraine. In both cases of marginality, an injection of a resource would give labour the potential to become economic agents.

The economic, social, and cultural emancipatory potential of capitalism does not function in most of the developing world, nor increasingly in the developed world. The route out of poverty is the creation of open markets for the economically marginalised to offer their labour. The effects of such an open market for hitherto marginal labour will be explored in the final section of the chapter.

There is an absence of a powerful international organisation with a mandate to articulate and address the structural conditions of underdevelopment. Unfortunately, the argument confirming the existence of labour marginality is still to be won, as there is no recognition of the problem of labour marginality in the main international organisations, from the World Bank to the ILO, albeit with the exception on occasion of the UN Economic Commission for Latin America and the Caribbean (CEPAL). The lack of acknowledgement of labour surplus—the fundamental structural condition causing poverty—in international organisations means projects and programmes are not dealing with the causes of underdevelopment.

We will now imagine a circumstance where the ILO inhabits the role in addressing labour marginality in the developing world. The ILO can be part of development programmes that focus on three factors leading to lasting development: (1) the provision of incomes rather than the provision of goods or services, (2) the role of integrating people into work to become economic agents that structurally create the basis for labour employment, and (3) upholding labour rights in new markets such that their empowerment lasts beyond the lifespan of the scheme. We will now explore a thought experiment of the operationalisation of one such scheme.

A Stones-For-Cash Scheme[4]

A model for a welfare scheme which could offer social insurance on the condition of work, and create labour markets in the process, would be the collection of "foam stones"[5] dropped from the sky in exchange for monetary values—a so-called stones-for-cash scheme. The broad parameters of the scheme are as follows: foam stones would be dropped in an area of labour marginality, these stones would have a convertible value to the local currency so that the more collected the more reward is reimbursed to the worker (albeit with a maximum per person), and the quantity

[4] The inspiration for the following scheme is taken from Elsenhans (1991).

[5] The material does not matter, as long as it does not endanger anyone.

dropped would be at a rate which the average collection made by the poorest would satisfy basic needs. The "group of gatherers would then proceed to exchange the collected money...with suppliers of goods in return for a basket of commodities" (Elsenhans, 1991, p. 281).

There are currently around 750 million people in the world earning less than $1.90 a day,[6] which is the definition of living in extreme poverty. Let's do a quick budget of the costs to potential donors of a global development scheme to raise everyone above the $1.90 a day threshold, thereby eliminating the worst sufferers of labour marginality. If the scheme was run over one year on the basis that an additional dollar would be provided for every one of the 750 million earning less than a $1.90 a day, this would amount to 750 million multiplied by 365 equalling around $520bn worth of stones dropped. Given the simplicity of its implementation, the administrative costs would only be a small percentage increase on that total. While a $520bn is a gigantic figure alone, it amounts to 1.6% of the world's GDP, less than the total external debt of the Debt Service Suspension Initiative-eligible countries which stood at a record $744bn in 2019 (World Bank, 2020) and the $700bn given directly to the banks by the UK government in 2008 alone (BBC, 2008). If the whopping policy response by governments to COVID-19 proved anything, it was that "politically impossible" is contextual. For example, running the scheme in Uganda alone would cost around $8.8bn over a year as per this simple calculation (World Bank, 2016).[7] As a disclaimer, we are not seriously suggesting dropping stones over half of the world simultaneously, but the preceding places the model's potential and its expenses into consideration.

The reward for the collectors will be money in exchange for the stones that they return. Given the collectors' marginal status, they will overwhelmingly spend the money on basic commodities of foodstuffs, simple manufactures, and housing, which in turn increases local demand in those

[6] For a running total of the "exact" daily number, see the World Poverty Clock https://worldpoverty.io/headline.

[7] The calculation is as follows: 34.6 per cent of Uganda's 35.7million population in 2013 lived below the $1.9 extreme poverty line, which is an absolute figure of 12.35m. If you were to give them all $1.9 a day for a year and add 2 per cent administration costs it adds up to $8,737,575,860. This figure includes babies, children, and pre-teenagers for the scheme which will cause it to be an overestimate on what is needed.

productive sectors (as opposed to rentiers spending on foreign niche products which are *unproductive*). Development begins to occur when "in order to increase their incomes, manufacturers and farmers will introduce innovations and go in for investments" (Elsenhans, 1991, p. 281), thereby beginning efficiency savings to stay competitive and accumulate. Assuming a decline in the number of marginalised people as a result of such a scheme, the stones being dropped will reduce. The scheme naturally ends itself when industries created based on the demand induced by the stones scheme begin to provide people with higher incomes.

The benefits of the stones-for-cash scheme are as follows: it will have a take-up by those most in need (those earning less than $1.90 a day); it has a wide reach overcoming geographical challenges given its rudimentary application; it overcomes any illiteracy in securing the income as it is a physical task which may be otherwise needed in completing forms; and it provides a ladder out of poverty and unemployment traps by reinforcing the incentive to work. The money would be received directly in a sum on the day of dropping to avoiding hoarding, and be non-withdrawable, non-discriminatory, and tax-free.[8] Current welfare payments either formally or informally struggle to fulfil that criteria.

It is administratively efficient, with overhead costs amounting to a high estimate of 2% of total expenditure, whereas "targeted" measures would be in the teens or twenties percentage costs of the overall scheme. Additionally, it also overcomes the inability to allocate resources efficiently across governmental departments, removing the risks of corruption, bureaucratic incapability and incompetence.[9] Everything except the low administration percentage will go directly into labour's pockets, which is the reverse of most development schemes.

The scheme is a fast and efficient way of escaping unemployment in the short-run, however, it takes until the later stages to create the motor of accumulation—namely, an increase in production. As Elsenhans explains, "Even though aid is initially directed at increasing consumption

[8] It embodies the basic principle that people should be taxed only on their surplus income after their unavoidable expenditure has been met.

[9] There is the potential for the scheme to be linked to skill-adding techniques of the unemployed which they might use subsequently for productive enterprises, if such scheme administrators have the capability and are not corrupt. Inherent in the proposition of this scheme is a criticism of existing foreign aid, such a scheme will bypass the buttressing of medium- and high-level incomes generated by foreign aid (whether by the development organisation or in the target country administration) in favour of the poorest.

alone, it generates investment in that producers holding 'assets' demand new investment goods to increase their own incomes" (ibid., 283), for example new machinery to produce homeware more efficiently. The fact that the market is artificial does not matter if accumulation effects result from it, which it will because it establishes the underlying mechanism for a sustainable development plan outlined above, namely ***hitherto marginal labour now has agency on a market.***

The largest cash transfer programme in the developing world which were triggered equivalent mechanisms than the stones-for-cash scheme is the 2003-present Bolsa Familial in Brazil. The state gives an allowance of 32 reais (about $19 USD) per child attending school to a maximum of five children to all families with below the poverty line of per-capita income below 140 reais (US $82). The scheme cost less than 1% of Brazilian GDP per annum yet coincided with approximately 28% reduction of total poverty reduction in Brazil between 2002 and 2012, with the number of Brazilians living on less than 70 reais ($41) a week falling from 8.8 to 3.6% (Centre for Public Impact, 2019). It shows that direct transfers raise the poor out of poverty the most by targeting reductions in the inequalities of consumption. This is in stark contrast to rent-dominated markets inhibited by political privilege where gains from productions are used for self-enrichment rather than reinvestment.

A Stones-For-Cash Scheme: Overcoming Marginality and the ILO Relevance

The stones-for-cash scheme may appear counterproductive given it would not utilise existing capacities in the developing world, and instead spends billions in foam stones to create an artificial industry. While there are plentiful resources in most underdeveloped countries to theoretically trigger such a development, as has been exemplified in the chapters on Brazil, they are trapped in rentism that strangles unleashing that potential. This scheme creates a new market which was not there before and is now open to all workers, and crucially, free from the dead-hand ownership of existing rentiers in closed markets. A new and open market is created which was not there before as no-one owns the resources with the exception of the collectors(/workers).

The earlier such a labour market is created in the developmental processes, as labour marginals transform into economic agents, the greater the chances for development to succeed. The power is being handed to the workers to decide what to do with their newly-sourced income. No one owns the resources (i.e. the stones, initially) except those who work to gather them. The scheme is truly Keynesian in its view that a problem of labour distribution has led to a problem of production and the solution is in empowering labour with a view to eventually initiate mass production.

It is also in essence a rent-weakening scheme because labour which was previously marginal and open to exploitation becomes empowered in markets the rentiers do not control. Once markets come to be dominated by rentiers it is extremely difficult to remove those privileges, as rentiers secure their interests through their connections and extended power.[10] Critics will point to the scheme not enacting vertical redistribution, however, in avoiding to do so, this makes it more politically viable by avoiding facing up to the power levers available to the rentiers. Such a scheme will still require government buy-in, but even with rentiers controlling all levels of government in recipient countries, their grip on the implementation of the scheme would not necessarily impede it as conditions on foreign aid is one of the few areas they do not have control over.

The programme's injection of a massive economic resource for general developments fits more to the remit and capabilities of the World Bank and IMF. However, it is our contention that if the ILO had its mandate expanded to address labour marginality, the organisation would be better placed given it does not have the tainted history of supporting schemes that thwarted development for decades and its make-up of labour as one of three pillars will be an imperative characteristic to solidify the gains for labour in the scheme. The ILO's convening power, position in the international sphere, and expertise on labour issues are better suited to promote such a vast scheme, including the subsequent possibility of enacting labour rights and welfare measures through its existing conventions. While this scheme will satisfy basic demands, it does not deal with the array of needs nor equity as a country begins to develop, that requires building institutions.

Labour has the potential to temporarily overcome its marginality in such a scheme, but long-term empowerment is always fragile. The mandates of the ILO, from defending the freedom of association, the right to collective bargaining, and the elimination of discrimination

[10] Examples can be seen across the world, from Brazil's coffee plantations, land ownership in the UK, oil fields in Kuwait.

at work, must be enforced by the ILO or the states themselves for development programmes to result in prosperity.

Conclusion

This chapter has discussed the role of labour in development, positing that underdevelopment is caused by labour marginality, or in other words, workers unable to find markets to avail themselves on. There is no acknowledgement of the labour marginality problem in mainstream development discourse, nor unsurprisingly in international organisations like the International Labour Organization. Enacting the ILO's present mandate is vital to facilitating piecemeal gains as it does at present, but it will remain in a bounded predicament if the source of endemic underdevelopment is not overcome, namely labour marginality.

For lasting development, labour schemes are required to transform marginals into economic agents in free markets where they can offer and withdraw their labour. A simple alternative employment stones-for-cash scheme was illustrated to show the kinds of open and free markets that need to be awakened to overcome the labour marginality problem. While the scheme is simply sketched, it represents the type of innovative and bold steps developing states and supporting international organisation like the ILO need to adopt in order to achieve economic development. In doing so, the scheme showed an example of triggering mass markets and mass consumption from creating an open market free from rent. These new markets will have the complementary effects of empowering hitherto marginal labour and weakening the power of rentiers.

Bibliography

BBC News. (2008). Rescue Plan for UK Banks Unveiled (8 October), Accessible at: http://news.bbc.co.uk/1/hi/business/7658277.stm.

Centre for Public Impact. (2019). Bolsa Família in Brazil (2 September), Accessible at: https://www.centreforpublicimpact.org/case-study/bolsa-familia-in-brazil.

Cullather, N. (2007). The Foreign Policy of the Calorie. In: *The American Historical Review* 112, no. 2: 337–364. Retrieved February 4, 2021. Accessible at: http://www.jstor.org/stable/4136605.

Donnenfeld, Z. (2020). What Is the Future of Poverty in Africa? Recent Trends in Poverty Reduction Could Prove Difficult to Maintain. In: *Institute for Security Studies* (2 March), Accessible at: https://issafrica.org/iss-today/what-is-the-future-of-poverty-in-africa.

Elsenhans, H. (1991). Reforming the Economic System of Bangladesh: Mayn Fields of Action. In: Hermann Sautter (Ed.), *Wirtschaftspolitische Reformen in Entwicklungsländern. Schriften des Vereins für Socialpolitik 209*. Berlin: Duncker und Humblot, pp. 109–133.

Elsenhans, H. (2021, forthcoming). *Capitalism, Development, Empowerment of Labour: A Heterodox Political Economy*. London: Routledge.

England, A. (2021). The Arab Spring 10 Years On. In: *Financial Times Weekend Magazine* (16 January).

International Labour Organization. (2021). About Us [Viewed 1 April 2021], Accessible at: https://www.ilo.org/global/about-the-ilo/history/lang--en/index.htm.

International Labour Organization. (2021). Conventions and Recommendations [Viewed 1 April 2021], Accessible at: https://www.ilo.org/global/standards/introduction-to-international-labour-standards/conventions-and-recommendations/lang--en/index.htm.

Mitchell, T. and Manson, K. (2021). China Sees EU Investment Deal as Diplomatic Coup After US Battles. In: *Financial Times* (1 January), Accessible at: https://www.ft.com/content/64ef5592-25b4-48c4-a70b-b42071951941.

Wilcock, N. and Scholz, C. (2016). *Hartmut Elsenhans and a Critique of Capitalism: Conversations on Theory and Policy Implications*. London: Palgrave Macmillan.

World Bank. (2016). *Uganda Poverty Assessment 2016: Fact Sheet*. New York: World Bank (20 September), Accessible at: https://www.worldbank.org/en/country/uganda/brief/uganda-poverty-assessment-2016-fact-sheet.

World Bank. (2020). *Debt Burden of Least Developed Countries Continues to Climb to a Record $744 Billion in 2019*. Press Release. New York: The World Bank (12 October), Accessible at: https://www.worldbank.org/en/news/press-release/2020/10/12/debt-burden-of-least-developed-countries-continues-to-climb-to-a-record-744-billion-in-2019.

CHAPTER 12

Fixing the Labour Surplus in Existing Economic Structures

Hannes Warnecke-Berger

As a matter of fact, the empirical observation on which the chapter under comment relies is not only actual but currently aggravated due to the COVID-19 pandemic. Global inequalities are a relevant issue in the global system, perhaps *the* most important issue currently at stake. But more than this, it is a historical issue, and apart from a couple of exceptions, structural unemployment and poverty have scarred the duration of the century. Inequality between economies and nations has further deepened (Korzeniewicz and Moran, 2009; Milanović, 2016), and when the case of China and its impressive course of development is excluded, global inequality between the Global South and the Global North increased from about 1:3 of per capita GDP at the end of the nineteenth century to around 1:80 in current times (Thirlwall, 2013). Furthermore, the North seems to have lost its function within the global economy as a locomotive of growth and employment and thus is not or no longer able to clear global labour markets. The North is unable to absorb surplus labour from

H. Warnecke-Berger (✉)
University of Kassel, Kassel, Germany
e-mail: hwarneckeberger@uni-kassel.de

N. Wilcock and E. Federzoni dos Santos (eds.), *Not Paying the Rent*,
https://doi.org/10.1007/978-3-030-78861-2_12

the South as the recent discussion on migration in almost all Western countries shows while migration controls are stronger and more selective than even before (Menjívar, 2014). South-North migrations are too slow to lead to full employment in the South, which was a distinguishing factor to the "age of mass migration" during the nineteenth century (Hatton and Williamson, 1998), when Scandinavian countries particularly gained enormously from out-migration to the New World. On the other side, labour markets within the West/North increasingly show structural deficiencies. Labour is increasingly deprived of organising access to economic surplus via real wage increases. The labour share develops in favour of capital and national labour markets increasingly dualise (Hassel, 2014; Baccaro and Benassi, 2016; Hein, 2013).

The labour surplus thus remains one of the most pivotal issues for the global economy in current and in future times. Since the discovery of the labour surplus by the early development theorists Paul Rosenstein-Rodan (1943), Arthur Lewis (1954), José Nun (1969), and John Fei and Gustav Ranis (1964), the expression of labour surplus has changed profoundly. Labour surplus models usually start by analysing agriculture. These models situate marginality within underperforming rural and agrarian production systems. Labour surplus initially became visible as "agrarian excess population" (Rosenstein-Rodan, 1943, p. 202). However, given the rate of urbanisation in many countries of the Global South (UNPD, 2019), labour surplus shifted from rural to urban and from agrarian villages to cities, particularly to the urban informal sector. Concepts such as "planet of slums" (Davis, 2004) or the "urban precariat" (Munck, 2013) exemplify this trend. The urban face of current marginality further imposes several complexities on the policies and political solutions proposed in the chapter. Before discussing the challenges, opportunities, and limitations of the political solutions proposed in the chapter, I will first exemplify some of the model specifies of the stones-for-cash scheme brought into discussion by Elsenhans (1996).

It was Keynes who pointed at structural unemployment as a major risk for advanced capitalist economies, inspired by the European and the US experiences during the Great Depression of the 1930s. In relation to the cash-for-stones scheme, Keynes (2018 [1936], p. 115) proposed the following to overcome unemployment:

> *If the Treasury were to fill old bottles with banknotes, bury them at suitable depths in disused coalmines which are then filled up to the surface with town rubbish, and leave it to private enterprise on well-tried principles of laissez-faire to dig the notes up again (the right to do so being obtained, of course, by tendering for leases of the note-bearing territory), there need be no more unemployment and, with the help of the repercussions, the real income of the community, and its capital wealth also, would probably become a good deal greater than it actually is. It would, indeed, be more sensible to build houses and the like; but if there are political and practical difficulties in the way of this, the above would be better than nothing. The analogy between this expedient and the gold-mines of the real world is complete.*

Keynes points to several issues that have been discussed intensively since, particularly in development economics. Firstly, in his vision, development does not relate in the first place to enhanced productivity, but by creating employment and aggregate demand through increasing private consumption. The root cause for crisis is labour surplus and structural involuntary unemployment. Labour is paid for independently of the productivity or the usefulness of its work. The efficiency of these investments in public work schemes can make a difference but is not necessarily decisive. Employing labour for socially useful purposes, however, can change the technological path of an economy. Labour can be employed for producing old "things" and products, such as fuel engines, or labour can be additionally employed for producing electric or hydrogen engines, sectors that today still appear as too expensive. Hence, tackling the labour surplus is not only related to overcoming unemployment but can have even positive impacts on the industrial structure, given that the technology is available and can be applied. Talk of a possible Green New Deal and overcoming labour surplus, therefore, can go hand-in-hand.

Second, the idea of resolving structural unemployment through initially non-purposeful practices that have large monetary effects related to demand and consumption is, however, linked to a specific investment and growth function. In mainstream neoclassical economics, as well as in Marxist political economy, wages and profits are caught in a zero-sum game: labour gains what capitalists lose, and vice versa. Higher real wages lead to less surplus available for investment. Keynesians confront this zero-sum game in highlighting the active role of money and in showing that money wages pay for labour flow into consumption that enhances profit expectations of capitalists and eventually drives net investment as well as net profits. In this Keynesian, and particularly Kaleckian adaptation, the maintenance of a certain level of investment is socially too important to be left to private business. Keynes and Keynesians are certainly doubtful against the capitalists' interest and capacity in maintaining the system overall. This is why Keynes thought that this issue should be the responsibility of the state, but without showing what exactly this meant and under which political conditions it should function. Keynesianism still lacks a proper political (state) theory.

A third consideration is that both Keynes and Elsenhans within their models assume that the productivity of the agricultural sector is at least as high to feed the marginal and marginalised population. Furthermore, in both models, the development of the agricultural sector is no longer important, as it is not recognised as a growth pole. During the 1970s due to the Green Revolution, many economies of the Global South reached food self-sufficiency. However, there are still many economies that need to import basic foodstuff and dependent on an import-based food regime (FAO, 2020). If food self-sufficiency is achieved, surplus labour at subsistence wages can be employed in any kind of activity, and given the possibility of foreign exchange control and depreciations of the currency, the goods produced from the surplus labour can be sold at any prices at the world market as long as intermediate goods are produced locally. Initially, the productivity of this labour force is less important than its total output.

Fourth, the unemployment equilibrium that Keynes had in mind, however, is different from the stones-for-cash scheme in a crucial way. Keynes recommends the Treasury to "fill old bottles with banknotes", as does Elsenhans (1996, p. 132) regarding international development agencies by helicopters effectively dropping millions in cash. However, in Keynes vision, the productive infrastructure already existed and "private enterprise on well-tried principles of laissez-faire" are able to jump in. Structural unemployment in this perspective is a short-term crisis scenario with the economy needing to be brought "back again" on the tracks of steady-state growth through political intervention. This is not automatic, however, as early contributions to development economics have shown. Development economics from early on made clear that a productive infrastructure, particularly in industry, needs to be build up and created in the first place. Either a capitalist class of entrepreneurs is simply not available, or, more complex, has access to surplus but does not want to or cannot reinvest this surplus because of tight markets and lacking demand for their products. The normal situation that the early development theorists described therefore is not a short-term problem of an otherwise functioning market economy, as would be the case for the small number of capitalist economies in Europe and the US, but a more fundamental, deep-rooted systemic problem in which capitalist logics do not function. In order to develop them, something apart from the unavailable capitalists must play their role, hence the invention of the development actor, be it the developmental state, international development organisations, or local non-governmental organisations. In effect, these developmental actors are compensations for the lack of really existing capitalists. After around one century of attempts for external development, these agents seriously lost their credibility. Instead of full employment and economic development, corruption, inefficiency and an ever-increasing labour surplus is the state of affairs. Hence, a certain "impasse" (Schuurman, 2000, p. 7) set in. This is the starting point of the current new interest in setting the stage for new development actors, either in the guise of local grassroots movements highlighted by post-development thinkers (for an overview, see Ziai, 2017), or "quasi-supranational" international organisations. Both are expected to be more oriented towards the needs of the poor and less prone to corruption and inefficiency. That all being said, their task remains the same: overcoming the structural equilibrium of labour surplus in the Global South. The chapter proposes the ILO can play this function with the objective of elevating the setting of labour standards, enhancing the empowerment of labour as well as representing a necessary counterweight of labour against capital. In the stones-for-cash scheme, this means that the ILO should set the framework, oversee the process, and provide the infrastructure. However, some doubts remain.

Firstly, the stones-for-cash scheme intends to create additional employment and raise private consumption through the transfer of money. As Keynes mentions, these investments do not have to be efficient. However, this depends on the threshold of the economic sectors external to the stones scheme that at some point should be able to absorb the labour force. Indirectly, the scheme assumes that at one point, labour when it achieves bargaining power and full employment will migrate to other sectors. The scheme alone, however, does not change the economic situation in this external sector if workers within the scheme do not buy a substantial quantity of products from this external sector. The model suggests that workers from within the scheme indeed demand products from agriculture and basic manufactured goods but estimated thresholds are important here. The scheme is mainly intended to supply a demand stimulus for the external sector, however that will depend on the level of wages paid, which is another obstacle altogether given it derives from donor countries. In general, an important issue therefore exists in interlinking both sectors. Again, this needs planning in the economic process, for directing consumption and creating forward and backward linkages, something that has failed so far in existing development strategies, particularly during import-substituting industrialisation during the 1960s and 1970s.

Second, the stones-for-cash scheme does provide additional resources to labour and enhances final consumption if money wages are spent and not saved. However, the scheme does not augment the bargaining power of the marginal labour force because in strict economic terms, the workers employed within the scheme still politically depend on the scheme as the scheme does not change their productivity, particularly because the external sector does not buy products made within the scheme. Here, political accountabilities shift from "national" rentiers to international organisations, such as the ILO. The political nature of the class struggle of labour against capital rests on the issue of productivity increases. Labour is able, due to its scarcity and its productivity, to make claims on the surplus. Labour scarcity means that capitalists must accept real wage increases in order to increase production. Labour productivity, in contrast, means that labour is potentially able to secure social reproduction independently from political bonds: political voice (Hirschman, 1970) as well as "structural worker power" (Silver, 2003, p. 13), or in a more general sense, economic citizenship that allows for the double-freed nature of labour, requires a minimum of productivity and subsequent productivity increases. The scheme is able to reach labour scarcity because it politically withdraws the workers employed within the scheme from the labour market and therefore functions as a minimal welfare state, although workers still have to work in collecting the stones. However, the scheme is not able to increase the bargaining power of labour vis-à-vis capitalists and rentiers. Instead, it creates its own rents since the remuneration of labour within the scheme does not depend on the intensity of work but on sheer presence at the workplace.

Finally, why should ILO do better than so many development agents before? The stones-for-cash scheme alone opens many possibilities for cheating and corruption, since the entire process is not under the control of systemic forces such as competition on markets within capitalism but under the domain of the political will of the organising institution. The ILO, like all other UN organisations, is just as vulnerable to political machinations and bureaucratic jams derailing good intentions. Therefore, there are clear limitations of the scheme. Labour surplus and low levels of labour productivity go hand-in-hand, but the scheme in its presented version is only able to mitigate labour surplus and perhaps only in the short run. That, however, does not necessarily influence labour productivity. Even if workers produce with technology for the local market, they need to compete with international markets at some point. The scheme, in order to guarantee even productivity increases and local learning, must be protected, and once again, the complexities of import-substitution return.

The scheme is based on the assumptions of agrarian marginality in rural areas. Theoretically, this still applies due to the mostly unequal distribution of land and the often low levels of productivity in agriculture as well as the dependence on food imports. However, given the historical process of migration from rural to urban areas, today's marginality is predominantly an urban phenomenon. In order to suit for the current global situation of labour surplus, the model needs to be extended as well as embedded into a broader rethinking of the role of economic structures. Embeddedness means that the scheme is able to generate both its employment and development effects if it works under the conditions of a relatively egalitarian distribution of income as well as an economic sector external to the scheme that is oriented towards the manufacturing of basic intermediary goods. The demand stimulus for basic manufacturing goods is higher if this additional demand is homogenous, and the external sector can increase quantities produced with only minor price effects. Again, the agricultural sector is crucial: with rising prices for foodstuff and rising real wages in the agricultural sector, the agricultural sector tends to buy products from the industrial sector in order to improve technology and productivity, another push factor and demand stimulus for the manufacturing sector. Relatively egalitarian agrarian reforms then must precede the introduction of those schemes. These reforms, however, usually fail because of the resistance of the rentiers (Bernstein, 2010; Janvry and Sadoulet, 1989). The scheme should be used not only for overcoming labour marginality and a demand stimulus for external economic activities, but additionally, *enhancing labour productivity*. An historical example is in infrastructure works, Germany in the nineteenth century employed around one million people in the construction of railroads and other infrastructure programmes that significantly absorbed the labour surplus and led to labour scarcity (O'Brien, 1983). The railroads sector, therefore, created forward and backward linkages through its boom in employment and interrelated previously disparate economic sectors.

The situation between advanced capitalist economies facing stagnation and downward pressures on real wages on the one hand, and the economic situation of the Global South where the structuring principle of the economy is rent rather than capitalist profit on the other, needs to be distinguished. Elsenhans (2015) forcefully shows this in contrasting a "convoy model of globalisation" versus a doomsday model he terms a "globalization of rent" (see Foreword). In the first case, the change of an entire technology path seems too expensive, both because advanced capitalist economies are externally locked into yet existing comparative advantages within the global economy, and internally, because these economies increasingly suffer from "secular stagnation" (Summers, 2014)—namely, stagnating real wages and the dualisation of labour markets (the divide between insiders in full-time permanent employment and outsiders in precarious work or unemployment). Usually, changing entire systems of technologies includes high complementary costs. Fuel engines against electric engines is such an example: driving a car necessarily needs a geographical network of gas stations. Changing the type of engine towards a more sophisticated type in terms of environmental protection not only changes the production technology of cars, but also needs to take into consideration the entire network of gas stations. In the case of environmental technologies, the technologies are already available and even proved and tested, but they still are too expensive to be introduced. The example of the German car industry further shows that corruption and the pressure on environmental standards are still perceived to be cheaper than following standards and introducing new technologies. Labour surplus employment schemes can fit into these phenomena as they create opportunities to cover the costs of complementary technologies and therefore significantly reduce the cost for changing towards more environmental technologies for the producers of the core technology. The general public, therefore, monetarily participates in alternating the technological path of their economy and creates incentives for the producers to shift their production interests towards greener technology.

If those models of green technological replication are as easily transferable to the realities of the Global South remains to be proven. It is sure, however, that in addition to the strict technological reasons, a number of other problems arise under the conditions of the non-availability of new environmentally friendly technologies. Firstly, qualification of labour matters within the schemes; if the technology is not available, it has to be developed locally. Environmentally friendly technology, however, is among the more sophisticated technology and usually capital intensive. Directing the development of technology within labour surplus schemes has enormous limitations. Secondly, the development of technology as well as the application and subsequent copying of technology takes time. The longer the scheme exists and the longer labour surplus prevails, however, the more likely the scheme develops a life on its own. Then, redistribution of economic rent towards the scheme as well as rent-seeking behaviour within the scheme becomes dominant and possibly undermines the overall objective.

These thoughts, however, open the possibility to think anew about the connection between development theory and environment. From this perspective, both Keynes' and Elsenhans' thoughts on how to tackle the labour surplus are highly actual, and more than ever, politically relevant.

Bibliography

Baccaro, L. and Benassi, C. (2016). Throwing Out the Ballast: Growth Models and the Liberalization of German Industrial Relations. In: *Socio-Economic Review* 54: 1–31.

Bernstein, H. (2010). *Class Dynamics of Agrarian Change*. Halifax: Fernwood; Sterling: Kumarian Press.

Davis, M. (2004). Planet of Slums. Urban Involution and the Informal Proletariat. In: *New Left Review* 26, no. 2: 5–34.

de Janvry, A. and Sadoulet, E. (1989). A Study in Resistance to Institutional Change: The Lost Game of Latin American Land Reform. In: *World Development* 17, no. 9: 1397–1407.

Elsenhans, H. (1996). Kein Ende der Großen Theorie. In: *Asien Afrika Lateinamerika* 24, no. 2: 111–145.

Elsenhans, H. (2015). *Saving Capitalism from the Capitalists: World Capitalism and Global History*. New Delhi: Sage.

Fei, J. C. and Ranis, G. (1964). *Development of the Labor Surplus Economy: Theory and Practice*. Irwin: Homewood.

Hassel, A. (2014). The Paradox of Liberalization—Understanding Dualism and the Recovery of the German Political Economy. In: *British Journal of Industrial Relations* 52, no. 1: 57–81.

Hatton, T. J. and Williamson, J. G. (1998). *The Age of Mass Migration: Causes and Economic Impact*. Oxford and New York: Oxford University Press.

Hein, E. (2013). *Finance-Dominated Capitalism and Redistribution of Income: A Kaleckian Perspective*. Levy Economics Institute Working Paper, No. 746. New York: Levy Economics Institute.

Hirschman, A. O. (1970). *Exit, Voice and Loyalty*. Cambridge: Harvard University Press.

Keynes, J. M. (2018 [1936]). *The General Theory of Employment, Interest, and Money*. Cham: Palgrave Macmillan.

Korzeniewicz, R. P. and Moran, T. P. (2009). *Unveiling Inequality: A World-Historical Perspective*. New York: Russell Sage Foundation.

Lewis, W. A. (1954). Economic Development with Unlimited Supply of Labour. In: *Manchester School of Economic and Social Studies* 22, no. 2: 139–191.

Menjívar, C. (2014). Immigration Law Beyond Borders: Externalizing and Internalizing Border Controls in an Era of Securitization. In: *Annual Review of Law and Social Science* 10, no. 1: 353–369.

Milanović, B. (2016). *Global Inequality: A New Approach for the Age of Globalization*. Cambridge: The Belknap Press of Harvard University Press.

Munck, R. (2013). The Precariat: A View from the South. In: *Third World Quarterly* 34, no. 5: 747–762.

Nun, J. (1969). Superpoblación relativa, ejército industrial de reserva y masa marginal. In: *Revista Latinoamericana de Sociología* 5, no. 2: 178–236.

O'Brien, P. (Ed.). (1983). *Railways and the Economic Development of Western Europe, 1830–1914*. Houndmills, Basingstoke, Hampshire: Palgrave Macmillan.

Rosenstein-Rodan, P. N. (1943). Problems of Industrialisation of Eastern and South-Eastern Europe. In: *The Economic Journal* 53, nos. 210/211: 202–211.

Schuurman, F. J. (2000). Paradigms Lost, Paradigms Regained? Development Studies in the Twenty-First Century. In: *Third World Quarterly* 21, no. 1: 7–20.

Silver, B. J. (2003). *Forces of Labor: Workers' Movements and Globalization Since 1870*. Cambridge and New York: Cambridge University Press.

Summers, L. H. (2014). U.S. Economic Prospects: Secular Stagnation, Hysteresis, and the Zero Lower Bound. In: *Business Economics* 49, no. 2: 65–73.

Thirlwall, A. P. (2013). *Economic Growth in an Open Developing Economy: The Role of Structure and Demand*. Cheltenham: Edward Elgar.

United Nations Department of Economic and Social Affairs, Population Division (UNPD). (2019). *World Urbanization Prospects: The 2018 Revision*. New York: United Nations.

United Nations Food and Agriculture Organization (FAO). (2020). *The State of Food Security and Nutrition in the World: Transforming Food Systems for Affordable Healthy Diets*. Rome: FAO.

Ziai, A. (2017). Post-Development 25 Years After the Development Dictionary. In: *Third World Quarterly* 38, no. 12: 2547–2558.

CHAPTER 13

Economic Development Through Social Movements

Edgar Federzoni dos Santos and Neil Wilcock

Modern history is primarily moved by the dynamics between three key agents. Firstly, the nation-state, and its monopoly of the legitimate use of physical force, has become the most evident driver of historical change since the seventeenth century. Secondly, the market, comprised of wealth-producing actors, has assumed a role that alternated between the leading player in society, and the nation-state financial sponsor. State and market usually form a symbiotic relationship in which one feeds the other's authority and, in many countries, the elites of each are barely distinguishable. The third pillar is society comprised of the non-elite citizens who have less entrenched institutional political and economic influence than

E. Federzoni dos Santos (✉) · N. Wilcock
Leipzig University, Leipzig, Germany

N. Wilcock
e-mail: neil.wilcock.07@aberdeen.ac.uk

E. Federzoni dos Santos
University of Vienna, Vienna, Austria

N. Wilcock and E. Federzoni dos Santos (eds.), *Not Paying the Rent*,
https://doi.org/10.1007/978-3-030-78861-2_13

state and market agents but invariably serve as the most significant source of power and value in a State.

Society furnishes the State with the soldiers and law enforcement personnel it needs for its sovereignty (power) and is responsible for the workforce and economic output (value). Additionally, society provides the taxes and consumers that the other two pillars require to exist. Nevertheless, and against all logical odds, modern history has been characterised by a variety of authoritarian rule, both political (all power to the state) and economic (all power to the market), that established themselves as the sole agents of progress, resulting in an allegedly homogeneous enterprise that excludes broader society (Favero, 2003). These dictatorships are not official government regimes, but instead, the de facto rulers of a time, as Eric Hobsbawm describes in *The Age of Extremes*.

With the advent of liberal democracies, society took a more pivotal role and flourished, if only belatedly, as a direct history-shifting agent. If development is chiefly a social matter, as opposed to naked economic growth, the state/market duality alone cannot lead to sustainable development. The popular manifestation becomes essential, as it will inform and shape statecraft and economic policy to assimilate in their agenda the topics that affect a nation's fate outside of the elites' ivory towers.

Upon recognising elites cannot be entrusted to maintain the development process, the next step is to acknowledge that it will only thrive if it is coherent with the social complexity on which it depends. In sum, elites and development depend on society, not the other way around. The masses are invariably more diverse in social terms than the state class, and by implication, development strategies must emerge from a patchwork of demand-driven policies that integrate and perpetually adjust for the many societal groups within an economy. In this context, single-interest groups and local communities are far more transformative and relevant for a country's economic success than in the past. Above all, harvesting the economic force that lies within these non-elite groups requires more than acknowledging their relevance: civil rights are indispensable.

It is important to distinguish individual rights from collective rights in this sense. The former represents civil and political rights developed since the seventeenth and eighteenth centuries when pre-modern caste systems began giving space to new ideas of equality of social and human rights. These rights are the foundation of free speech and protest. Collective rights, on the other hand, are twofold. The first upholds that everyone has minimum rights, and the whole of society is responsible for safeguarding these rights. The second concerns excluded groups' social and economic rights, those who cannot access their rights or those in need of additional protection. Indeed, the quest for a more egalitarian world, which the second aspect encompasses, has been a central principle in social movements for centuries (Silva and Richter, 2013).

The local space, or the space where common relations predominate, is the locus of the manifestation and recognition of difference as well as the negotiation or social construction of agreements. As a principle, there must be recognition of the existence of the different possibilities of power and wealth configurations at each historical moment and in each geographical place. Additionally, development must be centred on people, in their complexity and their fullness. Thus, civil participation is an essential presupposition of development. Finally, one must accept that state and market are fundamental but not superior to society in driving development (Favero, 2003).

Development is thus necessarily founded on relationships that construct and reconstruct dynamics between societal groups. As such, it requires cooperation and conflict management, which is a critical function of democracies. Development essentially fulfils each community's desires that allows them to acquire rights, more resources and strengthen their roles as political and economic agents. In this sense, development manifestly requires accommodating the various social demands, enforcing justice and inclusion, which has been the social movements' task. Indeed, there are myriad historical examples, some of which will be explored below.

Liberal democracies and technology enabled a surge of social movements in the twentieth century. One of the effects of the global diffusion of liberal ideals of equality and justice, along with the reach of social media as a tool for protest, is the emboldening of minority and single-interest politics. From anti-racism protests, calls for gender equality, respect for vocal minorities to radical action on the environment, single-issue politics constituting social movements have become a mainstream concern. While justice is necessary immediately for such causes, it is our contention that full emancipation cannot be reached without economic justice.

This chapter will argue that to reach full emancipation for a particular society, the social movements gaining prominence need to achieve economic empowerment as part of this ascension. Promoting economic empowerment should be concomitant with social movements' diffusion of liberal ideals of equality and justice. True emancipation for any single-issue involves equality in the widest sense, with progress in one positively influencing the next equality-minded movements.

A report by the Center of Strategic and International Studies (2020) entitled "The Age of Mass Protests: Understanding an Escalating Trend" found the number of mass protests globally has increased by 11.5% per year, on average, since 2009. A combination of factors from a global economic slowdown, worsening effects of climate change, and urbanisation, to increased access to information on corrupt government practices are causing an upturn in social movement activism. In March 2020, *The Economist* wrote "[T]he world has experienced more political uprisings in the past few years than ever before. In 2019 alone there were protests on every continent and across 114 countries—from Hong Kong to Haiti, Bolivia to Britain".

The Internet and smart phones have revolutionalised the way demonstrations are organised, promoted, and sustained.[1] With the uninhibited spread of information, both real and fake, deepening political divides, the trend of increasing mass protests and the social movements that inspire them is set to continue upward.

The focus of this chapter is the transformative power of social movements,[2] namely, the mobilisation of social forces around a specific cause. We will now discuss the main arguments for advocating economic empowerment as an integral demand of emerging social movements.

Social Movement Strengthening Themselves Through Capitalism

For those controlling capital and the output of an economy, the ultimate priority is to maintain that position. As a result, these privileged groups seek to undermine politics and policymaking intent on change, particularly transformative change. As politics bases its actions on the

[1] A full account of the factors and trends was published by Center of Strategic and International Studies (2020).

[2] A distinction is made here between social movements as a set of rituals for identifying and mobilising the public, and that of the professionalised class of social movements that policymakers refer to as support for non-governmental organisations (NGOs) and religious and private institutions.

management of the various realities in a particular locale and vicissitudes through time, it remains open to inspiring possibilities for change. Indeed, opposing transformation in politics requires countering politics itself.

Development is a political matter and comes charged with ideology like any other, and therefore, to take a quote of David Graeber (2016, p. 89): "…it is just something we make, and could just as easily make something different". In the past two centuries, social movements have been acting as the prime engine of political change and have managed to promote wealth redistribution, enactment of civil and labour rights, and replacement of governments around the world.

In the capitalist system, whose engine itself is accumulation, rather than maintaining concentration of capital, its most important enabler is the creation of mechanisms to multiply and distribute wealth. Mass consumption is a part of such mechanisms, and social inclusion resulting from it is the most significant of them. Development necessitates a recurrent recreation of politics and social relations so to accommodate for social innovations. It is, otherwise, a desire of those who lack justice or who are excluded from the economy and politics; it is their urge to be recognised as the pivot of a country and of the historical process itself (Favero, 2003).

In sum, social movements have the potential to boost prosperity through the empowerment of formerly dispossessed and vulnerable people by integrating economic empowerment in their movement's agenda. If successful, the socially and economically marginal will experience reintegration into the economic sphere—from labour marginals to economic agents.[3] The empowerment of labour leads to the expansion of the internal market and mass consumption, as mentioned, which is imperative for capitalism to deliver prosperity. Currently, this virtuous cycle is under threat: "We may live in political and economic systems also in the West which continue to exhibit formally many elements that we are accustomed to associate with bourgeois democracy and capitalism. It can, however, not be excluded that in reality we have already lost the social contents of capitalism and democracy because of disempowerment of labour" (Elsenhans, 2015, p. 134).

[3] Fully discussed in Chapter 8.

The role of social movements, therefore, becomes crucial not just for the interests they express but also for the freedoms capitalism may create. Past cases show how social movements of the past still contributed to wider emancipation despite economic empowerment not being the focus of its cause. For example, the abolition of the apartheid in South Africa meant those formerly vulnerable and economically disempowered due to racial discrimination could, as empowered economic agents, contribute learned skills to a higher-skilled economy. Likewise, just as women should be paid the same as men for the same job as a matter of morality and equality, achieving it will lead to higher wages for half of the world population, which is in the macroeconomic interests of all.

Ideally, social movements should aim at systemic, sustainable outcomes. This means that they should seek to contribute to founding, improving, and changing institutions within the government and society alike, with unions being of particular relevance. Worker movements, for example, should push for overall living wages, enforceable collective bargaining agreements, presence on company boards, fair shareholding entitlements for employees, among other actions that may empower specific categories of workers or the broad workforce. Overall, ensuring fair income contributes to workers being stronger economic agents, as well as avoiding labour exploitation, social exclusion, and marginalisation.

A case study of social movements integrating economic empowerment was observable recently in the aftermath of the initial Black Lives Matter protests. Economic justice for black employees was articulated in raising wages and employees forming unions to advocate for improved health care, sick leave, and other benefits. Richard Wallace, a "Movement for Black Lives" leader, said his organisation supports unions because they provide a pathway to more competitive wages and benefit for black workers: "You can't pay people minimum wage for a job, knowing it's not a living wage, knowing that [a plurality] of your workforce is black, and then come out and say, 'Black Lives Matter'…A collective bargaining agreement is the only ironclad way of ensuring those values that they're promoting in this moment are held onto in perpetuity until the contract is resolved" (CNN Business, 2020). Richard Wallace encapsulates this chapter's argument simple and profoundly by seeking justice and fairness through existing forces for inclusion on social as well as economic terms, namely labour empowerment, wages protection, and social inclusion. BLM is significant because it is not only targeting change in behaviour among individuals but recognising that "systemic racism" cannot be remedied (and punished) on an individual basis alone. Rather, "that the racism in America and in Europe is actually a product of the corrupted and distorted structure of power in those societies. That it is built into the system as it is presently structured... The HR response is that all problems in the system can be solved by getting someone to clear their desk – and ejecting them out of the building. What it never thinks is that maybe it's the system that's at fault" (Vice, 2021). Therefore, transformation comes from challenging the social, political, and cultural relations as well as the *economic relations* of a particular locale.

The latent potential of social movements was exemplified by the response in the Western world to the death of George Floyd. As the *New York Times* (2020) reported, "15 million to 26 million people in the United States have participated in demonstrations over the death of George Floyd and others in recent weeks. These figures would make the recent protests the largest movement in the country's history". The demonstrations point to an underlying thirst for change. With increasing inequalities, the worsening effects of climate change, and widening of disinformation, it is acting as a magnet for social movements. Joining a social movement has never been easier and "there have already been historical eras of mass protests and there is evidently a 'contagion effect' across borders" (Center of Strategic and International Studies, 2020, p. 21) which we are experiencing today (aided and abetted by a global culture of individualism in which people have multiple identities they want and need to express).

However, with the fragmentation of modern society and the increasing recognition of different identities, the danger of different social movements slipping into conflict or contraction of each other rises. In such a state, in-fighting caused by the intolerance of other single issues would effectively side with the status quo because those who would generally side with the cause are made out to be opponents.[4]

[4] In a response to a question whether appeals for racial justice and gender equality on the one hand and class-based organisation ran in contradiction, Noam Chomsky (2020) said: "I'm sure you recall that Martin Luther King, Jr., at the end of his life, at the point where he was sharply losing liberal support, was trying to organize a poor-people's campaign, Black and white, wherever you're from—you're poor, struggling, working people...All of these concerns interact....You can understand why, for some people, some of them are more important than others, but it's a matter of bringing them all together, because they're basically all on the same side".

The Case of the US Civil Rights Movement—An Example

Between the 1950s and 1960s, the US experienced a fierce, revolutionary social movement initiated by black Americans. The Civil Rights Movement swept the country and drew crowds of black people and others to acquire equal rights of treatment, opportunities, employment, education, and even to receive private and public services in the same places as white people. By 1955, when Rosa Parks, known as the mother of the modern-day Civil Rights Movement, inspired the Montgomery Improvement Association (MIA) foundation, thereby igniting the Civil Rights Movement activities, African Americans accounted for 10% of the US population or about 15 million people. Economic equality was central to the Civil Rights Movement's protests and general activities. Indeed, protestors desired justice, central to which was economic justice, as economic concerns contributed to fair treatment campaigns for black citizens in lunch counters, movie theatres, restaurants, and theme parks. Places that segregated black consumers were met with boycotts and protests, which harmed their businesses. Additionally, the desire for job equality was resoundingly dominant because this population was not allowed to partake in, contribute to, or benefit from the main economy fairly, regardless of their large consumer base (Wright, 2006a).

Prior to the Civil Rights Movement, black people were among the worst paid workers within the US labour market. Rarely did they take managerial and highly technical positions, partly because they were excluded from promotions and recruitment processes and partly because they were barred from receiving technical training. Their cheap labour was prey to exploitation and rent extraction. In reaction, black movements pressured federal and state governments for nine years and received an enormously aggressive pushback from society and politicians until the Civil Rights Act was enacted in 1964. The new piece of legislation put an end to centuries of formal, state-backed segregation in the country and was followed by complementary acts reinforcing this new position.

A large meta-study of economic data conducted in the late 1980s showed that the Civil Rights Movement also bore unheralded fruits (Heckman and Payner, 1989). As a remarkable example, South Carolina had one of the proportionally largest Afro-American populations in the US in the 1960s. Yet in 1962, black male workers represented just under 5% of the textile industry's workforce—the state's predominant industry—a scenario that had remained unchanged since the 1920s. By the mid-1970s, that number increased almost fourfold to 17%, and among black women the relative change was even higher, from a historic participation of near 0% in the textile industry to over 15% of labour integration in 1980 (South Carolina Department of Labour, Annual Reports). The trend consistently spread over to US and other states and sectors.

The Civil Rights Movement did not stop in the wake of the Civil Rights Act and other legal breakthroughs followed continuous popular pressure. In 1968, southern labour unions agreed that black Americans could be promoted to their "rightful place" within companies' hierarchical structures. By the 1990s, black participation in blue-collar jobs in manufacturing had risen from 15% to almost 30% along with inhabiting many of the higher-paying positions they had been historically refused (Wright, 2006b).

Beyond specific sectors, the overall personal income in states where the black population is above the national average has seen sharp increases. Nevertheless, in South Carolina, personal incomes as a national percentage stagnated between 0.8 and 0.9% between 1940 and 1963. Nevertheless, as of the Civil Rights Act's enforcement, that figure showed a sustained upward trend to reach 1.1% in the mid-1980s. While this seems a minor change, it is rather a growth of approximately 30% over 20 years following the preceding 20 years of stagnation.[5]

The Elementary and Secondary Education Act of 1965 represented another milestone, forcing schools to enrol black students. American economists were able to trace back income gains of the black population years later to these new educational opportunities (Smith, 1984; Smith and Welch, 1989). Indeed, more substantial human capital associated with greater access to the labour market generated a virtuous cycle of income and market growth.

In summary, data shows a "significant positive association between racial income levels in a metropolitan area and the returns to self-employment", being "no longer symptomatic of economic marginality" (Wright, 2006a; Black et al., 2001). In other words, the Civil Rights unlocked a cycle of events: black people conquered rights, gained access

[5] U.S. Bureau of the Census, Historical Statistics of the United States, Colonial Times to 1970 (1976), pp. 243–245; Statistical Abstract of the United States.

to the labour market with higher incomes, and ultimately created a more robust consumer market that fed back into employment and income.

Black Americans never reached full parity, nor was progress linear and constant, but the gains are not negligible. More importantly, the institutional, legal, and economic shifts did not occur through a traditional top-down process, in which Washington takes the initiative, passes the law, and cascades the results throughout the country. Instead, those shifts were of a societal nature, resulting from the massive, well-organised, and inescapable force that black movements sparked countrywide. One can undoubtedly say that the Civil Rights Movement was a great contributor to economic development in the US. Here, the order of the elements is essential: From a single-interest agenda, local communities opened up avenues for progress to the US' broader society by virtue of their personal plight.

UK Trade Unions

While the previous example outlined a social movement's widening enfranchisement towards economic empowerment of marginal peoples, the next example will outline the reverse—namely, when a social movement upholding economic empowerment is eviscerated.

Trade unionism is associated with enfranchisement of labour, from contractual limits to working days, the right to vote, to a host of other labour rights ensuring a greater share of economic output is distributed to the labour force. The institutional role of trade unions in bargaining for workers was critical in the development and maintenance of democratic capitalism. As Özlem Onaran et al (2015, p. 42) write, "Trade unions bring together the voices of employees to bargain for adequate wages and working conditions, which in turn impacts demand in the economy overall".

The UK has a strong trade union tradition, yet that tradition took a decisive turn in the 1980s in the face of Thatcher's neoliberal assault. At their peak in 1979, the trade unions in the UK had thirteen million members, but by the end of the next decade the leading unions of the Transport and General Workers' Union and the Amalgamated Engineering Union had lost 40% of its members (Gilmour, 1993, pp. 94 and 108). Empirical evidence shows this decline in the membership and efficacy of UK trade unions related to a declining labour share of income:

> [T]he dramatic fall in the union density in the last three decades in the U.K. has led to a 9.3 percentage-point lower labour share in GDP...[Unionisation] from its peak in 1975 to today, has reduced UK GDP by up to 1.6 percent. (Onaran et al, 2015, p. 3)

The decline of worker unionism in the UK has coincided with the long and seemingly irreversible decrease in workers' wages. Trade union membership declined from a peak of nearly half the workforce (49.9%) in 1981, to its nadir today (25%) while, not uncoincidentally, wages have been experiencing their longest period of wage stagnation since the Napoleonic Wars:

> For the U.K., the wage share [of GDP] reached its peak in 1975 at 76.2% and by 2014 had decreased by 8.9%, to 67.3%....the boost to demand from rising wages outweighs other impacts on profits and international competitiveness; growth in national income is driven by growing wages more than by growing company profits. *Declining union presence has, as a result, fed directly into lower growth overall.* [emphasis mine] (ibid., p. 9)

The weakening of the collective voice for workers in trade unions with a lower overall share of wages in the economy correlates with slowing economic growth—a trend set to worsen. The decline of UK trade unions shows the opposite of economic empowerment through a social movement, rather the degradation of a formerly powerful social movement upholding labour rights.

In the here and now, social movements can be complimentarily and supplementary to unions and can co-exist as they share the same underlying interests—when served with proper empowerment aims, honest leadership, and democratic organisation. Regardless of the complex reasons for trade unions' decline,[6] they are still relevant as the best protection for workers' rights.

[6] Occurred amid the transformation in the make-up of the UK economy from an industrial base with a high level of employee trade unionism to a rise in the service sector where workers are rarely unionised.

Requirements for Economic Development Through Social Movements

Mobilisation of a social movement should result in an agenda, which alongside the demands for fairer and just outcomes should articulate the demands of inclusion (in the fullest sense of the word) for the social movement. Inclusion is a necessity for social movements to have an impact on economic development, more commonly when the movement becomes normalised in the society within which it develops.

Inclusion is ultimately the same as the injection of resources in the economy. The argument for inclusion mirrors the model of dropping stones (see Chapter 8) in that social movements, through integrating economic justice as part of their agenda, promote a journey from exclusion to inclusion—specifically, labour marginalisation to workers on markets—by transforming the formerly dispossessed into economic agents. Inclusion also solidifies the existing labour supply because the threat of using an even more exploited population in the case of ill-discipline among those currently employed disappears.

Gains of any social movement that include economic justice will lead to factors important to development: access to education, a more robust labour force, and increasing production and consumption potential. At the earliest feasible moment, social movements should incorporate economic demands for the group upon which it acts—including higher wages, higher labour standards, stronger welfare protections, union representation on company boards—as part of a wider development agenda.

If extended widely, the inclusion agenda will start to address root causes of existing marginalisation. Labour rights are needed to create livelihoods and break the bonds of dependency and vulnerability, namely a lack of social and economic agency. Such exploitation cannot be overcome without fixing capitalism; otherwise, one merely mops the floor while it rains.

For capitalism to survive, there needs to be a balance of social forces between capitalists and labour, although the strengthening of rentism is tipping the balance towards social exclusion, from which it is long and arduous to return. The rise in inequality, of which long wage stagnation is a contributing factor, must be challenged as a mainstream political priority. Given their increasing role as political lightning rods in the modern world, social movements have a large role to play in rebalancing power in favour of labour.

Conclusion

This chapter has argued that with social movements on the rise in the modern world, the agenda should be widened for full inclusion of the social movement. That widening of the inclusion agenda to encompass economic injustice will start to address root causes of existing marginalisation.

Historical examples illustrate that social inclusion can produce the same effects as the injection of new resources into the economy. The Civil Rights Movement in the US fought against a series of inherent discriminations towards black Americans, and in doing so triggered a cycle of events. What began with acquiring basic human rights generated increased access and incomes in the labour market and ultimately to a more robust consumer market for all. The evisceration of the UK trade union movement, which explicitly aims to uphold labour empowerment, has shown the opposite damaging effects on labour and the wider economy. While in the present day, the Black Lives Matter social movement is challenging latent discriminations across US society, including marginalisation in the labour market.

It is incumbent upon the leaders of the social movements to overcome their instinct resistance to participating in the capitalist system and embrace the latent opportunity for full empowerment bound within their movements. These are the necessary steps if one aims to create a society of truly free and empowered individuals.

Bibliography

Black, D., Holtz-Eakin, D. and Rosenthal, S. S. (2001). Racial Minorities, Economic Scale, and the Geography of Self-Employment. In: *Brookings-Wharton Papers on Urban Affairs* 2001: 245–286.

Center of Strategic and International Studies. (2020). The Age of Mass Protests: Understanding an Escalating Trend (3 March), Accessible at: https://www.csis.org/analysis/age-mass-protests-understanding-escalating-global-trend.

Chomsky, N. (2020). Noam Chomsky Believes Trump Is "the Worst Criminal in Human History". In: *New Yorker Magazine* (30 October), Accessible at: https://www.newyorker.com/news/q-and-a/noam-chomsky-believes-trump-is-the-worst-criminal-in-human-history.

CNN Business Network. (2020). Workers Demanding Union Rights Plan to Walk Off the Job in Nationwide Strike for Black Lives (12 July), Accessible at: https://edition.cnn.com/2020/07/12/business/strike-for-black-lives-union-wages/index.html.

Elsenhans, H. (2015). *Saving Capitalism from the Capitalists: A Contribution to Global and Historical Keynesianism*. Beverly Hills, CA, London, and New Delhi: Sage.

Favero, C. A. (2003). Os movimentos sociais e a questão do desenvolvimento. In: *Informe GEPEC* 7, no. 2.

Gilmour, I. (1993). *Dancing with Dogma: Britain Under Thatcherism*. London: Pocket Books.

Graeber, D. (2016). *The Utopia of Rules: On Technology, Stupidity, and the Secret Joys of Bureaucracy*. Brooklyn: Melville House.

Heckman, J. and Payner, B. S. (1989). Determining the Impact of Federal Antidiscrimination Policy on the Economic Status of Blacks: A Study of South Carolina. In: *American Economic Review* 79, no. 1 (January): 138–177.

New York Times. (2020). Black Lives Matter May Be the Largest Movement in U.S. History (3 July), Accessible at: https://www.nytimes.com/interactive/2020/07/03/us/george-floyd-protests-crowd-size.html.

Onaran, Ö., et al. (2015). *Working for the Economy: The Economic Case for Trade Unions*. No 14083, Greenwich Papers in Political Economy from University of Greenwich, Greenwich Political Economy Research Centre.

Silva, J. B. and Richter M. L. (2013). The Role of Social Movements in Support of Social Economy: Enablers of Citizenship and Social Inclusion. In: *Universitas JUS* 24, no. 3: 77–92.

Smith, J. P. (1984). Race and Human Capital. In: *American Economic Review* 74, no. 4: 685–698.

Smith, J. P. and Welch, F. R. (1989). Black Economic Progress After Myrdal. In: *Journal of Economic Literature* 27, no. 2 (February): 519–564.

The Economist. (2020). Political Protests Have Become More Widespread and More Frequent (10 March), Accessible at: https://www.economist.com/graphic-detail/2020/03/10/political-protests-have-become-more-widespread-and-more-frequent.

Vice. (2021). Charlie Brooker in Conversation with Adam Curtis (11 February), Accessible at: https://www.vice.com/en/article/4ad8db/adam-curtis-charlie-brooker-cant-get-you-out-of-my-head.

Wright, G. (1999, revised in 2006a). The Civil Rights Revolution as Economic History. In: *The Journal of Economic History* 59, no. 2 (June): 267–289.

Wright, G. (Revised 2006b). *The Economics of the Civil Rights Revolution*. Stanford: Stanford University.

CHAPTER 14

Economic Emancipation in a Sustainable Society: Bridging the Gaps Between Economic and Environmental Justice Agenda

Thiago Elert Soares

Introduction

Social movements play a crucial role in the realisation of social, economic, and political rights in democratic societies. In a world of rising inequalities and lingering deprivations, they contribute to improving the living standards of vulnerable communities by driving civic engagement and influencing government decisions towards a more inclusive future. In this regard, the promotion of economic empowerment has been a key component in the agenda of social movements across the globe due to its potential to tackle economic disparities and contribute towards poverty alleviation.

Nevertheless, by straightforwardly supporting individuals' economic empowerment and, therefore, amplifying production and consumption potentials, social movements inadvertently risk neglecting the wider

T. E. Soares (✉)
Independent Researcher, Newcastle-upon-Tyne, UK

N. Wilcock and E. Federzoni dos Santos (eds.), *Not Paying the Rent*,
https://doi.org/10.1007/978-3-030-78861-2_14

consequences of unsustainable patterns of socioeconomic development for our planet and for the full emancipation of individuals themselves.

Against the backdrop of uneven distribution of risks and hazards from resource degradation, biodiversity loss, and the effects of climate change, in this response essay I argue that social movements focused on promoting economic empowerment need to incorporate the environmental justice agenda into their scope of action if they truly intend to generate socioeconomic and political emancipation. Besides contributing to sustainable development and long-term prosperity, the synergy between socioeconomic and environmental activism can increase civic participation, nurture strategic multi-sector coalitions, and strengthen social movements' capabilities to influence government decisions and policies.

To support this argument, this response essay is divided in two parts. First, I examine the rise of the environmental justice movement and the rationale behind connecting the environmental agenda with wider socioeconomic and political claims. Second, I analyse how the connection between environmental protection and social struggles contributed to the success of social movements in Brazil.

While the cases investigated here are country and context-specific, the analysis will also suggest overall insights into understanding why economic empowerment in itself is not sufficient to generate sustainable and equitable development and how social movements can be strengthened by combining the ideas of economic and environmental justice.

The Environmental Justice Movement

Although it is difficult to trace its emergence, the environmental justice movement gained prominence in the late 1970s and early 1980s in the US, when racial and ethnic minority groups started protesting against the uneven distribution and disproportionate exposure to environmental risks, such as toxic waste, pollution, and resource depletion (Agyeman and Evans, 2004, p. 156; Laurent, 2010, p. 3; Pedersen, 2010, p. 2).

For a long time, "environmental justice" was defined in terms of the distribution of costs and benefits within a society following John Rawls (1971) theory of justice. In this sense, the term focused on the problem of maldistribution—"the fact that poor communities, indigenous communities, and communities of color get fewer environmental goods, more environmental bads, and less environment protection" (Schlosberg, 2007, p. 4). Nevertheless, considering the evolution of justice theory and the inputs provided by further understandings of the causes and consequences of maldistribution, environmental justice can (and should) be understood not only in terms of allocation of environmental gains and losses but considering an expanded discourse of social justice. This entails connecting environmental justice with notions of political recognition (Young, 1990), participation in environmental decision-making (Gould, 1996), and the provision of freedoms and opportunities for individuals and communities to achieve what they value (Sen, 1999).

This broader definition of environmental justice is evermore necessary considering that the most vulnerable and impoverished populations within and across countries have proven to be more prone to suffer the impacts of environmental degradation as a consequence of unsustainable patterns of economic growth, industrialisation, and consumer practices. These communities also encounter additional difficulties in expressing their views and participating in local and global policymaking processes. For instance, the process of residential segregation in urban areas tends to push low-income households towards areas with deprived environmental conditions and infrastructure. Not surprisingly, socio-structurally weak neighbourhoods are usually located closer to highly-polluting industrial plants, heavy traffic roads, dumping facilities, and other health-threatening environmental settings (Hornberg and Pauli, 2007, p. 573). It turns out that, when compared to residents living in affluent areas, these communities also face the structural challenge of social and political exclusion, often holding less power to influence governments' decisions and to access strategic spaces to make their voices heard.

In Latin America, the expansion of economic reforms and structural adjustment programmes in the 1980s led to the emergence of rural-based movements concerned about the assault on natural resources—land, forests, water, and minerals—and the pursuit of social justice (Deere and Royce, 2009). The unequal distribution of lands, precarisation of labour, and dominance of export production instead of domestic agriculture increased rural poverty and indigence in the region (David et al., 2001, p. 42), driving rural social movements to protest against neoliberal globalisation. In addition to seeking basic rights for communities traditionally excluded from social, economic, and political power, these movements were increasingly dedicated to developing "sustainable livelihoods – ones that respect nature and traditional knowledge and are ecologically and environmentally sustainable" (Deere and Royce, 2009, p. 11).

As we can see, from its inception, the environmental justice movement has not only contributed to raising public awareness about the inequalities in terms of exposure to environmental hazards, but it has also concerned about challenges to social, economic, cultural, and political emancipation. This thematic synergy is central to the movement's success in engaging marginalised communities affected by lower levels of social and economic opportunities. After all, the environmental and economic fairness agendas share many of the same objectives and interests, often times contesting the same structures and actors within the capitalist system.

The Synergy Between Environmental Justice and Social Activism in Brazil

In the case of Brazil, social movements concerned about the country's unequal economic development trajectory began incorporating environmental questions into their mobilisation agenda also in the 1980s. Guided by a model of equitable growth which is based on the fulfilment of human rights, the improvement of the living conditions among the poorest and the elimination of social inequalities, social movements in the country have integrated pressing environmental concerns into the broader search for alternatives to the dominant neoliberal development system.

This was the case, for instance, of the Movement of People Affected by Dams (MAB, in the Portuguese acronym), which holds the electrical business sector accountable for profiting from the expropriation of lands from communities affected by the construction of dams. From its inception, MAB framed dam resistance as a land and peasant-based struggle. However, increasingly, the movement moved beyond anti-dam opposition to contest Brazil's dominant development model and energy strategy leading to environmental degradation (Thorkildsen, 2018, p. 356). By exposing the risks and threats associated with the building of dams and other energy mega-projects—such as deforestation, biodiversity loss, and disruption of ecosystems and communities connected to them—MAB articulates class, racial, and ethnic concerns with environment threats.

The same happened with the Landless Farmworkers Movement (MST, in the Portuguese acronym), which advocates for land reform in Brazil and denounces the agribusiness sector for destroying land fertility and biodiversity in the country by utilising chemical and mechanically intensive production techniques. Considered as one of the most important peasant organisations in the Americas (Rosset and Martínez-Torres, 2012, p. 4), MST has successfully scaled-up from a territorial struggle movement to a counter-hegemonic project of social transformation and remaking of nature-society relations. In the early 2000s, the movement introduced ecological concerns by encouraging alternatives to the corporate model of agricultural production, such as agro-ecological methods of agriculture that respect the environment and seeds that preserve biodiversity (Karriem, 2009, p. 322).

The impetus to connect the environmental, social, and economic debates culminated in the creation, in 1992, of the Brazilian Movement of Non-governmental Organizations (NGOs) and Social Movements for the Environment and Development, following the United Nations Conference on Environment and Development held in Rio de Janeiro the same year (Acselrad, 2010, p. 106).

By linking environment protection to overall economic development, social movements in Brazil have been successful in raising their agendas to the forefront of national discussions. This thematic coordination has been strategic in raising political and financial resources, strengthening capacities to implement projects (Domask, 1998, p. 3) and facilitating coalitions with grassroots movements and scientists providing vital support in the form of mobilisation and dissemination of information (Thorkildsen, 2018, p. 358).

Additionally, this integration of topics in a neo-conservationist discourse, together with increased institutionalisation and technical specialisation of activities, has enabled the environmental justice movement in Brazil to gain access to the state bureaucracy via political offices (Alonso and Maciel, 2010, p. 300). By operating at the centre of the decision-making process, social and environmental justice leaders have additional potential to convert civil society advocacy into policies and public projects.

This was the case, for instance, of environmental activists who were appointed for strategic positions at the Ministry of Environment, the Secretariat for Biodiversity and Forests, and the Secretariat for the Amazon during the presidency of Fernando Henrique Cardoso from 1995 to 2001 (Alonso and Maciel, 2010, p. 304). Furthermore, Marina Silva—a prominent grassroots activist leader in Brazil who was successful in associating environmental and social justice concerns for the protection of the Amazon region—rose through the political ranks engaging in the national trade union movement and the Brazilian Worker's Party (PT) in the late 1980s until becoming Minister of Environment under the presidency of Luis Inácio Lula da Silva in 2003. She later went on to run for the presidency of the country in 2010, 2014, and 2018 and, despite not being elected, her candidacies have contributed to strengthening discussions about the environmental agenda at the municipal, state, and federal levels.

Conclusion

Economic empowerment remains an essential part of the complexity of generating prosperity and alleviating poverty with social movements playing key roles in promoting this agenda. Nevertheless, it is becoming clearer each day that we must engender development paths in which individuals are able to meet their own needs without compromising forthcoming generations. Merely transforming marginalised communities into economic agents may have the short-term effect of expanding markets and improving productivity levels; however, it also accelerates consumption patterns and places additional pressures on the planet's already delicate natural boundaries. As we know, this prevents truly equitable and sustainable growth in the long term.

As long as vulnerable and impoverished populations continue to be unevenly exposed to environmental risks and hazards, they will remain unable to effectively participate in the wider economy and influence public decision-making processes. Environmental problems disproportionately affect underprivileged groups, which are more vulnerable to climate shocks and more dependent on ecosystem services for achieving acceptable standards of living. Hence, environmental destruction needs to be recognised as a compelling threat to *social, economic, and political emancipation*.

In order to truly contribute to promoting a sustainable livelihood model, social movements need to increasingly bridge the gaps between economic empowerment and environmental justice. By analysing the emergence of the environmental justice movement and its expansion in Brazil, I argue that the synergy between environmental and socioeconomic activism can contribute to strengthening civil society's capacity to meet its demands. Recognising these overlaps and tapping into the potential of combining both agendas can not only mobilise increased community support to both causes in sustained ways, but also take advantage of the political momentum and catalyse financial resources while opening channels for direct participation in decision-making processes.

In conclusion, socioeconomic emancipation cannot be made sustainable without considering the scope and impact of the capitalist production system in our planet. Rather than downplaying its importance, linking environmental and economic justice agendas can only strengthen the cause for sustainable economic empowerment. Social movements can thus play a more effective role in strengthening individuals' socioeconomic resilience and generating transformational change in a world where environmental stresses not only affect each and every one of us around the globe but is also a threat to future generations.

Bibliography

Acselrad, H. (2010). The "Environmentalization" of Social Struggles—The Environmental Justice Movement in Brazil. In: *Estudos Avançados* 24, no. 68: 103–119.

Agyeman, J. and Evans, B. (2004). "Just Sustainability": The Emerging Discourse of Environmental Justice in Britain? In: *Geographical Journal* 170, no. 2: 155–164. https://doi.org/10.1111/j.0016-7398.2004.00117.x.

Alonso, A. and Maciel, D. (2010). From Protest to Professionalization: Brazilian Environmental Activism After Rio-92. In: *Journal of Environment and Development* 19, no. 3: 300–317. https://doi.org/10.1177/1070496510378101.

David, M. B. de A., Morales, C. and Rodríguez, M. (2001). Modernidad y heterogeneidad: estilo de desarrollo agrícola y rural en América Latina y el Caribe. In: *Desarrollo rural en América Latina y el Caribe: la construcción de un nuevo modelo?* Bogotá: Economic Commission for Latin America and the Caribbean (ECLAC), pp. 41–88. Retrieved from https://repositorio.cepal.org/handle/11362/1662.

Deere, C. D. and Royce, F. S. (2009). Introduction: The Rise and Impact of National and Transnational Rural Social Movements in Latin America. In: *Rural Social Movements in Latin America*. Gainesville, FL: University Press of Florida, Vol. 38, pp. 1–29. https://doi.org/10.5744/florida/9780813033327.003.0001.

Domask, J. J. (1998). Evolution of the Environmental Movement in Brazil's Amazonia. In: *1998 Meeting of the Latin American Studies Association*. Chicago, IL.

Gould, C. (1996). Diversity and Democracy: Representing Differences. In: S. Benhabib (Ed.), *Democracy and Difference: Changing Boundaries of the Political*. Princeton, NJ: Princeton University Press, pp. 171–186.

Hornberg, C. and Pauli, A. (2007). Child Poverty and Environmental Justice. In: *International Journal of Hygiene and Environmental Health* 210, no. 5: 571–580. https://doi.org/10.1016/j.ijheh.2007.07.006.

Karriem, A. (2009). The Rise and Transformation of the Brazilian Landless Movement into a Counter-Hegemonic Political Actor: A Gramscian Analysis. In: *Geoforum* 40, no. 3: 316–325. https://doi.org/10.1016/j.geoforum.2008.10.005.

Laurent, É. (2010). Environmental Justice and Environmental Inequalities: A European Perspective. In: *Social Investment Seminar of the Institute for Futures Studies*. Stockholm, p. 21. Retrieved from https://inis.iaea.org/collection/NCLCollectionStore/_Public/47/006/47006484.pdf?r=1.

Pedersen, O. W. (2010). Environmental Principles and Environmental Justice. In: *Environmental Law Review* 12, no. 1: 26–49. https://doi.org/10.1350/enlr.2010.12.1.074.

Rawls, J. (1971). *A Theory of Justice*. Cambridge, MA: Harvard University Press. https://doi.org/10.2307/j.ctvjf9z6v.

Rosset, P. M. and Martínez-Torres, M. E. (2012). Rural Social Movements and Agroecology: Context, Theory, and Process. In: *Ecology and Society* 17, no. 3: Art. 17. https://doi.org/10.5751/ES-05000-170317.

Schlosberg, D. (2007). *Defining Environmental Justice*. Oxford University Press. https://doi.org/10.1093/acprof:oso/9780199286294.001.0001.

Sen, A. (1999). *Development as Freedom*. Oxford: Oxford University Press.

Thorkildsen, K. (2018). "Land Yes, Dam No!" Justice-Seeking Strategies by the Anti-dam Movement in the Ribeira Valley, Brazil. In: *Journal of Peasant Studies* 45, no. 2: 347–367. https://doi.org/10.1080/03066150.2016.1217842.

Young, I. M. (1990). *Justice and the Politics of Difference*. Princeton, NJ: Princeton University Press. https://doi.org/10.1086/293512.

Index

N. Wilcock and E. Federzoni dos Santos (eds.), *Not Paying the Rent*, https://doi.org/10.1007/978-3-030-78861-2

L

M

N

P

R

S

T

The manufacturer's authorised representative in the EU is Springer Nature Customer Service Centre GmbH, Europaplatz 3, 69115 Heidelberg, Germany. If you have any concerns regarding our products, please contact ProductSafety@springernature.com

Printed and bound by CPI Group (UK) Ltd, Croydon, CR0 4YY

30/09/2026

02225455-0003